# A Kidnapped Mind

# A Kidnapped Mind

## A Mother's Heartbreaking Story of Parental Alienation Syndrome

Pamela Richardson
with Jane Broweleit

Foreword by Dr. Reena Sommer

DUNDURN PRESS
TORONTO

Copy-editor: Patricia Kennedy
Design: Jennifer Scott
Printer: University of Toronto Press

Though this story is based on actual events, some names have been changed to protect the identity of the persons involved.

Library and Archives Canada Cataloguing in Publication

Richardson, Pamela
     A kidnapped mind : a mother's heartbreaking story of parental alienation syndrome / Pamela Richardson.

Includes bibliographical references.
ISBN-10 1-55002-624-0
ISBN-13: 978-1-55002-624-5


     1. Parental alienation syndrome. 2. Richardson, Pamela. 3. Mothers and sons--Canada--Biography. I. Title.

RJ506.P27R52 2006            618.92'852            C2006-901335-7

1    2    3    4    5        10    09    08    07    06

Conseil des Arts du Canada   Canada Council for the Arts

Canada

ONTARIO ARTS COUNCIL
CONSEIL DES ARTS DE L'ONTARIO

We acknowledge the support of the **Canada Council for the Arts** and the **Ontario Arts Council** for our publishing program. We also acknowledge the financial support of the **Government of Canada** through the **Book Publishing Industry Development Program** and **The Association for the Export of Canadian Books**, and the **Government of Ontario** through the **Ontario Book Publishers Tax Credit program**, and the **Ontario Media Development Corporation**.

Care has been taken to trace the ownership of copyright material used in this book. The author and the publisher welcome any information enabling them to rectify any references or credit in subsequent editions.

                                                                    *J. Kirk Howard, President*

Printed and bound in Canada.

www.dundurn.com

Dundurn Press
3 Church Street, Suite 500
Toronto, Ontario, Canada
M5E 1M2

Gazelle Book Services Limited
White Cross Mills
High Town, Lancaster, England
LA1 4XS

Dundurn Press
2250 Military Road
Tonawanda, NY
U.S.A. 14150

# Contents

# Acknowledgements

This book could never have happened without the spunky and talented young writer Jane Broweleit. She rolled up her sleeves and dug into the stacks and stacks of legal briefs, letters, affidavits, and documents that had absorbed twelve years of my life, taking my burning passion and driving force and getting it down, making it a reality. Jane co-wrote with me for over two years, lending her valuable intellect, her compassion and warmth, her humour and tears. For this story, Jane became me. It is my voice you have here, my heart, my despair, my tears and joy, but it is her conjuring that brought it to the page. It is a credit to her and her alone that *A Kidnapped Mind* is not a story only in my head and heart, but a book. We are forever bound because of that time — so much time — spent huddled in my library with endless cups of tea and coffee, or on the phone or e-mailing each other from all parts of the country, at all times of the day and night. Jane's commitment to this book was overwhelming. I give her this very special thanks.

There were many others. I know that I could not have endured writing such a deeply painful, honest, and ultimately cathartic book without the help of Ann-Marie Metten, an insightful and gifted B.C. editor, who worked with Jane and me throughout. She was more than just our editor, she was our "third eye." With Ann-Marie's crucial help, guidance, and tenacity, we sought — and I think found — the balance required to set the story free. Beverley Slopen, my agent, was consistently positive that she would find the right home for our work. She did, and I cannot thank Kirk Howard, Tony Hawke, Beth Bruder, Alison Pennels, and Barry Jowett at The Dundurn Group enough, with special thanks to the keen and meticulous eye of my editor, Pat Kennedy. My friends Sandy, Joan,

Lois, Molly, Dithy, Teresa, Catherine, Susan, and Leslie were always close, always encouraging and patient, and became the backbone I needed so often to stay strong. Dave's parents and mine were deprived of a beloved grandson, but cherished the times they did share with Dash. My brother Dave and his wife, Beverly, held me, both physically and emotionally, in their strong, loving arms during my years of struggle to see Dash and during my years of struggle to put it all on paper. My sons, Colby and Quinten, saw me sitting into the night on too many occasions, writing, editing, ankle deep in legal papers, totally immersed. And my husband, Dave — as throughout our life together — has been the solid rock I could not think about living without. Amy Thomas, our beloved Mimi, who looked after all of us and nurtured the nurturer. I thank you from the bottom of my heart.

As *A Kidnapped Mind* illustrates, many people turn the other way. I want to thank those of you who stood behind your words and allowed your names to be included in this book. Parental Alienation Syndrome (PAS) touches tens of thousands of people in this world, and none of them get off lightly. They — we — all feel the fallout. This is a non-profit book, with all proceeds going to The Dash Foundation, formed to help increase awareness of the damage that can be done by alienating a child from a once-loved parent. It is child abuse, and it can kill. I also wrote *A Kidnapped Mind* as the last gift to my wonderful, brave, brown-eyed son, Dash.

This, my darling, is for you.

# Foreword
## by Dr. Reena Sommer

Children enter this world completely dependent upon those — usually their parents — who are entrusted with their care. Parenting styles and the ability to parent may vary, but most manage this important life task quite successfully. Nevertheless, some children are failed by parents who are incapable of childrearing.

Mothers and fathers who are limited by physical or mental disabilities, poor health, alcohol or substance abuse, criminality, poverty, war, or other problems, often lack the ability, and at times even the desire, to invest in their children's upbringing. Children in these situations are either left to fend for themselves or are cared for by family members, friends and neighbours, or social agencies.

But another class of parents has also been found to fail at appropriately protecting, nurturing, educating, and guiding their children. Mothers and fathers in this relatively new and emerging group do not fit the stereotype of the deficient and ill-equipped parent. Instead, these parents are generally articulate, resourceful, and competent in all other aspects of their lives — except in the realm of parenting. In fact, these individuals might easily be mistaken for ideal parents, except to the properly informed, because they profess love and concern for their children. What sets these individuals apart from other dysfunctional parents is their overwhelming commitment to meeting their own needs first. In doing so, they destroy the relationship their children have with the other parent — at whatever cost.

A *Kidnapped Mind* by Pamela Richardson chronicles her son Dash's painful emotional descent, which ultimately culminated in his suicide. This is an extremely sad but powerful account of the circumstances involved in Dash's struggle to survive in an environment in which his father placed his own selfish need to punish his ex-spouse ahead of the needs of his dependent child. This was an environment in which Dash was held psychologically hostage for nearly eleven years of his sixteen-year life.

*A Kidnapped Mind* is more than a story about a mother's struggle to win back custody of her son following an acrimonious divorce and custody battle. Rather, it is a story of the emotionally damaging fallout that occurs when a child is robbed of his right to love and be loved by both his parents. It is also a story of the court system's ignorance toward children's needs and its unwillingness to look beyond the legal infrastructure in order to examine why a once healthy, happy, and well-functioning child, who experienced warm and positive relationships with both of his parents, systematically and without cause rejected one parent and denied himself the love and nurturing that would sustain him.

While Dash's experience represents the worst possible outcome of "Parental Alienation Syndrome," an increasingly common by-product of contested custody cases, it must be realized that countless numbers of children are suffering on an ongoing basis while they are in the care of parents who place more value on getting even with their ex-spouse than they do on the happiness of their child. More importantly, these same parents are deliberately and without cause consumed with destroying the bond that exists between their child and the other parent. Although Parental Alienation Syndrome remains controversial due to its politicization by special-interests groups such as Justice for Children and the National Alliance for Family Court Justice, which have a vested interest in proving it does not exist, it is nevertheless a phenomenon that professionals have observed with increasing frequency ever since the 1980s, when the courts considered joint custody as a better option following divorce.

I believe that *A Kidnapped Mind* will provide important insights into the needs of children of divorcing parents in a way that the theoretical or empirical contributions of academics have not been able to achieve. For this reason, *A Kidnapped Mind* should be required reading for all family-court judges, family-law practitioners, and anyone involved with divorcing families.

I applaud the strength, perseverance, and commitment that Pamela Richardson showed throughout Dash's life, and which endures now in her efforts to ensure that his death was not in vain. I am truly honoured by the opportunity to contribute to this excellent book.

Reena Sommer, Ph.D.
Divorce and Custody Consultant

# *Chapter 1*
# Torn Apart

In June 1990, in Vancouver, on a perfect day of twenty-three degrees, sunshine flooded bustling West Tenth Avenue, the street I knew so well. A breeze played with my hair and floated up and under the crisp linen shirt I wore. I was five months pregnant and holding the hand of my soon-to-be husband, Dave Richardson, as we walked with purpose toward the Cactus Club Café. West Point Grey wasn't my neighbourhood any more, but it had been for seven years, during my passionate but ultimately doomed marriage to Peter Hart. The marriage had become abusive, but from it had come my beautiful son Dashiell. It was along this active street just outside the gates of the University of British Columbia that I had pushed Dash in his stroller and, later, walked with him as a little boy. Every part of the neighbourhood was infused with him: story mornings at West Point Grey library, the bakery where we stopped for jelly doughnuts and fresh bread, buying tea towels from the country-fabric store. Dash smiled at everyone.

On our homeward route was Trimble Park. "Mommy, can you go under and send me to the sky?" he'd squeal from the swing, grabbing the chains and squeezing his eyes shut, bracing against the momentum as the swing flew high in the air.

"Is this high enough, Dash?" I'd laugh.

"No, Mommy, higher!"

As Dash rose high on the swing, I would stand in front where he could see me. I'd raise my arms and tell him I loved him by touching my two forefingers together and curling them inward while pressing my thumbs together to create a little heart. Dash and I had been saying "I love you" and "Goodbye" with that little heart since he was two years old. I'd made him heart-shaped sandwiches with a cookie cutter, and he loved them so much that I began making the heart shape with my hands. Soon he could curl his hands into the shape, too.

"I love you too, Mommmmmy!" shouted Dash.

It felt like another life, an eternity away. Dave glanced up at the cloudless sky as we walked along. "You know, if this weather keeps up, we should go away this weekend. To one of the Gulf Islands maybe. Do a bit of fishing, have dinner out on the deck."

"I love it. Which island?"

Dave laughed. "Whichever has the shortest ferry lineup!"

"God, let's avoid it altogether and stay home."

"Yeah, we'll go in the fall instead."

I laughed. "I have a feeling somebody doesn't know how busy life is going to get when the baby arrives in September."

"No more freewheeling weekends away?" Dave faked shock and horror.

"I'll let you see for yourself. You know, Dash is going to love Lake of the Woods this summer, Dave. Seeing your parents. The fishing, the diving and swimming."

"Do you think Dash is old enough to start learning about boats? We could start with the knots for tying up!" Dave added, his chestnut brown curls glinting gold in the sun.

Dave was boyishly exuberant about my son. They had touched each other deeply, the moment they first met. A few months after I fell in love with Dave, I asked him to come and join Dash and me for the evening at Whistler. We had been skiing there since Dash was four and a half years old, just after the separation. It was a great excuse to get out of town and a fun thing to do together. On our ski weekends Dash and I shared a room in a log cabin owned by friends of my father's. I rented the room for the season, and Dash and I went up whenever we could. Dave shared a cabin with friends that season, too. The evening they met, Dash had had an early dinner and I had given him his bath. He was in his cozy snowflake pyjamas when Dave knocked on the door. "Oh!" I exclaimed to Dash. "That must be for us! He's early, Dash!" I scooped him into my arms and walked over and opened the door.

"Dash, this is Dave Richardson. Dave, this is Dash."

Dave leaned over to greet Dash, and to my astonishment Dash turned and, without saying a word, put his arms straight out, to be taken into Dave's embrace. As Dash snuggled in, Dave said, "Hello there, Little Buddy. It's a pleasure to meet you. I've heard a lot about you from your mom."

Dash smiled. "You have?"

"Yeah, and you know what?" Dave said warmly. "I'm going to tell you something that may surprise you. None of my nieces and nephews call me Dave."

Dash took the bait. "They don't?"

"No, they don't even call me Uncle Dave."

"What do they call you then?"

"They call me Big D."

"Big D!" Dash repeated happily. Then a giggly, "Why?"

"Well, I don't know if you noticed when I came in the door . . . but I am BIG!" Dave stood up to his full height, lifting Dash with him to six feet four-and-a-half inches. "And 'D' is the first letter in 'Dave,' my name."

"Do that again!" Dash squealed.

Dave crouched all the way down and shot up tall again. Dash was jelly by then, high-pitched and happy. "So, if you like, you can call me 'Big D,' too."

For the first time since he'd fallen into Dave's arms, Dash looked at me. His big brown eyes sparkled. "Mom? Can I?"

"I think that would be wonderful, Dash. 'Big D' is a great name."

Dave walked over to the couch with Dash still clinging to him. I heard Dash say, "Hello, Big D," as if he were trying it out.

"Hello, Little Buddy," Dave replied.

"Do you like to play Snap?" Dash asked.

"*Do I like Snap?* I'm known as one of the best Snappers in the West!"

"Well, let's play!"

"I may be a bit rusty. Is that okay?"

That night Dave fell in love with Dash as though he were his own first child, and Dash became enraptured by this big man with the gentle voice, the natural teacher.

"Let's see if we can fly this kite as high as the clouds, Dash!"

"Big D! Big D! The kite's starting to dip!"

"Oh-oh. Okay. Wait a minute, Dash. Hold on to it!" And Dave ran over and slid like a first-base runner onto his knees next to Dash, grabbing the line and manoeuvring the kite back into the wind.

"You got it!" Dash cried.

"That was a close call, Doodle. Do you see how, if you have the kite in the right position, the wind will do all the work for you? Shall we let it go now? Yep, give it some line. That's it. There it goes. It'll be all right now."

As we walked along West Tenth Avenue, Dave's hand was strong and comforting in mine, but my unease nagged me.

"Penny for your thoughts?" Dave asked.

"I'm thinking about this meeting with Peter. Do you think it will do any good?"

Dave lost his carefree expression. "Well, it's not like he's responded to any of your faxes, and calling sure hasn't produced any results. We need to know when he wants to see Dash this summer, so we don't really have any choice but to meet with him, do we?"

"I thought that this way — meeting in a public place, with you along for support — Peter and I could decide how to split the summer." Mired once more in the stress of dealing with my ex-husband, I felt weighed down, unsure of myself. I lowered my voice. "Isn't this what he wanted? Custody? To be able to tell me where and when I see Dash? Why is he so nasty if he got what he wanted?"

"He's nasty because he's angry and he's angry because he's a lawyer and his reputation has been jeopardized," Dave said, a hard edge to his voice.

This had been a complicating factor since the beginning. When Peter and I split he was convinced *he* was the one who had been wronged and he seemed to act irrationally, doing things that went against the law and his legal training. During a routine title search in preparation for the divorce trial, my lawyer, Gerald Reid, found Peter had conveyed the matrimonial home to someone named Robin Williams. At trial, Justice Bruce MacDonald had not only found Peter guilty of illegally conveying the house but that Peter had faked the books and dates for the house transfer. As a lawyer, Peter knew the Law Society of British Columbia would eventually investigate this finding of fraud against one of its members. He had jeopardized his reputation by his own actions, but he blamed me, and when he wasn't blaming me, he was blaming my lawyer, Gerald.

I don't think this is about Dash at all," said Dave.

"Me neither. But I don't think it's about money, either. It's about control."

"Imagine how bad he would be if he *hadn't* been given Dash?"

"Yeah, well then I wouldn't be going to *him* for everything. He'd be coming to me, and I'd make sure we all stayed calm and focused on Dash and the future, not the marriage and the past. I wouldn't play games like he is."

Dave went quiet. Peter *did* have custody; he *was* playing games. Dave felt me tossing and turning at night as I worried about what Peter would do, about how things might never settle down the way we all needed them to. He remembered the first time he had met my ex-husband. Peter had rushed to tell him, "All I want is control, and all I care about is Dash's love for me." Dave and I walked on silently and I felt his hand squeeze mine. We were so lucky to have found each other, and I wanted to think about that, not Peter. The baby changed position, and with a smile I placed my hand on my hard stomach.

"Ah. He wants out, our little boy does," Dave said. A first-time dad-to-be, he reached across and patted my bulge tenderly. "He wants some of what Dash gets."

"Well, he's going to get lots of it," I said. "But today we have another little boy to take care of. Let's get through this meeting and get that summer schedule."

"Good," Dave replied. "Let's do it. It'll be okay."

"No, it probably won't," I said. "But Peter might behave better if you don't say anything."

This was hard for a big, protective man like Dave. I was the woman he had fallen in love with, but I had an ex-husband who tore strips off me on the phone, on the doorstep during Dash's changeovers, in front of Dash, in front of *him*, as though taunting Dave. *What are you gonna do about it, big guy?* Dave, a successful businessman, and Peter, a successful lawyer: one gratefully, joyfully, in love with me; the other filled with hatred. One who would do anything for me, the other who had Dash and could control us all with him.

"I won't say a thing, Pam. It won't help."

"I know this is tough for you, Sweetheart," I said, linking my arm through his.

"Yep, it is. But I understand why, and I'll do my best. I'll sit there with my buttoned lip and smile. Come on, let's just do this."

Off in the distance I saw Peter at the corner of Trimble and West Tenth Avenue. He was unsteady on his feet. He wore sunglasses, his shirt was half-untucked, his pants were rumpled.

"Oh, no," I said, slowing, pulling Dave back.

"Come on. It'll be all right."

"Dave, he's drunk." I felt deflated. "I know how this is going to go."

"We'll just have to see. Come on."


It had been a long and painful winter. Custody trials were supposed to set things right, weren't they? Like most people, I'd had an intuitive sense that court was a bad place to end up, and had begged Peter to consider mediation for our divorce. But he didn't want mediation. He was a high-flying criminal lawyer, sought out by clients who were charged with drug offences. His preferred arena was an adversarial one. I went into court as the besotted mommy. "Yes, Dash adores his daddy and Peter adores him. Yes, despite limitations, Peter has been a good father." But my testimony had ended with the issue that most concerned me. "I believe Peter will use Dash to control me. I believe Peter will use Dash to hurt me."

Early in 1989, mediation with Peter's criminal-lawyer friend Ross Senior had been a disaster. Peter had moved on to colleague Russell Trekiak, and I reluctantly hired Rosemary Nash, a family lawyer that our marriage counsellor recommended. Letters flew immediately and, by June 2, 1989, with Peter's new lawyer Barbara Nelson, we stood in front of Justice Douglas Wetmore.

By that time I had become increasingly concerned about Peter's drinking while Dash was with him. The weekend before the hearing,

Peter had arrived to pick up his son with a half-empty bottle of wine wedged between the front seats of his Jaguar. What I should have done was call the police, but I was too afraid. I knew it would make Peter even angrier if I got him into trouble, but, on the other hand, what if he had an accident while driving with Dash? Peter's drinking was one of the reasons I always had my nanny accompany Dash when he stayed with his dad.

My lawyer repeated my concerns to Justice Wetmore, who sighed and, in a fatherly tone, said, "Peter, will you not drink while you have the child with you?" He then ordered specific access and adjourned both of our interim custody applications.

My shock at Justice Wetmore's familiar and cavalier approach to Peter and his drinking was not lost on Rosemary, who broke an unwritten rule and wrote the judge to explain how I felt. I then requested a meeting with Justice Wetmore and Peter's lawyer, because Wetmore had chosen to seize himself of the matter, meaning we could only go back in front of him as our judge. Wetmore had agreed with Peter's counsel that psychologist Dr. Michael Elterman, who was well known to the courts as an expert witness in family matters, should do the custody-and-access report.

My meeting with Justice Wetmore never did take place. Instead the tension between lawyers began to build. Shell-shocked and numb, I watched their obviously biased presentations — arguments about what had been said, clerks' notes ordered to clarify, and orders redrafted. Dates to have orders resettled filled the months between June and September 1, when once again we stood in court. We had received Dr. Elterman's second and final report before the trial in August, and Justice Sherman Hood made his order. In 1989, the courts seemed wary of giving joint custody to parents who were viewed as not being able to get along. The psychologist's report had recommended joint custody, but, if a decision had to be made, then Peter should be the custodial parent, because, Dr. Elterman stated, Dash was more psychologically attached to Dad than to Mom.

Between the time Dr. Elterman's report was made available in August and our court date in September, I had tried again to meet with Peter, begging him to agree to joint custody for the sake of our son. But

Peter had no intention of agreeing to any such thing. He laughed when I brought up the idea, saying, "You must be joking. The report is in my favour and I know everyone down at the courthouse. I'm not going to agree to anything with you." It was that simple; it was that devastating. And Peter was right. Justice Hood ordered interim custody to Peter. More letters flew, as Rosemary battled to clarify Dr. Elterman's position. The matter was settled on September 27 and, within five days, Peter had refused to let me speak to Dash on the telephone. *It's already happening,* I had thought.

We each had nine months to prepare for the divorce and custody trial. I spent them enjoying my life, my new love, and my beautiful son, then just five years old. Peter found a new partner, a tough family lawyer. Nevertheless, he continued to brew up trouble. Peter flew into a rage with Dash's kindergarten teacher when she invited me to their class Christmas party. "How did Pamela even find out about it?" he demanded, because in his mind, as the interim sole custodial parent, all information flowing from Dash's school had to go through him. Peter phoned and told me, "I have the right to choose whether you are in the school or not, and I don't want you there."

I volunteered at Dash's school only one half-day a week (on Fridays, my access day), but Peter began telling the school, more and more loudly each time, that I was upsetting Dash by being there. Dash began to complain — though only to Peter, who quickly wrote it up and distributed it in affidavits — that I was "buggy" at school. Peter complained that I was alienating the teacher from him and confusing the school as to who was the custodial parent. My presence a half-day a week and my friendship with Dash's teacher was causing mayhem, apparently, and the only thing that would fix it would be removing me from the school. That would calm the situation, Peter contended.

"The situation *is* calm," I pleaded to the principal. "This is just Peter making an issue when there isn't one. Why doesn't he come and be a class parent, too? I just want to be with my son in his school environment, a half-day a week, the way I always have."

But Peter said I had to be stopped. I had "aggressively and unilaterally" involved myself with the school. My activities were "completely out of hand." The principal panicked, believing the school was going to become a battle zone between warring parents. "There is no war!" I cried. "It's not a war zone if only one person is fighting!" But the school wanted to neutralize itself. The principal called me into his office one Friday and told me to leave and not come back. Cast as one of two disputatious parties, in the blink of an eye I was gone.

An eczema rash on Dash's face flared up one day when he was with me, so I booked an appointment and took him along to see our pediatrician, who had looked after Dash from birth. Later that day Peter went barrelling down to the doctor's office to tell him that, as interim sole custodial parent, only he was to make appointments for Dash. I was not to be given any information about Dash's health, injuries, or illnesses without express permission. I was not to take Dash to the doctor. The doctor was astonished, but had to comply, because Peter's demand was perfectly legal. Peter would tell the court that he had acted so the poor doctor would have to deal with only one "anxious" parent.

Peter also flaunted his custody, accentuating how little power I had: I went to the school to pick up Dash for an access weekend, but was told he was in Mexico with his dad for a week. Apparently Peter didn't need my consent to fly Dash half a continent away. I kept thinking, *Once Peter moves on with his life and drops his anger, things will calm down. He won't need to stick it to me. He'll stop trying to upset and marginalize me. He's got the control he wanted and he has Dash — surely he's going to forget about me, that I left him, that I'm in love with Dave, or whatever it is he hates me for.*

But really nothing changed, not for the better anyway. Peter's anger peaked still higher. Though sometimes he was deathly calm, cold and impersonal, as if I were a telephone company he was calling about his bill, mostly he was enraged. "Fuck off, I hate listening to you," he'd say, or "I hate you. I want to push you off a bridge." Sometimes Peter would say nothing and simply hang up the phone as soon as he heard my voice. When he didn't, instead of getting Dash for me or discussing with me the things we needed to organize for him, he would harp on past grievances.

"But you got what you wanted! You got Dash!" I would protest. Then Peter would hang up. He was worse than I'd ever seen him.

Though alcohol had been a major factor in the breakdown of our marriage, at least then he used to hide himself away to drink. Now he was brazen about it, leaving slurred messages on my answering machine and sending scrawled, unintelligible faxes late at night.

Things were rotten in Denmark, but Dave and I agreed with Gerald, my lawyer, who had warned me before we went into our permanent custody trial, "You have an interim psychological assessment against you. We might vehemently disagree with Dr. Elterman and say he was biased and produce all your associates to say they felt rushed and ignored, but his report will stand and the judge will heed it strongly. So the *last* thing we do is talk negatively about the other parent, even if it's true."

"So we can't go in saying, 'Peter is manipulative. Peter is a drinker. Peter is abusive' because the court just doesn't want to hear it?" I asked.

"Right. We just can't play that game. We have to go in there talking about you, Pam, not Peter, and focus on the future, not the past. We have to stay above the fray, even if Peter doesn't, and we can't sling mud, because it'll only end up sticking to you. There is no question, Pam, that the court will see you as a good, fit parent. It's a tough fifty-fifty split." Gerald sighed. "The psychological assessment didn't condemn you, it just chose Peter. We don't know why, maybe because he put his hand up first, maybe because the court-appointed psychologist liked him better, maybe because he told him things that we will never know about. Who knows? It doesn't matter. We have to concentrate on showing that you are the balanced parent here, that you aren't angry, that you have moved on. Then we have to rely on the courts."

"But what about all the things Peter's been doing?"

"He's worked the 'grey' areas very well, and he's in the power position, because he has interim custody. Warring parents aren't given joint custody because, in the courts' view, they'll just keep fighting. They seek to appoint a 'boss.' It looks to me like Peter's doing all this to claim the title 'sole custodian.' Dr. Elterman told us all in his interim report that, if the parents don't settle down, he will recommend Peter for sole custody. So if it's made to look to the outside world as if you can't get along in all-important areas of Dash's life — his education and health and welfare — Peter will have created an atmosphere for the appointment of this 'boss.' That's the reality here. We've got an uphill battle."

Dr. Elterman's consideration of joint custody had been short-lived because of what he called the "ongoing conflict" between Peter and me. Look at these people, he seemed to be saying, they're still fighting. It was exactly what I'd dreaded. "Don't lump me into this. It's Peter who's fighting!" I wanted to plead. Giving Peter permanent sole custody, Dr. Elterman said, was "the only way to stop or minimize" the war. In Dr. Elterman's view it was Peter who "more closely resembles the idea" of Dash's "psychological parent." Dr. Elterman recommended that sole custody should go to Peter, saying that we were "two very good parents," but, while "Mrs. Hart is a good parent; Mr. Hart is an excellent parent." My lawyer asked him later in court, "Does an excellent parent attempt to exclude another parent from a constructive role in the child's education?"

"No," said Dr. Elterman.

"Does an excellent parent attempt to exclude the other parent from a constructive role in the child's health?"

"No."

It made no difference. Peter got permanent sole custody in the ensuing seven-day trial in May 1990. The "grey areas" had been successfully covered during the interim period. Peter lived in the matrimonial home. Peter had raised two grownup children (with the repeated emphasis on his son, Greg's, doctor-in-training status and his daughter, Lisa's, work as a nurse). He had secured the employment of Rose, Dash's nanny (though she had been my employee for four years). Peter still lived down the road from Queen Mary Elementary, the school, according to Peter, Dash had "been told all his life" he'd be going to attend in Grade One; I had moved to West Vancouver. Peter was going to start working from home.

Peter had convinced the court that he had single-handedly raised two children for the past eight years, even though I had lived with him and the family during all that time. Peter also convinced the court that he and his first wife, Mary Louise, had coparented well. But Peter had left Mary Louise, and when she remarried and moved to Washington State, he insisted the children stay with him.

Dr. Elterman had said I was a "good parent," and so did the court. The judge gave me 50 percent of Dash's time and believed Peter's reassurance that he would keep me fully involved in Dash's life. I took comfort in the fact that the judge hadn't so much found *against* me as it had found *for* Dash's continuity in his neighbourhood, with his nanny, in his old house. While I didn't believe that Dash's continuity equalled Dash's *stability*, the judge believed Peter would settle down once he was awarded custody.

I was home and five months pregnant when Dave returned early from work. I knew from the look on his face what he had in his hand. Knowing how upset I'd be, my lawyer had called Dave and asked him to bring the reasons for judgement to me himself. The court said that, if Peter and Dash moved out of the matrimonial home in West Point Grey or the nanny left, as access parent I could reapply for custody, but, for now, Peter had won. "I've lost *all* custody?" I asked, bereft. "Peter has *all* the power here? Oh, my God, Dave. What's going to happen now?" Dash was just about to turn six. What I felt as I held the custody decision in my hands was *fear*, mixed with great loss. My ability to parent Dash — or, I panicked, be a part of his life at all — had fallen completely to the mercy of the only man in the world who wanted to push me off a bridge. With little recourse and a perennial hope that the past was not the future, I had to set about making sure that Peter united with me to raise our son.

The trial had wrapped up two weeks earlier, and now Dave and I walked down West Tenth Avenue to meet Peter, the rumpled man wending his way into the restaurant ahead of us. Dave and I crossed the street and followed Peter inside. He was sitting at a table near the bar.

"Hello, Peter. Thank you for coming," I said mildly, as Dave and I sat down.

"Oh, it's you — the liar," he said, his voice already slurred, his red-rimmed eyes ablaze. He had ordered a beer and now took a long slug. I shot a quick look at Dave. *Don't respond.* He nodded imperceptibly.

"There's no way you're getting anything out of me," Peter told me icily.

"Peter, I asked for this meeting so that we can talk about summer, not the trial."

He ignored me. "That so-called 'fraud' will ruin my practice."

"Peter, that's not my fault. The judge decided what he decided. It's over. I need to talk about acc—"

"Not for me it's not. It'll never be over for me. I'll never sign that order. I'll never say that was fraud." Peppered throughout his barrage were ancient themes: I was an "actress" (I had been a model in my 20s, and was a Vancouver television personality when I had met Peter). I had "fooled the courts." I was a "fucking bitch." Twenty-five times he said it in the Cactus Club Café: "You're a fucking bitch." People turned and glared at the three of us. Oblivious to all, Peter just raised his voice higher. "Why all the rush on this, anyway? Yeah, I need a break, too, you know."

"Well, I thought we could talk about your plans, so Dash and you can do what you want and I can work out my holiday time, too."

"Plans, plans, plans. That's all I ever hear from you is plans. What do you want anyway, all of July?" Peter asked, then exploded into laughter. "What is Richardson doing here anyway? What has he got to do with anything?"

"He's just here to listen, Peter, so you don't have to worry about him." I felt myself buckling under the weight of this man's hatred and irrationality. "You won, Peter!" I eventually exclaimed. "You got custody. You got what you wanted! We need to put this behind us. I came here to work out summer access with you."

"That trial was all your doing. I can barely stand to look at you."

"Okay, Peter," I said miserably, "we're leaving." I smoothed my shirt over my tummy and manoeuvred out from behind the little table. Dave still hadn't said a word, just as he had promised. We were out onto the street before he finally spoke. "I'm glad that went so well, aren't you?" he said, lightly.

I smiled crookedly. "I'm so sorry, Dave."

But he forced a laugh. "Hey!" he said. "It goes with the territory! I don't know how you kept your cool." Dave may not have liked my strategy of non-confrontation, of trying to neutralize Peter's aggression by not responding to it, but he *respected* it, he respected *me*. And this is where the foundation of our love lay. Despite the abuse, my misery and frustration, and the knowledge deep in my gut that Dash was going to suffer for his father's blistering anger, I felt safer than at any other time in the past ten years. I may not have come away from the meeting with a summer access schedule, but knowing that Dave would be there for me, in whatever way I needed him to be, was the rare and precious cargo I took home that day. And I did get my four weeks of summer with Dash. It took another half-dozen phone calls to Peter, but I got them. We went to Lake of the Woods and had a great time.

That September, Dash was our best man at an intimate garden wedding. My best friend, Sandy Cameron, and her husband, Terry, my dad, Jim, my brother, Dave, and his wife, Bev, celebrated with us. My mom was visiting relatives in England, a trip long planned. Dave's parents were on the phone listening to the service from Winnipeg, with champagne glasses in hand for the toast. Dash wore a soft sea-blue shirt and neat black pants. He shone as he posed for photographs, grinning widely and proudly, signing his name on the marriage certificate with a face heavy with concentration. He told me how he wanted to make sure he wrote his name perfectly on the lines. "You've done it beautifully," I told him. At forty-one, I had my son with me, I was marrying a man whose beauty and generosity endure in the same abundance today, fourteen years later, and I was eight days from meeting Colby, the first of two beautiful baby boys Dave and I would have together. Though I still reeled from the court's decision, I had a family, I had love — I had a whole world. "Custody" was just a word for the paperwork, I decided. What happened in our *lives* was what counted.

But losses began to accumulate. I discovered that, along with my ban from the school, I wasn't called when Dash was sick. Peter was called, and if he wasn't home or the nanny didn't answer the phone, Dash stayed at school in the sickroom. Because I had to go through Peter for school notices, I never got any. I didn't know when sports days were, or Dash's school plays. While missing the events of Dash's school life was bizarre and upsetting, what was far worse was losing my ability to continue the natural bonding that takes place when your child knows you are actively involved with his school. The child feels loved and cared for and generally does better at school when the parents participate. I knew what it was to be an active member of Dash's school community. I had been involved for his two years of preschool and then kindergarten, and when I lost all that, I was keenly aware that there was no way to make up or substitute for it. On what planet would a school want a loving, committed parent excluded from school? I knew no other parent who was so cut off from their child's school life, and I felt dirty and stained, a marginal person, a lurking pariah. *A bad parent.*

But I never drove by the school to try and catch a glimpse of Dash, or grab an illicit cuddle with him, or try secretly to meet with his teachers for news. I never pushed anything. I was the picture of propriety. I didn't skulk. I couldn't do anything that accorded with the view of me that Peter had put out at the trial. I couldn't be seen in tears — the over-emotional madwoman. I couldn't screen out Peter's drunken calls — the judgmental socialite. I couldn't accuse him of telling Dash terrible things about me, which I knew he was doing — the paranoid loose screw. I had been tainted. As in politics, Peter had framed the issue — me — and I couldn't get in front of the debate again. I had no standing to argue. In my private life I lived in a beautiful house in Kerrisdale, I was married to a wealthy business-man, but in legal terms I was the woman who had lost all custodial rights to my child, a punishment I thought was only meted out to crack whores and deadbeat dads. So I had to act the very opposite of that reputation and incrementally restore myself by being who *I* was, not who Peter said I was.

I wouldn't have cared what Peter did if he had just trained his sights on me. But I was never so naïve as to think Peter could — or wanted to — leave Dash out of it. That little boy represented the best means of getting me to do whatever Peter wanted. In Peter's growing preoccupation with diminishing my role in our son's life, Dash became the ultimate lever. Six years old as of August, Dash had to see it all, hear it all, witness everything. If Peter was to be the one parent Dash had, Dash himself had to believe that life would be better that way. Knocking me down, morning, noon, and night, was Peter's chosen method of achieving that end.

One Friday afternoon, when I was at their door to pick up Dash for the weekend, with Dash standing right next to him, Peter snarled, "Get off my steps and go and wait in your car." My face flushing with rage and frustration, I walked back to the car and got in. I would not bite. For Dash I acted as if it were okay. I smiled brightly when he jumped in the car, and we both pretended that I wasn't the only person in the world who wasn't allowed on their doorstep. I had become a fool, too: rather than "Mommy" or "your mom," in their house I was "Yo-Yo Head" and worse, "Pam." I had become a casual acquaintance. The first time Dash called me "Pam," he did it with such naturalness and nonchalance that I nearly choked on my coffee. "Pam, Daddy wants to talk to you," he said, handing me the phone. When Dash and I were settling in later to read a bedtime story, I asked, "Does Daddy still call me 'Pam' when he's talk-ing with you?" and he became so serious that I regretted bringing it up.

"Sometimes 'Pam,'" he said very quietly. "Sometimes other things."

"Like what, Dash?" I asked.

"I don't think you'll like it, Mommy," he said in an unhappy little voice. "He calls you the F.A."

I crinkled my forehead in confusion and said nothing, so Dash went on. "He calls you the Fucking Asshole, Mommy."

Shock crept over me, thinking of what it must feel like to hear that kind of talk about your mother. With my heart hammering, I pulled Dash closer and asked, "How does that make you feel?"

"Very sad, Mommy."

*Very sad.* Another mom with a child in Dash's class called me one afternoon to tell me she had just seen Dash sitting alone on the school steps, crying. When she had asked him what was wrong, Dash had replied with an astonishingly grown-up, "It's personal." When he burst into tears in my arms a little while later, saying, "Mommy, I have a bad life," his distress was so overwhelming that my first thought was to steal Dash away.

Another Friday afternoon, Dash jumped into my car grinning and wiggling two loose baby teeth at me. All weekend he toyed with them, making a crunching sound as he used his tongue to push them out before sucking them back in. They were Dash's first teeth, and losing them was a special occasion. By Sunday night they were hanging halfway out of his mouth on a thread of pink gum, and Dash finally asked Dave if he would help him get them out. They found a soft facecloth and, with a couple of gentle twists, the little teeth came free. "I can't wait to go to bed!" Dash shouted. "The tooth fairy is going to visit!" He put the teeth into a little cotton-wool bed I had made.

"Why don't you call your dad and tell him you've just lost your teeth?" I said blithely.

"Yeah!" he cried and ran to the phone.

As I dialled the number for him, I told Dash he should take one of his teeth back to his dad's house so the tooth fairy could visit him there, too. Dash had already thought of that. He wanted two loonies for his teeth, not just one! He pressed the receiver to his ear and waited for his father to pick up the phone, his mouth set in a gap-toothed grin. He wore his joy so openly.

"Dad, I lost those two teeth!" he shouted into the phone, but he got no further than that. I watched, horrified, as Dash listened without speaking for a full minute, his face collapsing. Peter demanded to talk to me, and Dash stepped aside, shaken. "You have Dash's teeth!" he shouted. "*I'm his custodial parent!* You had no right to take them out! Dash is to deliver *both* teeth back home on Monday afternoon!"


Greater and greater interference flowed into our lives. After the trial, Peter told me he had a new phone number for the house, so I took it down and began using it, but found it curious, and then maddening, that the phone was rarely answered. Weeks passed. Night after night I would dial the number to talk with Dash, but increasingly simply couldn't. Instead of hearing Dash's happy voice, my ears would fill with endless ringing, an answering machine clicking on, or, later, a fax machine. I often sent a note saying, "Please turn off the fax machine, I am trying to get through to Dash," but the machine's shrill scream continued to mirror my inner one. I was ashamed to realize that I felt intimidated by the barriers Peter put up and, mindful of aggravating the situation by calling too often, I limited myself to three attempts a night. I don't know if Dash ever knew that I had called; certainly he never called me back. When once or twice a week someone did answer the phone, I was unprepared and unnerved. Once, when I hadn't spoken to Dash all week and actually got Peter,

I begged him to get Dash to call me, but Peter said calmly, "It's not my fault Dash never calls you back. Dash doesn't *want* to call you, and I'll be damned if I'm going to drag him to the phone and force him to speak to his mother." Stung, I hung up and stared at the phone. Dash didn't want to call me? Why? He was six years old.

On the nights I couldn't get through, Dave would come into my den and instantly know. "Oh, well, no one's home," I would say, trying to sound casual, but my smile would be wobbly and my eyes would threaten tears. A whole year of this passed; then one day I was looking over Dash's new soccer schedule — which another child's mom had faxed me because Peter had not — and by chance I saw that the number listed as Dash's home number was not the "new" one Peter had given me after the trial. A plummeting, sick feeling hit my stomach. I scrambled to the phone and dialled the number listed on the schedule, and Peter answered immediately. He was shocked to hear my voice. "Get off this line and use your own!" he bellowed, and I knew then that my number was a dud. *This man truly wants me to fall out of Dash's life*, I thought, for the first time articulating the fear that had lingered near my heart for a year now. My hope that the future would one day be normal lay shattered, in that moment. I was paralyzed. *Where does this end? When a child is in the hands of someone who calculates this way, how does it end?*

Using the main telephone number I now spoke to Dash more often than before, but the evasions continued. Once Peter picked up the phone and said, "Dash isn't home," but Dash, having picked up the other extension, quietly said, "I'm right here, Dad." *What is this doing to him? Calls from Mom are bad?* The hang-ups went on. The shouts to get off the line. Peter had his own version of events prepared in an affidavit: "Anytime the Respondent has called our home and asked to speak to Dashiell, she has been accommodated. . . . Dashiell has been advised of his Mother's call, and encouraged, *very much encouraged*, to return the call." Some months were worse than others — that August I was able to speak to Dash only once — but on average it was about once a week. Dash had become increasingly uncomfortable on the phone. Sometimes, in the middle of a sentence, he would suddenly lower his voice and whisper, "I love you," then hang up, leaving me clutching the phone. "Dash? Dash are you there?" Other times he was buoyant and cheerful and I wondered, *Is Dash alone in the house?* I wanted our lives to be *normal*. Why weren't they? I wanted to call up and say, "Hi, Dash! There's a great show on TV tonight I think you would love!" or "Don't forget your rollerblades this weekend. Big D is going to take you around the seawall." Having to orchestrate everything ten times over crushed my spontaneity. It crushed *me*.

Peter's new wife, Suzanne MacGregor, had been my great hope. When she moved in and then married Peter in April 1991, I saw her as a sober person, a professional woman, a *tough* woman, who wouldn't let Peter get away with bad behaviour. That hope had been crushed quickly, too. When Peter was too drunk to drive over and pick up Dash, Suzanne came instead, but wouldn't say a word about Peter's drinking that would help me. She later told the court Peter never drank. The reason she drove over to get Dash was because of the "problems" at exchange times. She was sparing Peter and Dash the upset. On the stand at the second custody trial in 1996, she would say he drank so little, in fact, that one of her pet domestic peeves was his "half-finished" beer bottles left in the fridge. She wrote her own florid affidavits about how happy Dash was and how great a parent Peter was. I often wondered if it was through Suzanne's intimate knowledge of the family-law personnel in Vancouver that Peter learned exactly what to tell Dr. Elterman that would gain him the recommendation he needed. Who knows? Suzanne and Peter's son, Greg, who still lived with them, certainly gave powerhouse performances belittling my role as Dash's mom and turning blind eyes to Peter's growing parental flaws: the drinking, the *telephonus interruptus*, and his unhealthy preoccupation with Dash — and me. I could understand a son's loyalty from Greg, but I couldn't understand how Suzanne tolerated having to share Peter's attention with me. How much time did sending faxes and leaving abusive messages for me take up in their lives? How much time at the dinner table was absorbed by their strategies against me? Why did Suzanne tolerate Dash being the centre of attention that they all huddled around? Was it because I was believed to be every bit as dangerous as I was made out to be? Greg, who had lived happily with me for seven years while his father and I were married, testified at the trial that I was enraged, demanding, and impossible to live with. With an icy hostility, Suzanne refused all my attempts at reconciliation and pleas from Dave — as the other step-parent — to work together. She refused countless offers to come in out of the cold and have a cup of tea when she came to pick up Dash — staying in the car or outside the front door instead. Christmas drinks were turned down. I was never invited to share Dash's birthday or go trick-or-treating with him. There was no "in" for me with which I could turn their heads back to rationality. "Just let me be Dash's mom!" I wanted to tell them. "I'm no threat. I don't want anything from you — just my son on my appointed days and the ability to speak to him on the phone." But I guess I gave them a common enemy, and living their lives preoccupied with their version of Dash's welfare became a glue that bound them together.

With Peter's household so ordered, he set his sights on ours. Peter sent letters telling me I was manhandling Dash. He sent letters accusing Dave of intruding into his relationship with his son. We received faxes on Mondays telling us we had "interrogated" Dash all weekend. At our house Dash had always been encouraged to talk about and ask about whatever he wanted, but within weeks of the first of these accusations, Dash clammed up. He stopped telling me things — normal things, six-year-old things — about his life, about school, about his father and Suzanne. Conversations that included the phrase "your daddy," no matter how innocent, provoked visible suspicion and discomfort in Dash. Something as probing as "Are you going away with your dad for the long weekend?" was an ordeal for him. Our exchanges were filtered through the prism of his newly complex relationship with his father, and it crystallized in an utterance that, once spoken, came thereafter with alarming frequency. Dash and I were in the kitchen. I was unpacking the groceries, we were chatting away happily.

"My dad and Suzanne are going out for dinner tonight," Dash said out of the blue.

"Well now, that's a really nice thing to do on a Friday night," I said, reaching up high to put away the tea. "There are some great restaurants near you. Where are they going?"

Dash lashed out immediately. "It's none of your business," he said.

I was stunned. In "none of your business," the child molester's "Let's keep this a secret" rang in my ears. In Dash's words — so alien to a six-year-old — I finally realized that whatever went on in that house was completely private, with Dash, too, now complicit. Most things became none of my business: whether he liked his new teacher, what he had done on the weekend, trivial and harmless details, guarded like state secrets. Dash came to believe that innocent inquiries from his mom and stepdad about his day and his life were "interrogations" to get "dirt" to take to court. Dash went home and told his dad, "Yeah, they did. They questioned me *all weekend*."

We "abused" Dash, too. Peter wrote a vitriolic letter telling us that I had yelled at Dash and grabbed him by the testicles in anger. It brought ice to my veins. *How far will this man go?* Peter knew better than anyone that I never, ever, used physical discipline with Dash (nor have I ever with my other children; it's a parenting style I am dead against), and no court in all the subsequent years of accusations believed for a minute that I ever laid a finger on him. So Peter turned his gaze on Dave. As a man and a stepfather he was a far easier target. Peter sent letters declaring that Dave "had better stop abusing Dash," but he never informed family services or the police or Dr. Elterman that Dash was being abused at our home. Dash began to say Dave was "mean" to him "all the time," although when we asked him, in desperation, what he meant by "mean," it came to such crimes as "He takes the big piece of pie for himself and gives me the small piece."

Tension flowed daily through our lives, as I'm sure they were meant to. Dave's increasingly visible frustration with the abuse charges was reasonable, his outrage appropriate. He wanted to do something, anything! But I told him, "You have to suck it in, Dave. We're dealing with a sick man. We've got to stay non-confrontational. Just as we can't deviate from the court order, we have to do everything right. We can't give Peter anything to use against us. He has Dash. He has the court's nod. We have nothing here."

Dave knew my approach was the only choice we really had, but he couldn't always accept his inability to act. The accusations were deeply personal and highly offensive. We often rehashed our positions over dinner or in front of the fireplace. "This is bullshit!" he would half-shout, holding the latest "abuse" affidavit. "Dash doesn't think this! Why is he telling Peter these things?" I hated these flare-ups, because I was often exhausted from having fended Peter off myself, or from trying three or four times to get through to Dash, or from just being a new mom on the go all day. I didn't need to fight Dave as well, but his feelings were real and I never, ever, shut him down. Ironically enough, instead of avoiding the issue, engaging it allowed us yet another forum within which we worked on and tended our marriage.

"We've been here so many times," I said, trying to calm him. "Peter *wants* us to fight about this. You know that, I know you do. So we need to stay focused on the real issue here. You know this is Peter. Dash is telling him what he wants to hear, not only because Peter rewards him for doing it but because Dash is insecure otherwise. Remember 'Mommy, I have a bad life?' He's not talking about the price of yen, he's talking about a life that's scary sometimes."

"I know. But, Pam, I mean . . . God!" he said, running his hands through his hair. "How can I not defend myself? Isn't this slander or something? I love Dash!"

"Dave, listen to me. Dash has to do this. You threaten Peter because Dash loves you so much, that's it. It's not you. It's not *about* you. We have to keep seeing Dash and trying to give him a normal life that way."

"Peter's telling Dash what to think."

"Yes."

"He's telling him what to feel."

"Yes. So we have to be his safe harbour. We have to stay out of Peter's battle."

"Okay. I know. I do know this. It's just so frustrating to be behind the ball all the time. Waiting instead of acting. Reactive instead of proactive."

"None of this is how I *want* to play this, Dave. It's how I *have* to play this."

"Ah," Dave said softly. "The art of war."

"The art of war."

Dave was quiet for a moment. "Pam, I don't think he's ever going to change," he said carefully.

Tears came immediately to my eyes, and I sat up straight. "I can't go there, Dave," I said firmly. "I can't. Because if I believe that, then I lose Dash."

At my reality, Dave slumped. His anger evaporated and he composed himself before my grief and reached out and touched my arm. "So I should step back?" he asked.

"No, don't step back. Above all Dash needs to know that we love him, no matter what. Just let go of your expectations of him. Let go of the history you had with him. Don't demand anything of the relationship and don't take any of this personally."

"It's impossible not to."

"It's not impossible, but it's really hard. I've had to do it, too. We have to give them nothing to write affidavits about and nothing they can pressure Dash with. Your disappointment overflows sometimes; it's not helping. Your *need* is visible, and it makes Dash worry about loyalty to his dad."

"I know. It's just so—"

I touched his face with my open hand and he stopped and closed his eyes into it. "Dave, this isn't about us. Dash *loves* you. He just can't show it. I need you to put aside your relationship with him. The most important thing is that Dash has time with *me*. I'm his mother and I have to try and parent him from here. I need you to just kind of filter in and out. Apply no pressure to do things. Can you do that?"

Of course he could. Dave made a graceful exit from the tattered remains of what had once been a delightful, easy friendship, because he had no choice. He had been made a wedge eroding my already fragile relationship with my son, so to help save Dash and me as a unit, Dave stopped inviting him to putter about with him in the garden for hours on end, talking about plants and trees and nature. He stopped taking Dash skiing. He waited for Dash to come to him, and he waited patiently, but it was a devastating, utterly unnatural adjustment.

It broke my heart, too. Their relationship had been so beautiful to watch. Dave's embrace of Dash had solidified my feelings for him as a partner and the future father of our children. I knew I would never again see Dash rip open the curtains at our Whistler cabin and hear him call to Dave, "Come on, Big D! Let's get our skis on!" By the time the accusations began, when Dash was six, they had become soulmates, and when Dave moved into the background, a big piece of him died along with the relationship. He looked physically crumpled by his loss.

Other people had to drop out of Dash's life, too. My best friend, Sandy Cameron, had been a fixture in Dash's life from the day he was born. She had been there his whole life. He understood my relationship with Sandy and loved her because I did. Sandy had been my best friend for most of my life. I don't remember a time she wasn't on the other end of the phone for me, or sharing my lunch-hour or, with her husband, Terry, enjoying one of the many dinner we had together. Inevitably we would be pregnant together, and we gave birth to beautiful baby boys three months apart, Dash in August and Warren in October. Warren had his mother's amazing blue eyes and his father's blond hair, and Dash had my big brown eyes and tawny blond mop. As young mothers, Sandy and I met for walks in the park or at the beach, pushing our strollers, drinking coffee from Thermoses. We talked and talked. We wanted our sons to be best friends and, with no effort at all, they were, together for every birthday, Christmas party, Halloween, Thanksgiving, and as many play-dates as we could arrange. Sandy and I looked on with wonder and pride as we watched our boys grow and learn together.

Sandy was there when I despaired over my marriage to Peter. She was at one of our dinner parties when he went to the bathroom four times in an evening, coming back to the table with white powder under his nose. "Vitamin C," Peter explained. She was there for me in June 1988, the morning after Peter finally exploded into violence and threw me against the kitchen wall. When I got away, he grabbed the back of my dress and threw me into the den, slapping, punching, and kicking me. He banged my head over and over against the den wall, and with shock and mortification, I felt a warm burn down my legs and knew I had wet myself. I went to see Sandy the next day, after my doctor documented my injuries and wrote a report I filed away and tried to forget. My head, buttocks, arms, and legs were covered in bruises. Sandy was less horrified than deeply, deeply wounded for me. She knew how much I had loved Peter. She hugged me hard. She just said, "I'm so sorry." I pressed no charges and I stayed with Peter for another six months before I had the courage to leave him. Sandy was there, with my mother and my brother, Dave, at the West Vancouver house I rented. Again, she hugged me hard and helped me unload Dash's teddies, books, and his little pine stool. Warren came for our weekends in Whistler, and the boys skied all day and collapsed in their beds at night. When Dash started to hesitate in his relationship with Dave, and later with me, we held up Warren as an enticement for Dash to come and enjoy himself. Whistler weekends became fraught for Dash, but, with Warren there, Dash could say to his father, "I have to go, Warren is coming." Dash hid behind Warren, at least for those first couple of years. By the time Dash was seven or eight, all four of us — Sandy, Terry, Dave, and I — would use whatever we could to get Dash to spend time with me. Warren was Sandy's gift, but soon even he was cast aside.


After isolating Dash from many of the people he loved, Peter began pressing the most valuable part of my relationship with Dash: our time together. By the end of Peter's first year of sole custody, he was cutting my access indiscriminately, using dozens of semi-plausible reasons. Peter would take Dash on trips and bring him back half a week late, erasing my Wednesdays or weekend access days. He would cancel or shorten Dash's time with me in order to get him to doctor and dentist appointments that didn't exist. Dash was, for the most part, still the happy, cheery child he always had been, and he never questioned these cancellations or expressed disappointment. They came so often, maybe he was simply used to them. I never even mentioned the irritating, curious cancellations to Dash, but it was hard to keep up appearances. Once Peter wanted Dash home early in order to take him to a birthday party, but when I dropped a gift around to the birthday boy's house (instead of dropping off my child, whose father insisted on driving him to each and every party or sleepover), his surprised mother told me that I was five days early for the party. I could only get out an idiotic, "Oh! I must have got my dates wrong!" before lurching for the sanctuary of my car, my blood boiling. And although I never tried to keep Dash with me, and I never lobbied Peter for makeup time when he picked up Dash, my antennae was wired. *Is this deliberate? Anger is one thing, but these sabo-*

*tages of our time?* I saw what was happening but tried desperately to see the other side. I second-guessed myself even in the face of overwhelming evidence. It was hard not to start obsessing about the numbers. Four hours here. An afternoon there. Two evenings here. A whole weekend. Lost. As Dash spent time doing anything with anyone but his mother. *Are my lost hours and days just coincidences, part of the life of an access parent?* I asked myself. Dave's frustration would rise. "You are the only parent giving up access time, Pam. Peter *never* loses time. He doesn't even give you makeup days. He offers you time you are supposed to have with Dash anyway."

I discovered through another mom that Dash finished school at noon every second Friday, so I called Peter and asked if I could pick him up at one or two instead of the usual four o'clock on those Fridays. I got a flat out "No." Instead Dash stayed with his nanny until I arrived at four. Sometimes on Friday afternoons Peter would call and tell me that Dash didn't want to see me until Saturday, unaware that I had just spoken to Dash, who was planning on me coming to get him that afternoon.

Sometimes Dash was whisked off for hamburgers just as I was due to arrive; other times he waited eagerly for me at his door and sprang out and hugged me excitedly, leaping into my car and holding my hand tight the whole drive back to our house. At the same time that Peter wrote in one of his countless affidavits, "Dashy is happy, content and exuberant in every aspect of his life, except when it comes to these access visits. Dash wants to visit every second weekend and he doesn't really like mid-week visits, at the end of a school day," Dash would be in my car, chattering away merrily and blasting questions at me about what was planned for the evening or weekend.

Still, when I drove over to pick up Dash for our access time, I often found no one home. I'd wait for a half hour or so, fighting back tears and rising frustration, then drive home alone, rehearsing my ever-unspoken questions: *Why doesn't he think about what this does to Dash? Why, when Dash lives with three professional adults and a nanny, can no one respect the access order and have Dash packed and ready to go when I arrive? Where are they? How will this end? When will I see him next?* The first of many times Suzanne took on the role of gatekeeper and refused me access to Dash, I turned on my heel, brushed away hot tears, and called my lawyer from the car. He told me to go home and then sent a fax to the Hart house, saying I would be arriving again at seven that evening to pick up Dash. Breaking out of his background role, Dave volunteered to go. He needed to do something. I had come home in tears yet again. When Dave arrived at seven o'clock, Peter and Greg were standing guard at the door.

"Go away, little boy. You're not getting Dash," Peter sneered.

"Get off our property," Greg said. "You're trespassing and we will call the police if you don't leave." Peter wrote an affidavit. "Pamela complains of a denial of access. Her accusation is false. At no time have I denied access. I have conducted myself, regarding access, in a manner that is quite the opposite. I have been flexible and generous." Dave had worn a little recording device that night, and the whole exchange was on tape. But what could we do? We might have a tape, but they had Dash.

Once, on a hunch, when Dash wasn't at home when I arrived to get him, I drove to a local park and found him playing there with his nanny. My heart leapt to see him, as it always did, and I parked and walked over to them. Dash called out, "Mommy!" and grinned from ear to ear when he saw me. When I got to him, he reached up for a hug, then hung his arms around my neck and snuggled in.

"Oh, it's so *good* to see you!" I said, as Dash twirled my hair in his fingers. He smelled of dirt and soap. He was divine. "Brown eyes to brown eyes, Dash." That was the way I always got his attention. Dash looked at me, smiling, expectant. "Guess what? It's our weekend together. Do you want to come over?"

Rose, the nanny, flashed a glance at Dash and shifted uncomfortably on the park bench. The seven-year-old boy whose father wouldn't "push him out the door" to see me shrieked "Yes!" waved goodbye to his nanny, took my hand, and ran all the way across the field with me to the car.

# Chapter 2
# The Disappearing Boy

Dash loved his dad, he loved me, he loved Dave, and he loved Suzanne. What Dash wanted most in the whole world, as he told Dave when they saw a shooting star a year earlier, was to have all four of us living together in the same house. All the people he loved, together. Dash wanted what every child from a broken family wants: to not have to choose between his parents.

But a year after the first custody trial, Peter enrolled Dash on a soccer team that played their games on my Saturdays and trained on my Wednesdays. Peter made himself the team's coach, a position of authority and a new way to pull on eight-year-old Dash's loyalty. Now, when Dash wanted to ski with me on weekends, he had to answer to not only his father, but his *coach*. *What do you mean you're skiing with your mother this weekend? Well, what about your team? What about your coach? Gee, Dash, you're letting us down, kiddo.* I wasn't asked if Dash could play soccer on my weekends and practise on my Wednesday access nights, and I found out about it only because Peter refused me access after I arrived at the house to pick up Dash one Friday night, citing "Dash's first soccer game" the next morning.

"Couldn't you at least have asked me, Peter?"

"Jesus Christ, here we go. What are you complaining about? You should be happy Dash is playing soccer. Don't be so selfish. This is for Dash, not you or me."

"It's great that he's going to be playing, but—"

"You want him to be happy don't you, Pamela?"

"Peter, you know I do. That's *all* I want."

"Good. Oh, and by the way, because I'm the coach, Dash wants to stay with me tonight, to get to the game together in the morning. You know, to carry the balls and whatnot."

*So this is it.* He told me that my weekends with Dash would now begin not on Friday after school, but on Saturdays, after their game. It was all I could do to get back to the car. *I'm losing a night a week for the whole soccer season.* As always, I needed to check my paranoia with Dave. "If Dash really wants this, maybe I *am* being selfish by wanting to be with Dash on those Fridays?"

"Pam—"

"Dash is a boy growing into a man. Maybe he really does want to spend Fridays with his dad to get ready for the game? Colby may want the same thing one day. I don't know."

"Maybe. But we've seen a lot the last few years, Pam," Dave said.

"You think he's making Dash choose between time with me — 'Geez, what a drag that you have to be with your mom this weekend, Dash' — and the enticing package of dad and the soccer team?"

"That's how it looks to me."

"But what if it's not? What if it's just what happens when boys from split families want to play soccer?"

"Well, what would Sandy say? Would Terry pull this if they split up and he put Warren on a soccer team?"

"Nope. And Warren wouldn't care who got him to soccer as long as one of them did."

"Right."

"What do I do then? Go to court and say, 'Don't let this man coach soccer'? That's madness. So what? What do I do?"

"I don't know. I really don't. Peter's always a step ahead of us."

"Dash will suffer if I do something involving the courts, and if I do nothing I lose a night I may never get back. Which is worse for Dash?"

As my shoulders slumped, Dave reached for my hand. "Look," he said, "at some point Peter's going to be left behind, talking to himself, plotting and planning with no one listening, least of all Dash. It'll be okay. Just keep going over there and getting him."

So I did. I went every Friday, and when I could get him, which was every few weeks, we went together to his Saturday games. Despite Peter's malevolent looks in front of all the other moms and dads, I gave out oranges at halftime and cheered and clapped from the sidelines, watching my beautiful eight-year-old running his heart out on the field. The delight of it all didn't last long, though. Peter ignored my weekly requests that he send along the soccer uniform with Dash those times he came with me on Friday nights, so I called the league and got an extra team jersey, shorts, and socks. I picked up a pair of soccer boots, too, to make sure Dash could get ready at either house on Saturday mornings. When Peter found out he demanded that I hand over the uniform. I refused. He repeated his demand; I refused again. Then, when I was out one morning, he told Colby and Quinten's nanny, Mimi, to immediately go through Dash's drawers for "every sock and short." She was told to put them in a bag on the front step ("Get them out there!" Peter had yelled), where he would pick them up immediately. Mimi had had enough runins with Peter to know first-hand how angry and difficult he could be. Despite her strength of character, Mimi was no match for Peter. He intimidated and frightened her. Mimi knew exactly what it meant to be gathering up Dash's soccer clothes and giving them to Peter, and she was in tears as she did it. She knew the reason I had got them in the first place. I wasn't there to protect her from Peter's demands, and she couldn't refuse him. Peter said Dash wanted "to wake up on Saturday morning, at his home, put on his uniform, shin pads and choose his foot gear. He wants to be here when we receive phone calls early Saturday morning from other teammates, and when I speak to other coaches. He wants to be part of the team. Remember, his father is the coach."

*Ah, yes, the coach.*

"Imagine yourself as a little eight-year-old girl being dressed in your tutu and pointe shoes and delivered to a dance session by your father when your mother is the instructor?" he continued. My gut screamed. *This is not right. Why should an eight-year-old boy be made to feel bad for not being with his dad to get dressed for soccer? Peter is a grown man! Why does he do this to his son?* I watched Dash on the field and saw a boy who just wanted to have what other children had. He wanted to play soccer; he wanted to ski. He wanted to see and love both his parents. He didn't want to choose.

Two Saturdays later, Peter called me early and demanded that I bring Dash back to his house immediately, but I stood my ground. "I will get Dash to the game, Peter," I told him, but he hissed, "If you don't have him over to my house by 9:30, I'll make sure you never get any access. I'll never let this rest, and I'll fight you to the end."

Under the pressure he was receiving from home, Dash crumbled. How could he say, "Isn't it my weekend with Mom?" without letting "their" team down. I think he tried. In the same way I used Dash's little school friend Myles to get Dash to come over, Dash used him to try and stay — "I've got Myles here." But within a couple of months, Dash was able to tell me firmly and to my face that he had "the right to decide" where he spent his Friday nights, and he wanted to spend them with his dad.

Through soccer, Peter obliterated the ski weekends in Whistler and nearly all my Friday nights with Dash. I would often lose Saturdays and Saturday nights, too, because, regardless of the fact that Dash was supposed to be with me for the weekend, Peter would arrange a post-game play-date for Dash with a teammate, which would drift into the evening and more often than not become a sleepover. Spending time with Mom, already a grossly devalued exercise, was quickly forgotten amid all the fun.

More people fell away. Like those with Sandy and my brother, Dave, the wonderful relationship Dash had with my mother disintegrated. For a whole year before she died, two months before my third son, Quin, was born, when Dash was eight, he showed no interest in seeing her, but I couldn't believe it was really true. This was not the boy who just a couple of years earlier had chattered noisily on the phone to his Gramma, then waited at the front door for her to arrive and take him hand in hand off to the park. When he stayed the weekend with his Gramma, every few weeks in those early years, Dash would lead me to his bedroom there and show me the project they had started that day — a Lego town, or a complicated colouring book — or he'd take me to his teddy bears, all lined up on the shelves of his bookcase, and tell me in great detail what each one had had for afternoon tea with Gramma.

"This big one, Tufty, eats a lot of food, Mom. He's a greedy guts. Gramma said he needs to exercise and watch what he eats, so I gave him my banana today and I ate the muffin Gramma made."

"Well Gramma knows what she's talking about, Dash. Hey, perhaps you should take him jogging in the park with you!"

"No, Mommy. Bears don't go jogging," he said seriously, pulling Tufty's sweater over his swollen and misshapen tummy. "Ooh. I think his ear needs sewing. Look, Mom."

"Gramma will fix him."

"Let's go ask her." And off we'd go.

My brother's children weren't born until Dash was five (Colby was a year later again), so Dash had Gramma's time and attention all to himself. His comfort with and enjoyment of his Gramma came from spending such a lot of time with her. It was a privilege my father did not quite share. My parents had divorced when I was eighteen, and though they remained close for the rest of their lives, it was Gramma who got the bulk of Dash's attention. Dash loved his Grandpa to bits, but Gramma was the constant in his life. They would eat boiled eggs and soldiers for lunch and then while away whole afternoons playing board games and cards. They'd spend Sunday mornings preparing and cooking favourite meals like French toast with icing sugar. "Gramma lets me sprinkle it on myself with the big shaker!" he would tell me slyly, as though it were naughty. Then they would do it all again for dinner. The litany of little joys I heard when I came into the house after their days together, I can still hear today. "Mommy, guess what! Gramma taught me a game today. Crib! It's so much fun with her and guess what, too, guess what? I won!" "Gramma says we're going to the toy store next week to get some more playdough, because we ran out. You know what we do, Mom? We get out all her cookie cutters and make shapes!" "Do I get to sleep over again soon, Mom? Gramma says it's time to make the Christmas pudding. I have to stir it and I get to make a wish! Can I go, Mom?" "No, Mom! I can't tell you the wish! Gramma says if you tell anyone, the wish won't come true. Not even you!"

But slowly, in those first two years after the trial, Dash grew distant. He would be uninterested in speaking on the phone with her, and it became disheartening to try and convince him to say hello. Much as I tried to keep his relationship with Gramma alive, even when Dash wouldn't see her, he eventually showed so little interest that I stopped doing so. When my time with Dash became sporadic, I had to focus on things that would interest and please him, so he would enjoy himself enough to want to stay and then come back. Those early relationships, with Warren, with Sandy, with my brother, Dave, and with my mother, so infused with history and meaning, faded out until there was nothing left but a dim memory attached to a name.

The effects of not being free to look forward to seeing me, or to talk happily in his home about our time together, to see the people he had loved so much, or to soak up the love Dave was so desperate to give him started to show. At school Dash ran over to the window of his classroom, three storeys up, and threatened to jump out. "There is no reason to live any more," he said to his friend Dorio, "and if no one was here, I'd jump." I didn't even hear about this until years later. Level-headed Dorio pleaded with Dash not to jump and desperately listed all the reasons Dash should live. Dash told another friend around the same time, "My life is a mess." Was the suicidal threat a cry for help or a prank? Who knows, but a girl who knew Dash at that time told me years later in a hushed, angry, voice, "You can bet there would have been no support at home over that incident. His dad would have yelled at him, telling him not to do stuff at school that would reflect badly on him." Peter still claimed far and wide, usually in the form of a florid letter to me or a random affidavit that Dash was "happy, confident, doing well in school, and well cared for." He wrote that description weeks before Dash ran desperately to the classroom window. Suzanne had written, "Dash is the happiest child I have ever seen. He is enthusiastic, playful, and has a wonderful sense of humour and fun. He whistles and sings around the house." Their lawyer friend, Dave Martin, believed Peter's "incredibly balanced guidance" allowed Dash to "thrive." But Dash wasn't thriving — he was regressing, rebelling, and retreating — by no means all the time, but often enough to jar me. It was worse when he hadn't seen me for a couple of weeks, and better when school was in session, but there was no pattern to it. We never knew until we saw Dash whether he would be his old self or this new, malcontent version.

Dash had been well loved as a baby and had grown into an engaging and easy-going young boy. But now I caught sidelong glances from him that contained silent, inexplicable resentment. His eyes betrayed discomfort and confusion. He said strange things that repeated his father's view of me. He told me I didn't have a "real job," and he began to compare us with his father. "My dad's garage is bigger than yours," he would say, or "My dad's cabin is bigger than yours," "My dad has a boat and you don't." Instead of telling jokes or clowning around at the dinner table like he used to, he often had outbursts and banged his silverware on the table to protest the late arrival of his food. He had a new and strong aversion to even the tiny amounts of structure I tried to impose, shouting, "I don't need one!" when I suggested we get him a haircut and "I don't need it and I don't want it!" when I asked him to have a shower after a muddy soccer game. No parent in the whole world has had a child that doesn't do those things now and then, but with Dash it was so peculiar, because it was simply *not the Dash I knew.* Dave and I threw a dinner party one Saturday night to say farewell to some friends who were moving to Rome. Dash knew them and I had told him I would spend all my time with him before the guests arrived, but Dash flew into a rage anyway. He demanded I make him a different meal. "I don't want to be here if there's going to be a dinner party tonight," he told me aggressively, refusing his second dinner, too. He called home, and Peter and Suzanne dutifully arrived within minutes, despite my pleas to not let Dash play us off against one another. They didn't even take Dash home. They took him to the dinner party *they* were attending that night.

That was an extraordinary blip, but for the most part changes in Dash's behaviour were hard to spot: they were inconstant and inconsistent. We all saw the change in him, but it was impossible to describe to anyone else, and we second-guessed each other, too. I forced myself to under-react and concentrated on just loving Dash, to try and counter what I had long suspected he was getting at home — manipulations of his needs, plays on his loyalty. I watched him like a hawk and made mental lists of the things he had enjoyed before that didn't seem to matter anymore. He told me he was "never homesick." He didn't seem to care about whether or not he saw me and never appeared upset that we had missed a night or a weekend together. He shrugged it off. His reasons for cancelling time with me were always vague. "I have friends coming over," he might say, but when I asked, "Who?" he would say, "I don't know," or "Oh, I haven't made the arrangements yet." I would tell him I was disappointed to not be seeing him and he would just say, "I'll see you soon. It doesn't matter, Mom." *It doesn't matter. Don't worry. It's okay.* Why was it okay with him that he lost all this time with his mother and people he cared about? He didn't say *a word* about it. He asked no questions about it — *ever.*

I saw in Dash a boy in distress. His emotional skin was getting thinner. When two-and-a-half-year-old Colby knocked apart the Lego house Dash had painstakingly built, Dash screamed at him, burst into tears, and hid behind the couch. It was a real shock because Dash had always been a resilient little boy. Another time he snapped "Where's my food?" but then followed it with, "Mom, after dinner, can you massage my back?" To others, Dash looked fine. Even his "tantrums" could be considered "age appropriate." What child doesn't act out? He never became wild-eyed and crazy. He didn't say anything *really* outrageous. "Dave ruined Daddy's business," something he said a number of times, isn't *that* bizarre. I could have rationalized Dash's lack of concern about his relationship with me, I could have rationalized his intense loyalty to his father, the way he kissed his father's floor when he came back from visits with me (Suzanne and Peter described this in affidavits). Dash, they wrote, would say, "Home Sweet Home" as he did it. I could have rationalized his nicknaming himself "Peter," his desire to be a lawyer "like my dad," and even his threat to jump from a three-storey building. Children say crazy things. Children cry. Children get insecure. Children cling more to one parent than the other at various times in their lives. They are often indecipherable and unfathomable, Dash especially so because his parents' separation had been so hard. But I knew Dash. I had raised him, twenty-four hours a day, for just under five years, until the separation. What I saw simply didn't fit with the personality of the boy I had nurtured. Dash had been high-spirited, not a hell-raiser. He had been inquisitive and thoughtful, not desperate and needy, overwrought and sad. In my wildest dreams I could never have imagined him being "okay" with hardly speaking with me on the phone or not seeing me as much as he should have. Dash had held his arms wide open to the world and the people in it. Now he had shut all these people off. I didn't believe his lack of caring had been established on its own. It wasn't bred in; it was forced in, and the fit was bad because there was no *reason* for any of it.

But I was stuck in the far bleachers trying to watch the game. Within two years of the trial, eight-year-old Dash was going weeks and weeks in a row without seeing me. He lived in an emotional environment in which seeing me had become almost impossible for him to pull off. I saw coercion in his eyes, in his apathy. With no information from Dash and less than no contact from Peter unless it was to tell me to lay off or "be responsible," I worked, in a surreal vacuum, treating each tear, each moment of Dash's rage, each rude, dismissive phone call or each missed visit with a mother's understanding and kindness. I simply loved him, and used the only resources I had: the phone and those nights I saw him. I treated Dash's distress, in every aspect, laughter and tears, with love and acceptance. *Tend to him* was my mantra.

I had no idea what went on in that household, and I had no idea what was happening at Dash's school, although living in a close community with friends who had children at Queen Mary, I heard things. I knew Dash was late for school at least once a week and, worse, that he went home for lunch and often didn't go back to school for his afternoon classes. I read Peter's ceaseless stream of affidavits saying that Dash "runs down the block to school each morning, chirping like a bird. He runs home at noon for a hot lunch. He runs back to school for the afternoon, similarly chirping away." I compared that description to what Dash had said to one of his classmates (whose mother told me). His dad "wouldn't care anyways" about whether he was at school or not, he claimed.

Dash had slid into being a child of the community, a child that other parents knew about. He seemed to manage his life so that he was home as little as possible. Dash had a lot of friends, and he inveigled himself into more dinners and sleepovers than most other children, but it wasn't noticeably alarming because Dash was a charming child and his friends' parents enjoyed his company. They did worry, though, that no one at home seemed to care about his comings and goings.

I wondered what they thought of me. Did they believe everything Peter was saying? Did they say to themselves, "Where is this boy's mother? Is she a drunk, like Peter says? He says she has problems, that's why we never see her around." There were no limits to what Dash was allowed to do, except when it came to me. Dash roamed the neighbourhood, going from friend's house to friend's house, but he didn't see me. Other parents wondered why Dash was so outspoken about his father, why Peter was Dash's only proclaimed "hero." They wondered who did his washing and bought him clothes, because he always looked slightly bedraggled. I still have a pair of Dash's old sneakers. Once white leather, they had gone grey with ingrained dirt and grime, the toe of the right one was completely separated from the sole, leaving Dash's sock-clad foot, too big for the shoe, hanging out in the Vancouver rain; the sole of the other was ripped and the upper torn. They looked like the shoes of a street kid, but Dash was eight years old and living in a five-bedroom house in West Point Grey with two lawyers and daily help. When I managed to get hold of Dash long enough to take him shopping, he would say at school the next day, quietly, "Yeah, my mom got me these" when other kids pointed out his new gear.

I had thought for so long — hoped really — that everything would get better. Peter would forget about me and get on with his life. Or Suzanne would get tired of his angry obsession and tell him to shape up or get out. But our appeals to Suzanne had roundly failed. Dave and I had tried dozens of ways to connect, but they had only bound her more tightly, more angrily, to Peter. "If I see one word of this conversation in an affidavit, I'll sue you," she had said during a phone call Dave made to her to see, as step-parents, if she would cooperate in Dash's best interests. Those first months in which my hope had been realistic had now stretched into three years. and my belief that Peter would get over his anger had become frustrating to Dave and my family, and tiring for me. I had to analyze the problem.

I made lists and mulled them over in the middle of the night. How much of Dash's behaviour was normal for a boy his age? How much of it was because he hadn't seen me that week or that month? How much of it was because anger flowed through the Hart household like lava? How much of it was me, my "overprotectiveness"? I would get down on myself as the clock ticked toward midnight. *I tend to obsess about things. I'm probably just obsessing now. Maybe the experts were right to choose Peter over me. Have I so misjudged Dash's needs that he clings to his father? Dash is my first child. Have I done a bad job?* Then I'd swing back the other way.

*Surely the five years Dash and I spent together meant something.* You can't pour your heart and soul into a child, spend every day with him, introduce him to music and food and have him nurtured at your breast, and have it go this badly. I had given him everything I had to give, all my security, all my confidence, all my love, and he had responded to it as children do. He had been happy. Most of the time he *was still* happy with me. When I saw him. I mulled it over and over and over. I read books on parenting. I talked to other moms about what I should expect from an eight-year-old boy. Each weekend when Dash didn't visit, or did but was withdrawn or angry, I would go to sleep with only one thought in my mind: If Dash was living with the parent he most needed to be with — Dr. Elterman's "excellent parent," Dash's "psychological parent" — why wasn't he thriving? Why was he running from place to place and avoiding his father's home? Why did I never hear from him except when I called? Why didn't he need his mommy? Why was Dash's tolerance for ordinary discipline so low that, at the first sign of a rule, he ran off and hid behind the couch? Why had Dash's entire personality changed so radically in the space of three years?

But I could mull all I wanted. I needed help. I had to talk to someone who knew more than me. I made an appointment with a prominent Vancouver child psychologist, Dr. Norman Goodwell, and told him everything. "I don't see my child much. There was an ugly trial and the father hates me. The whole household seems to be hostile to the idea of my parenting this boy. The father has sole custody, and Dash is rebelling against me in queer, uncharacteristic ways. I don't know how to maintain order in our house — I have two little babies now — without disciplining him. And I can't discipline him because he goes home and says we've abused him, and I don't want to punish him because I really do think he's a boy in a lot of pain. What should I do?"

"Why do you think he's in a lot of pain?" Dr. Goodwell asked.

"There is so much anger and poison in his father's home. I'm this, I'm that. Dash isn't free just to love me and he isn't allowed to forget that there was a trial between his mother and his father and that his father won and is all-powerful. I think it's changing Dash's opinion of me. I think he's suffering under it."

I saw Norman Goodwell half a dozen times in that initial period. I talked freely about the new and old Dash, and at great length about my marriage to and divorce from Peter and about his anger, which seemed to consume everything in its path. It had consumed our marriage, it had consumed Dash's relationship with Dave, and it was consuming Dash. I was his mother. I saw it. I wasn't getting my access and couldn't dilute Peter's poison on the days each month I saw him.

From our handful of sessions Dr. Goodwell came to believe that Dash was suffering from "loss of attachment," a reaction to being separated for long periods from a parent he loved, was bonded to, and wanted to be near. This "defensive detachment" was Dash's psychological response to his periods of separation from me. Dr. Goodwell said his most stringent resistance would probably be immediately following and immediately preceding a period of separation from me, and I almost leapt out of my chair to say, "Yes, yes, that's exactly what happens! He shuts down. It takes hours to settle in with us when we first get him, and his acting out usually comes when the time is approaching for him to go back to his father." Dash wasn't rebelling, Norman Goodwell told me — at least not in any traditional sense. He was getting sick. Defensive detachment was a disorder, a form of psychological distress.

"Get your access," he told me. "This can't be turned around until he regains regular time with you. In the meantime, I agree that he should not be disciplined — this boy is in pain and he needs your love, not punishment. With one hand on each of his shoulders, ask him to look into your eyes when you want to speak with him, but don't do anything that will give him an excuse to step even further away from his pain. That's what he's doing. Each separation from you threatens and frightens him, so he withdraws from it. We all do that. So keep doing what you're doing. Provide boundaries. All kids need boundaries, so keep providing them. Above all, get your access."

Dr. Goodwell relieved me from my humiliation as a rejected mother and relieved me from the depressing feeling of *not knowing* what was happening to my son. Still, I was jolted when Dr. Goodwell told me, kindly, but bluntly, "Pam, you must do whatever you can to reverse the condition here. Otherwise the inevitable result will be the functional loss of you as a parent to that boy." *Dash will have no mom.*

The love between parents and their children runs deep, and each time Dash visited I saw that the easy love Dash and I had shared for years was never far away. We'd built a bond in Dash's first five years that I didn't believe could simply be set aside. Every book I had read on parenting — and, since Dr. Goodwell, on "detachment" — told me that those years are the glue. They mould a child, the experts say. As well as I knew Dash, he knew me equally well, regardless of what his father had taught him to think. When I was with him, it still felt as if we were old friends, friends who don't speak often but who slip into each other's special groove when they are together. So as much as I cried, and I did, all the time, I also smiled, filled up with love at my memories of him. I believed that my connection was always going to be deeper than the lack of interest Dash often projected. In those moments I believed I could protect him. I could be his light.

I kept calling. "Dash, I'd love to see you this weekend. Do you think you'll want to come over?" "Dash, I haven't seen you for three weeks. How about a movie on Sunday?" I coaxed Dash over by promising him that we wouldn't do anything he didn't want to do, we wouldn't go anywhere he didn't want to go, we would do whatever it was he wanted to do. It wasn't the way we would have chosen to raise Dash and it was nothing like the way Dave and I were raising Colby and Quinten, but we had to do what we could to get him to stay. If Dash had begun to believe that my family was noxious in some way, then, because he was a little boy, I had to ease the pressure on him. He was eight. I needed him to feel that he could stay, for a day, perhaps for a night, every couple of months, or for meals and other close family times. I kept saying to Dave, "This isn't parenting," but in fact I think it was. I was managing a child who lived in an emotional war zone, and I had to do it to stop it from sinking him. It had taken a bewilderingly long time to get it: much as I wanted everything to be "normal" — it wasn't. Much as I wanted to simply be Dash's happy soccer mom, the first thing I had to do was bind up my damaged son's wounds. I might be the original Pollyanna, but Dave and I had eyes. The anger and paranoia that existed in that house was corroding the most beautiful parts of that young boy: his natural trust, his capacity for joy, and his ease.

So Dave and I decided to lead by example and show Dash how healthy, loving families lived and operated. It let me keep my pride as a parent and stopped me from ever sniping at Peter or his parenting methods. He was sick, and that was the end of it. We shifted the focus from Peter to us and from Peter to Dash and just tried to live our lives without anger, criticism, and conditions. I believed that Dash would one day see the difference and, before he did, he would *feel* the difference and want to see me more because our home was gentler and safe. Through Norman Goodwell I gained the knowledge and confidence to parent Dash in unconventional ways. Life, when Dash was with us, centred on him. Dave and I refused dinner invitations if Dash was supposed to be coming over; our friends quickly understood. I called Sandy and borrowed Warren; if he couldn't come I'd call my friend Myrna Halpenny, whom I met when Dash and her son Myles both attended Queen Mary Elementary. I still had some parental pull, and I used that as well as other things. I rounded up local playmates in the neighbourhood. I told him we would make his favourite chocolate cake together. Or I'd tell him "Colby was asking about you and says he really wants to see you" — anything special or exciting we could think up, we did. It couldn't be anything extravagant — there were no circuses staged in the back garden — because it had to look normal, *be* normal. We watched hockey games, made cookies, played video games, and went to movies. Although we were naturally inclined that way anyway, now whatever we did, we did as a family unit. We ate all our meals together, laughing and joking. Those times I sensed that Dash needed time alone with me, Dave would take the boys off somewhere. At other times we all stayed home together and tried hard to make sure Dash not only enjoyed himself but felt our love and care for him. I never let him leave without making plans for our next visit or arranging a time I would call him. I sent him home with Ziploc bags of fresh cookies or a new glitter pen, a set of puffy stickers or a photograph of us all together. If I asked him to stay over and he squirmed and said, "No, I don't think so," then I would say, "That's okay." If I asked him when he wanted to go home and he said, "In an hour, Mom?" then I would say "No problem, Dash." I'd drop him off with a big hug and kiss, and as he walked up the path to his door, I would make our little heart shape with my fingers and thumbs.

When I wasn't with Dash or engaged with trying to be with him, I put my head down and tried to raise my two baby boys and be a good wife to Dave. Staying healthy became a priority and, while I have always been an athletic person, I worked out with renewed vigour. I had to be strong. I was the captain of our ship, and I couldn't neglect my marriage. It was in my car that I tried to work through my distress so as not to involve Dave too much or let it have any more of an impact on our family life than it already did. I would neither give Peter the satisfaction of driving wedges into my family nor put aside my two little boys because my relationship with my eldest was dizzying and preoccupying. Through my family I was able to focus on what was important. Anger was not important; I had seen first-hand how destructive it was. Grief had to be temporary, because we were all still alive and had needs. I was forced out of myself by the demands of my family, forced to be on when I sometimes wanted to be off, forced to stop crying when I thought I would drown in my tears. I *immersed* myself in my life instead of stepping out of it, and I kept going forward, always forward.

I sat at my desk a lot and stared at the wall or got in the car and drove around, ostensibly running errands, focusing on the little changes I could make in Dash's life. I dreamed up things to send him and organized great family vacations I thought might entice him. I called him as often as I dared, and sent little cards and notes in the mail, baked cookies and left them on his doorstep. I kept trying to arrange access days with him and, when I had done all I could do for him that day, I lived the other half of my life. I sent Dave off to work with a kiss, played with the boys, worked in the house with Mimi, our nanny, went to the gym, picked up the groceries, took the boys to the park, and had a bottle of wine chilling in the fridge and dinner in the oven when Dave came home in the evening. I had structure and I was surrounded by love, places to pour it and places to get it. I found strength in Dave's gentle arms and in the healthy, happy giggles of my little boys.

But Dash's absence was sometimes unbearable, because the reality was that he lived so far out of my life he could have been on Mars. By the third anniversary of Peter's sole custody win, it felt like nothing I did in the tiny pockets of time I saw Dash and in the marginal ways I could reach out and touch his heart could solve our problem. It could apply triage, it could help, but it fixed nothing, because the problem came from Peter's home, and the two of them lived side by side. But as one of Dash's old school friends told me recently, "There are two parts to a kid's life: his home life and his school life. So even if his home life was a disaster — and it was for Dash — the structure at school kept him up and moving in the right direction. We kept showing him the way." His peers helped moor him. Most had known him since preschool and cared a great deal for him, and they knew his home life wasn't like their own. So when he said or did something inappropriate, or acted out, the group guided him back into line. "Gee, Dash, don't do that, that's dumb," or "Come on, Dash, quiet down." A school friend told me they kept trying to make Dash "stay normal." Did Dash know he was starting to seem *abnormal*? Or that his life was one other kids pitied? That taint would have been profound.

I kept seeing Dr. Goodwell. Our conversations had progressed from specific techniques for dealing with Dash's behaviour and state of mind to talking more and more about Peter's influence. We talked about his anger and his interferences. I told him about how Peter whistled loudly or played the guitar next to Dash when he was on the phone with me. We talked about the glares and hostile stares he gave me from the soccer field and how Dash, after only a few games, stopped coming up to me at halftime like all the other kids did with their moms. We talked about how Peter said Dash never acted up at their house but did at mine, and how curious that was, and we talked about the constant presence of alcohol. I showed Norman Goodwell the illegible faxes Peter sent me, filled with drunken ravings: I was being "irresponsible," I didn't respect "Dash's wishes," "Dash wants" this and "Dash wants" that. Dr. Goodwell came to believe, as I already did, that Peter *fully supported* Dash's distorted relationship with me.

"Pamela, defensive detachment often has a second element to it beyond the distress of a sudden or traumatic separation. The actions of the other parent play a *huge* role," Norman Goodwell said. My antennae shot up. "When a parent pulls on a child's loyalty," he continued, "when he treats the relationship with the child as exclusive and doesn't acknowledge the other parent's existence or the existence of a relationship between the child and the other parent, when he forbids or discourages contact with the other parent, the child's sense of separation is wildly exacerbated. This is what I think is going on here."

Peter was showing Dash what to think. I tried to focus on what Dr. Goodwell was saying, but blood was pounding in my ears. *This person is telling me what I have felt for three years.* I was not nuts. I was not over-protective. I was not over-emotional or obsessed with my custody loss. My child was in distress and *that's* what I was responding to. It didn't make any difference any more whether the destruction of Dash's good feelings for me was Peter's deliberate plan or just the accumulated actions of his sickness — what mattered was that it was happening. This was *child abuse*, and of the three of us I was the only one capable of turning it in another direction: Dash was a child, Peter was sick. I was the only healthy one, and I had to get the situation under control, because it had already gathered its own head of steam.

"You have to get your access in order to help your son," Norman Goodwell repeated. "Whatever you have to do, keep going."

I cried in the car driving home (always in the car, so often crying) but these tears were sharp and jagged, filled for the first time with not just pain and grief, but relief. My love for him could fix my son.

# Chapter 3
# Crushed

I had had Dash with me for three hours, but in that precious time Peter had called three times to harry the boy. "Are you ready to come home, Dash?" Then, "Be ready at seven o'clock, okay?" Then "I'll be right outside at seven on the dot, Dash." I collected three further messages on my answering machine, and in each Peter was increasingly sarcastic, his voice more and more slurred and incomprehensible. By the time he had left his last message, Peter was so drunk that I dreaded Dash going home. I called Peter back as soon as I got that third and most aggressive message, but got only his answering machine. Had he already left? I hung up and tried again, but got no answer. I looked out the window to see a taxi at the curb and walked quickly to the front door. Peter waved dismissively at the taxi as he wove down our pathway. "I was just having dinner with a judge. And before you accuse me of anything, my car's at the mechanic's."

I didn't speak. I kept our exchanges short when he was like this. Peter reeked of alcohol, and I turned away from the smell. He handed me one of his scrawled notes, which I glanced at quickly but didn't read.

"Where's Dash?" he demanded.

"He's inside. Wait here, please, Peter."

I flew downstairs to the playroom where Dash was watching television. I sat down with him and began a conversation I had been meaning to have for years. I couldn't keep putting him in cabs and cars and sending him off like this.

"I was just thinking, do you want to stay the night?"

But Dash never stayed overnight anymore, and he knew it. "Why, Mom?" he asked, suddenly wary.

"To tell you the truth, Dash, I think Daddy's been drinking tonight, and sometimes when people have too much to drink they can get, well, a little out of character."

He stared at the television again but said nothing, his face a mask.

"I'd really like you to stay."

"I'm going with my dad," he said quickly, automatically. I knew he would and I kept my voice calm. "Dash, can't you stay just one night? I'll drive you home first thing in the morning, I promise." *Please, Dash.*

I turned the television's volume down low and stayed close to him, speaking very quietly, conscious as always about snaking carefully around his loyalty to his father. Dash didn't look at me. "Dash, your father has a problem with alcohol." At this hefty charge, Dash betrayed no response at all. He didn't bristle. He didn't even seem surprised. "It's no different than diabetes or cancer," I continued. "It's a disease, so don't feel badly about what I'm saying."

Dash fiddled with the zipper on his fleecy vest.

"But I am concerned," I continued, reaching for his hand to try and remind him of *our* bond, as well as the one to his dad. "I worry about Daddy picking you up and driving you around, because people don't drive as well when they've had too much to drink. Everyone's the same."

"He's fine," Dash said resolutely. "He doesn't drink that much."

"Well, you're certainly entitled to your opinion. But you're my child, too, and I want you to stay here tonight."

"I'm going with my dad." Dash got up off the couch. "Where is he?"

I looked at his eight-year-old face and saw how hard it was then. His getting up had broken the spell I had begun to weave, and pushing it would fail and send him further away. I resigned myself to him leaving, because I wasn't going to fight with him and I wouldn't make him stay. I wouldn't risk losing what marginal influence I still had over him. I tied it up with my standard pitch. "Okay, Dash. I understand and I'm not going to argue with you. But you're my son and I love you. I want you to be safe, and I'm never going to stop trying to make sure you are."

"I know, Mom," Dash said, climbing the stairs. He walked past his dad, got into the taxi, and shut the door quietly behind him. And while his father berated me as he walked back up the path, Dash refused to look at either one of us.

The next week I tried to pick up Dash at four o'clock Wednesday, then at four o'clock Friday. I waited. And waited. Outside his house. No child appeared. This time I cracked. Still shaken from what had happened the week before and my bird's-eye view of my total inability to protect my own son, I dialled my lawyer, Gerald Reid, as I drove away from Dash's house.

"Gerald? It's Pamela."

"Pamela. What's happening? It's four o'clock. You're at Hart's home?"

"I just left. Dash wasn't there. No one's home and I've waited fifteen minutes. Colby's with his nanny, and she has to get home, and I've got Quin in the back seat."

I heard Gerald sigh, exasperated, a little bit sad.

"How much more of this do I have to take?" I asked.

"Go home, Pamela. If you like, I'll send them a fax saying you'll be there later."

"No, don't. Not tonight. Dave's mom is visiting from Winnipeg and I have to get home and start cooking. There's no guarantee I'd get Dash anyway. Just leave it tonight."

"Are you sure?"

"Gerald, I'm never sure. You keep telling me things will change: Dash will grow up; Peter will settle down. Well, *when* will they? Norman Goodwell says they may not."

"Pam—"

"This has gone on for three years. You keep telling me that, if Peter doesn't settle down, he'll do something that will allow us to go back to court. Fine, I watch and wait. But, Gerald, why does anything have to happen? Why can't I go back and simply ask the court to enforce its own order?"

"The court is not going to enforce this order because it feels stuck between a rock and a hard place. Hart will keep saying he tries to get Dash to visit but that Dash only wants to see you when he wants to see you. The courts don't know how to handle that. Hart will say Dash shouldn't be forced to visit if he doesn't want, and he'll say that Dash's been clear on this."

"Dash has been clear? That's absurd! Why would a court take the word of a young child who has been coached to believe that he has to choose one parent over the other? Peter is using this boy. Those words aren't Dash's. Those feelings aren't Dash's. That's abusive, Gerald. That's *abuse*." My voice caught. *This is the truth I live.* I shook it off and tried to focus. "You say we can't go in with 'emotional abuse'? That it's the hardest thing to prove?"

"In my experience, yes."

"Well, I know Peter's putting words in Dash's mouth, Gerald. Why does he not want to visit? None of the reasons make sense because they are not real reasons — they are Peter's."

"But Peter has custody, and that's what makes it so difficult to argue this successfully in court. Like it or not, he's the court's first recourse. We will have a better chance if we have other reasons to add to the interference with your access."

"So the more we throw out there, the more something will stick."

"Yes."

"Then what else can we go in with? I just want Dash to get his time with me. Peter keeps saying 'Leave him alone, he's fine, he's thriving, he's happy,' but how can he be? Dash is eight years old, not eighteen. It's important that he sees his mother."

I always worried that my lawyer would grow tired of my urgent calls from the car outside Peter's house, the endless faxes he sent to Peter's lawyer, or Peter himself, trying to set up access visits that mostly failed. I worried that I was too time-consuming, that my case was too ugly and stressful.

"Pam, we have to go in loaded. We can't go in with a complaint they can label frivolous."

"But that's what I mean! Why would these people think that my not getting access to my son is frivolous? Ask any mother, Gerald, any parent. This isn't frivolous. Dash has two parents, he should be able to *have* both parents. I was given generous and specific access times that, for a range of reasons, I am being denied. Where is the 'frivolous' here?"

"Peter will tell the court what he tells you when you complain. He'll say it's what Dash wants."

"I'll never believe that what Dash wants — or at least what Peter thinks he wants — is more important than having a relationship with his mother. At some point Dash will be an adult and all this will really matter. *He has a mother, Gerald.* So what do we do? How many of Peter's affidavits do I have to read that say he 'chirps like a bird,' when others tell me, and I see myself, that he clearly doesn't? How many times does Peter get to turn up on my doorstep drunk and take him home? One day they're not going to get home, and I'm going to have to live with that. I haven't been able to stop this, Gerald, and I'm this boy's *mother*. At what point am *I* being negligent by not going back into court?"

We both paused. I hadn't even taken a breath. I had pulled up in front of my house and sat there, wanting to finish the conversation before I went inside to my family.

"I just want my son to have a normal life again, Gerald. I want him to have a normal relationship with both parents. I want him to want to see me. He has never given me a valid reason why he doesn't want to visit, and I've never done anything that would justify his not seeing me. Children of divorce don't do what Dash is doing. They want peace. They want stability. They stick close to both parents, and they don't choose one over the other. Norman Goodwell says this is something different and unhealthy, and I believe him. If Dash really was thriving without me in his life, then it would be easier to accept, but he's not. Peter's attitude toward me hasn't moderated one bit since we split up; it might even be worse because of the substance abuse. I don't know. Dash isn't doing well at school, but he's always been a bright child. Elizabeth tells me — that's Elizabeth MacKenzie, her daughter is in Dash's class at school — that his teacher wants to meet with me but isn't allowed. Dash is having serious problems, the teacher says. He hardly attended school last month. He had the flu for two weeks, Peter said. Two weeks! Then he went to Mexico for another two weeks. The drinking is getting worse and the more Peter drinks the less he is able to stop himself from badmouthing me to Dash. Myrna told me that, when she went to pick up Myles a few weeks ago, Peter answered the door slurring and disoriented. He'd spilled red wine all down his shirt and tried to laugh it off. She doesn't let Myles play there any more." I paused.

"Is Peter still leaving those messages?" Gerald asked.

"Yes. Or I talk to him and he's slurring his words or saying things like 'This is Bert's Beanery' and laughing to himself."

My frustration was clouding my thinking and, above all, through this, I had to think. If I *felt*, I'd be done for. "Gerald?"

"Yes, Pamela?"

"If I don't do something, then I'm saying it's okay, and it's definitely not okay. Nothing about this is okay. I've tried to do this alone, but I think the only way this will change is to go back to the courts. They made the decision in the first place that Dash should be with his dad. I know Peter will use it against me and it'll make me and Dave — and you — and Dash targets again. I know that he will involve Dash, but I don't have any other choice aside from just watching myself fade out of my son's life, and I won't do that. I want to go back. I want my access," I said quietly. "I want this fixed."

My lawyer breathed deeply; when he spoke he was matter-of-fact. "Then we have to do it properly. We have to have more than an ex-wife's concerns. You've lost that battle, twice: first at the interim custody trial and then at the custody and divorce trial. Your word against his on the alcohol question will never get us anywhere, no matter how many corollaries or slurring, incoherent tapes you have. If we go to court with anything less than hard, third-party evidence, we'll be wasting our time. Peter has been given custody, twice. He had the psychologist's support, twice. He's brilliant in court and has a team of people to vouch for him, including his new wife, Suzanne MacGregor, and he has Dash working with him." I felt myself getting smaller and smaller as he listed the obstacles we faced. I was exhausted just listening to him. I knew the path ahead would be dangerous. Because Peter involved Dash so heavily in his power plays, if I went back I had to win. Otherwise the household that was perpetually prepared for war would finally find its battleground.

"Having said all that," Gerald continued, "I agree that court is the only recourse we have if we want Peter *forced* to get Dash to see you, and of course it's the only place we can go for a custody change — if and when you want to look at that."

If court was all we had, I had to start getting our ducks in line.

Putting alcohol and abuse on the table was a major departure from my legal strategy. At every turn I had presented to the court the real me, as an antidote to the Pam that Peter repeatedly placed before it — the emotional, aggressive, blaming, frivolous, litigious *angry* woman. So, even as my gut argued for it, I held back. "We have to keep out of the fray," Gerald had said, and the advice was sound. But Dave had begun to question that strategy, and I now agonized over it. I *had* tried once, at one of our earliest pretrial hearings, to put the issue out there. I had told the judge about Peter arriving to pick up Dash with an open wine bottle in the car and Justice Wetmore's indulgent "Oh, c'mon, Pete."

The tolerance of Peter's substance abuse by the legal boys' club had long frustrated me. At one point, Dave and I went to a party in West Vancouver and, as we mingled, separated for a time, Dave was introduced to a group of four men. It came out after a few minutes that one of the men, David Gibbons, was the lawyer Peter had recently hired to represent him in a case he was bringing against Dave and me, accusing us of trespass, eavesdropping, and violation of privacy, because we had taped phone conversations. (Dave and I had all but left the charges in the hands of our lawyer, because it seemed so silly. Peter taped us, we taped him; it was a wash.) The lawyer shook Dave's hand and said with a smile, "I didn't know you were *that* Mr. Richardson," and when Dave looked at him quizzically, the lawyer went on. "It'll be difficult to pursue you aggressively now that I see what a decent fellow you are," he said.

"Well, thank you, David," Dave said. "But I'm no match for my wife when it comes to decency. That's why all this seems so unwarranted."

"You seem to be a good person," Gibbons said warmly. "What's caused the animosity between you, Pamela, and Peter do you think?"

"David, I don't want to be disagreeable, and I know he is your client," Dave replied, "but I've long thought of Peter as the most self-destructive person I have ever known. His cruelty toward my wife seems to reflect some deep-seated rage."

The lawyer nodded, not giving anything away, but was clearly interested, and, when Dave saw that his audience was neither offended nor in shocked disagreement, he continued. "I think he's fundamentally a really angry person and we both believe he has problems with alcohol that lead to our difficulties with him."

Dave paused, and the lawyer replied, "Yes, Peter's problems are common knowledge."

Were *Dash's* problems common knowledge? How could Peter *flaunt* his indiscretions so? The dichotomy between the real world and the world represented by the legal system staggered me anew every time. Not getting my access wasn't enough to take to court, yet any mom I spoke to was horrified that my court-sanctioned relationship with Dash was being impeded the way it was by the custodial parent. Peter showing up drunk and dishevelled to take Dash home wasn't proof enough to take to court, yet Peter's colleagues knew all about it. There were no consequences. Peter was allowed to be as bad as he wanted to be. I had lost my patience. If I had to make a case the courts would understand, then so be it. *None of us should be living like this, least of all Dash. I will play the game and the result will justify the journey.*

I made an appointment with Dr. Barry Beyerstein of Simon Fraser University, a tall, bespectacled man, whose twenty-two-page résumé established him as an expert in biological psychology and psychopharmacology. He was my expert on what drugs do to bodies and minds — and children. I needed him to tell me if my truth about Peter was in fact borne out by objective fact. I knew what I had lived with during my seven years with Peter, and I knew what it was to see Peter staggering to crosswalks and down my driveway, but I did not know the true extent of Peter's involvement with alcohol at this point, and I didn't really know whether my son was living with a problem drinker. I was acutely aware that I described a different Peter than the one his wife, Suzanne, wrote about. How much of that disconnect was my particular set of distresses surrounding the separation and Dash's custody and how much was Suzanne's standing as a family lawyer and future judge? If Peter was an alcoholic, then what sort of environment was Dash in, physically, emotionally? Was he being neglected? Did alcoholism *constitute* neglect? Was the danger just in my imagination? Would this be enough to take to court? I wanted an expert to give me some answers I could make sense of and use.

Dr. Beyerstein and I talked for a long time in a room filled with papers and books while drinking hot coffee one rainy afternoon. I told him my story. Over the course of the dozen years I had known Peter, I had seen him mesmerizing, charismatic, endlessly charming, and boyish, but also deeply paranoid and highly secretive. After Dash was born, Peter became increasingly aggressive about his privacy. "That's what closet drinkers do," Beyerstein said. When Peter was away, he locked his home office and did not let anyone in. But occasionally I had cleaned the room and found half-empty liquor or champagne bottles in his desk drawer. Now Peter was completely unconcerned about hiding his drinking. The fact that he was now coming drunk to pick up Dash was for Dr. Beyerstein a signal of potential substance abuse. The last place a person with normal inhibitions would show up drunk would be on the doorstep of an ex-wife whose concerns had, within the community at least, been well publicized.

I showed Dr. Beyerstein Peter's scrawled faxes. When I saw them alongside the "normal" letters that Beyerstein had requested "for control purposes," they resembled the writings of a lunatic. They were long and loopy, repetitive, and filled with sarcasm and aggression. They contained basic grammatical mistakes that were absent in the control letters, and the prose and presentation differed markedly. "They were not," Dr. Beyerstein wrote later, "what I expected from someone accustomed to writing tightly reasoned legal briefs." He dismissed "mere haste or fatigue," and said that the letters appeared to be written by "someone without full control of his fine motor movements. The volume of material in Mrs. Richardson's possession suggests that the state that produced such writings was not infrequent."

Dr. Beyerstein got out a tape player and slipped in one of my answering-machine tapes. Peter's "normal" voice filled the little room. "Pamela, it's Peter. I just want you to know that I'll be there at seven o'clock to pick up Dash. Make sure he is ready for me." Erudite, crisp, controlled, curt, even polite. Normal. Then I played Dr. Beyerstein ten of the messages Peter had left on my answering machine over the past couple of months. The messages, many recorded during the day, featured Peter rambling, repetitive, and uninhibited. Beyerstein made note of Peter's difficulty in calming his temper, his threatening tone of voice, and the speech errors

— slurs, slips of the tongue, strained overpronunciation, overuse of "filler" words like "Okay." I played Dr. Beyerstein the exchange Dave had recorded the night he tried to pick up Dash for me. Dave had told Peter when he answered the door, "I just want you to know, Peter, that I am wearing a recording device," and the response, "Go away, little boy. You're not getting Dash," sounded shocking in the cold light of Dr. Beyerstein's office. Peter's "social disinhibition was very high," Dr. Beyerstein wrote,

> possibly because his state of inebriation was greater or because Hart simply did not care that there would be a record of his contraventions of normal standards of social propriety. Either way, this sort of childish behaviour and lack of judgement is suggestive of a high blood alcohol level. He comes across as crude, taunting and gratuitously offensive to someone merely trying to facilitate young Dashiell's visit with his mother.

The report Beyerstein wrote up and sent to me was a technical breakdown of what I had been dealing with for a dozen years in far simpler terms: an aggressive, inebriated man. Drinking, for Peter, was "a pattern, rather than a freak occurrence," Dr. Beyerstein wrote.

> The taped conversations, the various faxes, the consistency of the other parts of the story related to me by Mrs. Richardson and her general credibility are sufficient to raise doubts about the advisability of the present custody arrangement.... The adverse consequences for a child in that milieu are such that when allegations of this sort are raised they should be thoroughly investigated. I would urge the court to take Mrs. Richardson's allegations seriously and to investigate them thoroughly for the good of young Dashiell.

The scrutiny, probing, and harsh judgement of me that had come with the custody trial and from Dr. Elterman had awoken me from my naïveté. I had never before concerned myself with whether or not I was "believed" about anything. I'm a pleaser by nature, so I often cared if I was *liked* or not, but *believed*? Who has to worry about that? But this feeling comes to life when you're under the microscope, and when the court-appointed psychologist has taken a dislike to you, believing that your passion and concern for your son are signs of pushiness, impression management, and elitism. I would have forgotten all about Dr. Elterman's judgement and his damaging reports and the court decisions that were based on them if I had got the access the court had ordered. I didn't care that I was seen in a particular light by a system I neither understood nor particularly trusted. But I cared very much that their judgements had left my son in the care of a man whose anger and dysfunction had led to a whole host of problems, beginning with my lack of access and extending to Dash's psychological health. Beyerstein's report wasn't much, because Peter would no doubt argue hard against it, saying I had bought myself an expert witness, but Beyerstein's wholly positive reaction to me as a human being and a mother, and his confirmation of things I had long suspected to be true, gave me much-needed validation.

Allowing the questions about Peter's alcohol and drug use to be swept aside at the permanent custody trial three years earlier had created two big problems: When I brought the issue up in court this time, Peter and his lawyers would almost certainly consider it an attack and attack me back with the same kind of character assassinations they used before (I was a high-rolling party girl, never at home — and Dave, a man who's never tried anything more than the odd joint in university, was a coke-head). Worse, the judge might ask suspiciously "Why now?" and toss it out. Would Peter say, "Did I suddenly become an alcoholic?" Would the judge think I was grasping at straws? Looking for a winning angle? If so, how would I answer that? If I said I relied on passive legal strategy, then I was blaming someone else for a strategy I had thought hard about and agreed to. Saying "It's worse now" seemed feeble, even though it was true. Peter's drinking *had* escalated, as all the literature says it so often can. When we were married, Peter was not weaving around drunk during the day. He drank at night, while I slept upstairs. I only saw *signs* — the empty bottles, his absences from my bed, and the flimsy excuses that went with them. I figured I would cross that bridge when I came to it. For now, I had to get my evidence together, because if I was going back, I had to go in with both guns blazing. I had real concerns about Dash's care, and I wasn't going to be passive any more. I hadn't aired my marriage's dirty laundry in court yet, but I had come to the crossroads. Continuing to wait to bring forward relevant evidence would soon make me negligent toward my own child.

My lawyer, Gerald, had suggested, months earlier, that I think about hiring a private investigator to watch Peter, but I had been hesitant and then had shelved the idea. If I was found out, then things could get even worse. Peter might even be on the lookout for such a thing. While we were married he had secretly taped us eating dinner together. He left tape recorders running when I had girlfriends over. He planted bamboo in front of his den window in our early years together, so "no one can see in." He kept the blinds closed and locked the door of his den when he was inside. The idea of hiring a private investigator might blow up in my face, but now I wanted to try. If she saw Peter ferrying Dash around in the car while he was drunk, we could use it. Although Peter had been picked up twice for driving under the influence, he had not been convicted either time.

Hiring a private investigator turned our life even further away from "normal." I called her only when I knew Peter had been drinking (because we had spoken or he had left messages), and either I had Dash and he was coming to get him or he was dropping Dash at my house. Neither of these things was regular, so there wasn't all that much investigative work to do, and I didn't hold out inordinate hope that we would get anything we could use. Sometimes Suzanne drove Peter over to get Dash. They would both wait in the car until Dash came running down the path to them. Sometimes Greg came with Peter instead of Suzanne. Sometimes Peter came in cabs. Sometimes he came alone but didn't act as if he were drunk. The investigator would park on his street and watch the house, and when they drove away she followed him to mine. She saw little things. Peter banged his Mercedes into the gutter outside my house as he was parking, left his window rolled down during a downpour. He berated me on my doorstep for seven documented minutes. Turned up again to my house in a taxi. The investigator discovered that Peter's 1969 Mustang was licensed to an address that didn't exist. These were trivial things, though, nothing we could use. I wasn't really surprised, and at least I'd tried.

Meanwhile Peter's increasing paranoia paid off. He discovered the surveillance and quickly informed Dash that they were being followed. Peter swore an affidavit saying that he had found in his car a "recently drilled hole in my console where a bug had been placed but since removed." Its purpose was to intercept his phone conversations, he said. Dash insisted that I had put a bug in his dad's car, even though the investigator hadn't gone near the car and would never in a million years have bugged it. "My dad proved it to me," he told me on the phone. There was a drilled hole in his dad's Mercedes, Dash told me emphatically, the purpose of which was to house a "surveillance camera."

"But Dash, there isn't a bug, and there isn't a camera."

"There is. There's a hole. And there's a microphone in the car, my dad said so."

"Why would I bug your dad's car?"

"To dig up some dirt on him."

"Well, it wasn't me, and I really hope you can think about that and believe what I'm saying. I do not know why there is a hole in your dad's car. It seems like an unusual thing to have happened, to have found a hole in the metal of a car. I guess it would have had to have been drilled, but I don't know how that could have happened with the car sitting right in front of your house. Surely you would have noticed."

"I'll have to ask my dad. But there *is* a hole and it's there to bug him, I'm sure."

Getting caught "spying" gave Dash yet another reason to distrust me. After three months with nothing but a big bill, I let the private investigator go. Looking at our paltry evidence, I began to slide away from the idea of going back to court. I began to comfort myself in strange ways that later smacked of rationalization: *He's not dead. He's eating. He's going to school, where he's surrounded by healthy adults and his peers. He's seeing me once a month or so. When he does, he seems all right.*

Still, I had been all but wiped out of Dash's life. Peter had air time in my marriage, much as I tried to shut him out of it, and sometimes he *hurt* my marriage, as Dave and I disagreed or I picked on him in my frustration or when I cried and he couldn't comfort me. I wasn't super-woman, and my loss and frustration *did* sometimes distract me from my other children. We were hardly bouncing through life without a care in the world, and my household had become distorted. Waiting for Dash. Trying to pick him up. Avoiding conflict with Peter. There were my tears, Dave's anger, and Colby's confusion when Dash missed long-await-ed visits. "I made his favourite dinner," Mimi would say sadly, and there at the table would be Dash's special table setting — folded napkin and childhood bunny cup — sitting out waiting for a boy who so rarely arrived to use it. Mimi bounced back every time, as Colby did, as I did, but it wasn't easy. I kept Dash with us, though, even when he wasn't and hadn't been for weeks. It was important for *my* family to know that he still existed as a brother, a stepson, and a son. "Remember the night Dash got into Breeza's doggie bed?" I would say brightly, referring to our black Lab, and Colby would recall it with a smile and a snort. When we got a new roll of film developed, we would pore over the prints, and Dash would be in our house again, even just on paper. Colby would shout hap-pily, "There's Dash!" We all loved him and waited impatiently to see him and welcome him when he crashed back into our lives.

Through our love and our efforts and my vigilance, my family and I stayed healthy. Where Peter was obsessed, angry, and fixated on our mar-riage and divorce, both of which were long, long over, we had all moved on to greater joys, hoping, as we *always* did, that Dash would join us some-where down the track. Peter wouldn't win. He couldn't even diminish me, because in a perverse way his plan had already backfired: he had given me the forum — excruciating pain, long-term heartbreak — within which I was forced, like a character in a book, to sink or swim, live or die. Through the experience of being that hated, that toyed with, that debased and humiliated, I had stepped up and become a better person. I was more patient, more tolerant, more confident, a more grounded wife, a better mother. I hadn't always been patient in my life. I hadn't always chosen well. But now I lived each day and embraced every moment I was given, with my three boys, with Dave and my family and friends. I wasn't going to lie down on a couch and pass my years in a fog of depression. I wasn't going to forget about Dash. I wasn't going to toss my marriage. I had a *life*. I wasn't going anywhere.

Much as my family buoyed me, though, it was still *me* who had to drag myself out of bed every morning; it was still me who sat outside Dash's house every Friday night and wrote letters and sent care packages filled with Easter eggs or socks and boxers. In many ways, I was in it alone. I tried to find ways to quarantine my despair and horror to keep it from infecting the other half of my life. Compartmentalization is what the psychologists call it, but I just called it survival. My gratitude for life, and for what I had, almost always outweighed the trauma I felt about what I didn't have.

Almost always. I didn't have many places where I was willing to peel back my skin, but in the office of my therapist, Bob Armstrong, I did. I had started to see Bob to help deal with the stress I faced. I'd make an appointment when my reserves were running low, or when I needed to run through my plans or ideas, or just grieve in a safe place, somewhere that wasn't home. Dave, my brother, my father, my best friend, Sandy, and wonderful Mimi were the ropes I leaned against between bouts, but it was to Bob that I laid it all out — the moments of hopelessness and heartbreak I never wanted anyone else to see. He saw my tears, my rage, helplessness, and fear.

"I never, ever forget that I am missing huge parts of Dash's life. I worry about him needing me and me not being there to comfort him when he feels afraid or is hurt. I think about what it must have been like to be a prisoner in a POW camp, to have your children taken away from you. I think I know how they must have felt.

"I try to keep it from Dave unless we need to talk about something specific. I have brought *grief* into our marriage, and pain. And I don't feel good about that. Dash is *my* son, and I have to be the one who deals with Peter and the lawyers.

"I've learned to compartmentalize, because I literally cannot take the reality of what is happening any more. As a parent, to not be able to protect and comfort your child from *any* harm, let alone harm done by the other parent, is a form of exquisite torture.

"Bob, sometimes I feel so trapped. Who can understand what I live? How many parents can relate to this? It's like some secret, underground club to which no one would ever want to belong, and yet if you're there you can't leave it. That's my real world, and no matter how successful I am in all the other areas of my life — it's always there.

"Then I remember how lucky I am. I don't have to worry about paying the rent, I'm not alone, I'm healthy, I have a beautiful family. I close my notebooks and fold up my papers and notes and walk back to the other area of my life. Without my family I couldn't do all that I have to do to be with Dash and it makes me alive and gives me the strength to go on."

While Bob Armstrong was there for *me*, Norman Goodwell was still my point man on Dash. He completely understood my deep, almost-phobic reluctance to go back to court unless I was guaranteed a win. The adversarial system was, in his mind and mine, the last place to resolve custody and access disputes. "It's a crapshoot every time," he said. He had seen cases go horribly wrong and children suffer as cases dragged on for months, with parents taking the black-and-white positions that the adversarial system forces upon them, with hired-gun lawyers taking fight-to-the-death oaths for their clients and refusing to negotiate or compromise or consider the welfare of the child as paramount. When that happens, war comes to children's homes. It had come to mine.

The legal system was a crapshoot, but at some point all that had happened to Dash was going to cause him irreparable damage. Like me, Norman Goodwell wanted to avoid court, but we both knew that the situation wasn't getting better. He had believed right from our first session, two years earlier, in 1991, that Dr. Elterman had done a poor job of assessing Dash's ideal custodial situation. Dr. Goodwell viewed Dr. Elterman's two reports as superficial and illogical, and we had long argued that there was no reason for Dr. Elterman to have wanted a sole-custody situation for five-year-old Dash and that there had been no logic behind his nomination of Peter for the job — beyond the house, the nanny, the school, and the spurious definition of "psychological parent."

"Either Dr. Elterman declined to report things that were unfavourable to Peter or he allowed his conclusions to be coloured by his own prejudices," Norman told me. "I can't see how he came to his conclusions based on the things he reported.

"Whatever route you're going to choose, do it now. Your window is closing. If you don't re-establish your relationship with Dash within the next couple of years, he will attach to his peer group instead, and you will have no control and no ability to guide or influence him."

When a batch of legal documents was placed in my hands by a process server a little while later, I reeled. Peter had applied to change the access order to formally remove my Friday nights. "It's a ploy," I told Gerald later that afternoon. "'Dash wants to know where he'll go to soccer from.' But I've already lost those nights. Dash goes with Peter — always. Peter wants it on paper, so I'll never get them back." Although I didn't see Dash overnight anymore, symbolically — emotionally — I still had my Friday nights, because they were written into the access order. Dishonoured and useless though the order was, the days were there. If Peter won his application and set the loss in stone, I would never see Dash again on any Friday nights. Soccer season would come and go and it wouldn't change a thing, because it was never the real reason. The visit was. Soccer was simply the wrapper in which the interference had been packaged. Peter's application panicked and galvanized me. Peter would push and push until I had nothing, even on paper.

I called Gerald. "I don't want Dash to live like this," I told him. "Let's go to court. I need custody."

He drew up and filed our application. Later I got a message on my answering machine: "Pamela, it's Gerald Reid. I am hoping you might come down to our offices this afternoon. We need to talk to you about something that happened here over the Christmas holidays. Our office has been firebombed again."

The first time my lawyers' offices had been firebombed was a year or so earlier, twenty-four hours after Peter had applied to the court to expunge my Wednesday access evenings, because Dash had asked for the change and Peter had "agreed to support him." Peter hadn't told me or my lawyer about the application, but by coincidence, Gerald's partner, William Morton, happened to be in the courtroom on another client's case when Peter's motion was called. He rose to object and ask that the motion be adjourned because I wasn't there, but in the end it wasn't necessary, because Peter never showed up and his application was dismissed. Peter had called me the morning the motion was to be heard in court, so slurred and incoherent I had hung up in frustration. That night, a Molotov cocktail was found underneath a window outside the heritage house that contained the law offices. No investigation had ever linked Peter to the bombing, but at the time the possible connection had worried us all. The timing of this one was just as alarming.

I drove downtown to the law offices of Morton and Reid and met with both of them, because they had done significant double-duty on my case. Peter had been representing himself for many months, and because of this had much closer contact with my lawyers than he would normally have, and he spent much of his time personally attacking Gerald. He constantly relived the old trial themes and the judge's finding of fraud against him, which he blamed, when he wasn't blaming me, on my lawyer. (It was Gerald who had found Peter's illegal conveyance of our marital house while preparing for the permanent custody trial.) Peter's animosity toward Gerald became so personal that we had decided that switching from Gerald Reid to his partner, William, a QC, might neutralize Peter and allow us to move forward. The two of them sat me down.

"The Vancouver Police arson investigators say that the bombing was not a random attack," Gerald said. "You think this is Peter? Or someone for him?" My skin crawled. I remembered when Dave and I moved to our Kerrisdale home. Peter had been so threatening and unpredictable that, on the weekends we skied in Whistler, we had hired a security company to watch our house.

"We are concerned about your file." William leaned over and relit his cigar, by now a familiar and almost comforting movement to me. He took a moment before he spoke again. "My secretary has been here thirty years, and now she is frightened to come to work. She is considering leaving, and I just can't lose her." *Oh, no,* I thought, *they're letting me go.* Sudden panic rose in me. We were in the middle of renewed court proceedings. How could I just change lawyers? How would I do this? "We've been in touch with another family lawyer. His name is John Fiddes."

"Oh, I know John Fiddes!" I brightened. "I knew him years ago." Living as neighbours in West Vancouver, we had become friends. I had even cooked him the occasional roast-chicken dinner.

"He's agreed to take on your file."

"Okay." I gnawed on my lip, not quite believing what was happening. I glanced over at the secretary who had threatened to leave and felt a pang. *I'm sorry*, I wanted to say.

"The Vancouver Police Department has advised us to take extra precautions about our personal security."

"My God." *I have two young children at home.* "I'll talk to Dave." I nodded, struggling to work through all the thoughts in my head. "William, I will talk to John first thing tomorrow morning. We will probably have to put off our court date, right?"

"Well, you and John should decide that. Both Gerald and I will make ourselves available to go over the files with him, but yes, I expect he needs some time to absorb all the material." He pointed wryly to the legal files that pertained to my case. They had been brought out and placed in brown legal boxes, as if already waiting for the moving van. I left their offices in a daze.

After that, Dave stopped parking in underground car parks, and once again we hired a security company to watch the house from dusk till dawn when we were away. Although the police never came up with a culprit, William Morton and Gerald Reid had no more problems after they let me go.


The notice of motion asking for custody sparked one reaction I *did* expect. Eight-year-old Dash flew into the fray. His rage was swift, his hostility palpable on the phone. I tried to keep my nerve, but I was left shaking after each exchange. Even though I had spent three weeks persuading Dash to come on a ski weekend with us, he called the night before we were leaving and demanded to know if we were still going.

"I want an answer," he snarled. "It's simple, are we going to Whistler or not? Because I don't want to go."

"Okay, Dash. We'll stay here, if that's what you want."

"I don't believe you."

"Dash, I *promise* you. We'll stay here."

"I won't come."

And he didn't.

Dash kept up his hostility and distance from me, and I kept trying to bridge it: I called, every day, telling him I wanted to see him, I loved him, I was there for him. When Peter wrote me a letter saying that Dash had decided he wouldn't visit me until I called off my application, my resolve only grew firmer. *This is sickness.*

Dash retaliated still further. "I don't want to see you. I don't want you to come and pick me up on Friday," he said angrily. "This is your warning. Goodbye." Days later, Peter had a courier deliver a handwritten letter. "I will not be visiting until the custody stuff is over. Dash." I panicked. *Dash is in a worse position than ever. What am I doing?* Whatever it was that Peter did to make Dash respond like that, to be able to say those things, terrified me. The cruelty seemed limitless. He was orchestrating and manipulating Dash in exactly the ways Norman Goodwell had predicted. *Will pulling out of court stop it? Will anything change?* I didn't know. These thoughts preoccupied my days and nights. I would find myself doubting myself, adjusting my strategy, becoming exhausted, and wanting to rescind the whole thing. But in the end I knew things were never going to improve if I just kept taking notes and letting my child slip through my fingers into the unknown. So I didn't pick up the phone and call my lawyer and pull out. I went instead to Bob Armstrong to let it all out, and continued to drive faithfully to Dash's house each week to pick him up. He was never there and even my meagre phone conversations with him vanished. I knew I was hurting him, and I knew I was making things worse for him where he was, but as a parent I had to stay strong. I was the only one willing to bear the pain of helping him. I wouldn't pull out.

Months passed.

The length of time I waited outside Peter's house for Dash to appear depended on how strong I felt on the day. Five minutes, usually fifteen, now and then a half-hour. I watched the front door the whole time for my son to appear. I didn't read. I rarely made phone calls. I just waited and watched, believing each time that Dash would soon come out and jump in my car. Sometimes I knocked on the door, a knot in my stomach in case Peter or Suzanne answered, but mostly I stayed in the car. It had been nearly four months since I had last seen Dash when one afternoon I knocked and got lucky. Rose answered and told me where he was — at the local community centre, playing floor hockey. I drove straight there with Colby and Quinten, and we went inside to find him. At a faceoff Dash looked up briefly and saw us, before he raced for the ball. We waved and cheered for him. Colby screamed, "Dash!" but he didn't even look at us in between plays. Crushed that he could ignore us like that, I pushed it down as best I could and forged ahead. When the game finished, I stood up, gathered the boys, and walked over to intercept Dash as he came off the floor.

"Hi!" I said brightly. "It's four o'clock. Time to come with us for the weekend."

"No," he said blankly. "I can't." Dash's friends looked on in disbelief as he turned away from me and trudged off. I went after him, with Colby skipping along beside me, his hand grasping mine, Quin on my hip.

"Dash, please come with me," I said softly. "Just for a few hours. You can bring your friends. I'll make us all something yummy to eat. We'll hang out. What do you think?" Dash didn't stop walking, but he slowed right down as he passed my car. He didn't turn around, but I leapt at the opportunity. I piled Colby into the car, fumbling with the car's safety buckles, strapping Quin into his baby seat, and I didn't stop talking. "It's been so long since I've seen you. Why don't you come with us for just a little while? Just for the afternoon. Dash? Just a couple of hours? We've got lots of things to show you: new photographs, toys, new games for the PlayStation. Will you come?"

Dash shook his head and, after a second's pause, continued on his way. His back was hunched; his bag looked heavy and was dragging down his right shoulder. I wanted to take it from him. I wanted to take him away. I begged him to come. "Please, Dash. Please come with us. Please come." I wanted to grab him and put him in the car and drive off, just to get him to our house with me. I knew he would melt there, he always did. But I wouldn't force him. I wouldn't give Peter another thing to rail against, and I wouldn't put Dash under any more pressure. I had tried hard today, but it hadn't worked. Colby began to cry, because tears were streaming down my face. When Dash disappeared, I leaned back on the car to wipe my face with the backs of my hands. I got in the car and pretended to the boys that I was fine. But I was devastated. I had totally failed to reach him. I was now someone this child was warned about: *Don't get in cars with strangers.*

And yet Dash was never completely gone. That May, when the court application had been in for nearly six months and a court date was just around the corner, Dash and I had a conversation that was as fun and animated as any of our chats were, as any "normal" son and mother would have. We talked for ages, and I filled him in on what was happening in my world with Dave and Colby, Quin's toddler antics, the last of our Whistler trips for the spring season, and our upcoming summer plans. Dash raved about his spring-break trip to Mexico, where he had boogie boarded and snorkelled with his friend Vecco. Our talk rolled in waves, flowing happily and spontaneously. Dash was excited to show me a video of him bungee jumping and, much as I cringed that he had been allowed to do such a thing, I never missed an opportunity to craft a connection and a visit.

"Dash, I wish I had seen your jump!"

"Mom, you would have loved it!"

"Would you bring over the video and let us watch?"

He went quiet immediately. "Soon," he promised soberly. "I'll come soon, Mom."

When I saw the video, weeks later, the camera pulled back from a tight shot of Dash, who was concentrating hard on the instructor, to a wide shot that would capture Dash's jump from the high platform. There in the corner of the shot was Peter, siting in a deck chair, reading. The camera stayed on the wide shot as Dash readied himself to jump, but Peter didn't lift his head from his book, not once, not even as his son jumped off the platform with a rope tied to his legs. The image of neglect seared on my brain, and I saw it whenever I imagined Dash struggling with his homework or going off to a sleepover without a packed bag or to school without lunch. Maybe I was wrong. I wanted desperately to be. But I didn't think I was.

The next week, Dash and I had another exuberant phone conversation, at the end of which we agreed to hang up on the count of three. It was something we used to do when he was a little boy, and when we did it that afternoon, I could tell he was smiling wide — as I was. Little things meant everything. As always, I had tried to arrange a day for

Dash to be with me. "As soon as you're ready. You know I'd love to see you." Dash had replied immediately, "How about Monday?"

It was three days away. I sent Peter a fax, my usual method, telling him that Dash and I had spoken, had agreed to spend some time together the following Monday, and that I would be there to pick him up at half past three in the afternoon. Peter's response, as I later learned, was to take Dash for an ad-hoc visit to Dr. Elterman. I wasn't told. All I knew was that I was supposed to see Dash at half past three. After his session with Dr. Elterman, though, Dash wouldn't dream of visiting me. Ignorant of the visit to Dr. Elterman, I bustled about that Monday, whipping up some of Dash's favourite things, and just as I was upending the banana bread on racks to cool, Peter called. My shoulders slumped when I heard his voice. "I got your fax, but Dash hasn't mentioned this visit," he said. "I can't imagine he'd want to see you, so I'm going to have to check it out."

I sighed. "Okay, Peter. You do that."

I patted the warm loaves absently while my heart sank. *Dash isn't coming.* He hadn't walked through our door for six months.


Two weeks later, at the end of May 1993, lawyers for both sides and Peter and I finally stood before Justice Donald Brenner for a fifteen-minute preliminary hearing. The judge expressed concern at the extent of the estrangement between Dash and me and his slipping progress at school. My friend Elizabeth MacKenzie had told me Dash had been placed in a special learning program at the school, because his reading and spelling were well below his grade level. Like earlier judges, Justice Brenner was concerned by my lack of information about Dash's educational life, and immediately ordered Peter to hand over copies of all Dash's report cards and school attendance records. (Peter would give me nothing for another three years. The one faxed report I had received from Peter just weeks earlier had the attendance portion mysteriously absent.)

I wanted to get a chunk of stipulated summer access from the preliminary hearing (which I got without a serious fight) and an order that Dash be psychologically evaluated. I wanted the judge to order an expert to spend time with Dash and sort out what he really felt. With a big sigh,

Peter got up and explained that Dash didn't need an evaluation — the estrangement between Dash and me had been caused by my "harassment" of the two of them. Dash had a perfect life in Peter's home, and his regressions, strange behaviour, and moodiness at my home and at school were, variously, my fault (for not leaving Dash alone), the court's fault (for allowing my frivolous custody application to be heard), and his teachers' fault (for picking on Dash: "Why don't you people just leave the kid alone?" Peter told them). With Peter's strenuous denials and the wildly divergent stories he and I each told about the state of Dash's life, the only way Dash was going to be evaluated and helped was if the court ordered it. Peter would never send Dash voluntarily. He claimed that "We don't believe in psychologists," but the truth was that having a psychologist assess Dash would uncover the true depths of his "bad life." Dash had become hopelessly estranged from me on his father's watch. So, despite the fact that Peter had whisked Dash off to see Dr. Elterman, upon Justice Brenner's order that Dash be psychologically evaluated, Peter gave a theatrical lament, "I shudder to think what Dash's reaction to this will be. I don't think it's going to be pleasant. When he hears of this he is going to be resentful, very resentful."

*We mustn't upset Dash, we mustn't get him angry. He'll never visit her again if we upset him. Hush now. Don't let him hear us talking about him. He'll be mad. Who was this Dash that Peter thought he knew so well? Nine-year-old children don't decide these things for themselves.* I looked over at Peter briefly. *What had he done to our child? And what more would he do?*

"Well, then, Dr. Elterman should do it," Peter said.

*No!* I wanted to slam my hands down on the bench seat. *Anyone but him.* My lawyer, John Fiddes, looked over at me with a hard expression. *He knows it, too.*

"Dr. Elterman knows the child. He's done two reports," Peter continued. "Justice Hood relied on Elterman's first report in granting me interim sole custody, and our divorce trial judge, Justice MacDonald, relied on Elterman's second report in granting me permanent sole custody. He knows the case and is the logical choice," Peter said.

In desperation I looked at John, who stood up immediately and argued that Dr. Elterman had not been a balanced evaluator and that "fresh eyes are needed here." When the judge said we should find a psychologist both sides could agree on, John offered up the name of Dr. Leslie Joy. Not many psychologists did court-ordered assessments, but she was qualified and available, and someone none of us had ever met. My heart beat wildly as I recognized the feeling of a court hearing starting to go my way. For perhaps twenty seconds my hope hung suspended in the air. Then Peter delivered his final blow. Speaking for the boy who had told me definitively after his first meeting with Elterman in 1989, "I don't like that man," Peter declared that Dash would *refuse* to see anybody but Dr. Elterman. "Dash," Peter proclaimed, "trusts Elterman."

My teeth were clenched to keep my jaw shut against what I wanted to say: *The person who trusts Dr. Elterman, Peter, is you, not Dash.*

"It is doubtful that Dash will speak to a stranger at this stage," Peter continued. "It would be irresponsible and cruel to subject him to any such attempt, and it will likely be fruitless anyway, as we believe Dashiell will refuse to take part."

Could the judge see what was happening here? Why would Dash care who he saw if it was court-ordered? He wasn't even ten years old. It was *Peter* who didn't want Dash to see anyone other than Dr. Elterman. After two court-ordered assessments and several ad-hoc meetings Peter could probably guarantee the outcome by now of any report Elterman did. The bias was entrenched. Dr. Joy was unknown and a risk. "Dash won't see anyone else" meant "I won't let Dash see anyone else." Would the court sanction this manipulation? No, it didn't. Whether he actually understood what was happening in his courtroom or not, Justice Brenner gave us the order we wanted: Dash was to see a psychologist for a full assessment, and the assessor was not to be Dr. Elterman.

Our first win.

In the end it didn't matter what the judge had ordered, though, because the system gives people like Peter every loophole they need. Peter didn't like the court order, so he simply ignored it. With no penalties, why not? Lack of consequences was the key to his success. School reports, attendance records, access, summer access — all had been mandated by judges and ignored. For the next month and a half Peter and his lawyers stonewalled us, ignoring my lawyer's letters and delaying their own for days, refusing our requests for them to either agree to the appointment of Dr. Joy or to put forward other names. Every day was precious, but we got nothing. In early July, exasperated, we went back to Justice Brenner, who this time wrote a specific order: Peter was to get Dash forthwith to Dr. Leslie Joy for a full psychological evaluation, news I sailed along on for a couple of weeks — until Peter changed tack. He wrote to Dr. Joy and welcomed her to her task of "dealing with the reasons behind the child's reluctance to visit." My lawyer faxed me a copy of Peter's letter and I stared at it blankly. *What is he doing now?* His voice filled with frustration, Dave deciphered it for me. "Christ, he's trying to limit the inquiry, Pam. It will bring back a useless evaluation."

In framing Dr. Joy's role as he did, Peter started with the assumption (which he must have hoped the psychologist would take at face value) that Dash really *was* reluctant to visit, an assertion I had never believed. Dash's "reluctance to visit" was the result of a bizarre home life that had encouraged him to dump his mother from his life. We needed the court's "full psychological assessment" to be a thorough look at Dash's home life and emotional health and the custodial arrangement as it related to it — not Peter's truncated inquiry.

The shenanigans were a pain, and evidence to me of Peter's continuing desire — and ability — to manipulate the legal proceedings; but hanging over me like a cloud was the one thing that distressed me more than anything else: Peter's immersion of Dash directly in his battle with me. It was Dash won't do this, Dash won't do that. He had always been told far too much about the "court battle." I had tried so hard to shield Dash, but Peter had submerged him. He was showing Dash all the court documents. All the affidavits, all the accusations. Though he publicly considered it "Dash's right" to know, in my mind, focused through my work with Norman Goodwell, it was just another way he set up the black-and-white good parent/bad parent scenario that had been the signature of the past four years of Dash's life.

Because Dash wasn't with me enough, or free to see me as I was, and because I never spoke to him about what was happening between his parents, or in court, Dash got only his father's story — his anguish, my betrayal. It kept Dash hyped and paranoid about me, maintaining a high level of hostility in their household. I was the villain; Peter was the benign knight looking out for his son. It was a made-up fantasy scenario, but their *folie á deux* relied on it. *Dashy, you wouldn't believe what she said in court today. She thinks you need to see a shrink! Well, don't worry, son. I'll get this all sorted out.* Although positioning and involving the children is common in divorce, to me what Peter was doing was child abuse. Dash's intimate knowledge of every letter, every legal document, the presence of process-servers, his father's dinnertime rantings over the latest legal salvo, all immersed Dash and forced his loyalty vice ever tighter. It was only going to get worse from here. I had hoped, when Peter did it in front of Justice Brenner ("Dash will refuse to see anyone but Dr. Elterman") that the judge would see it, but all he did was order Peter not to tell Dash about what was happening in court. Why would Peter discontinue something that worked so well for him? Now Dash was given a new locus for his torment: the order that he was to see a psychologist and spend two weeks with me over the summer.

I had crossed my fingers and willed him to be brave, but, sure enough, Dash called the night before he was to begin his court-ordered time with me.

"Don't you come and get me tomorrow. Do you get it? Don't come over!" he raged. "Do you understand? I'm not coming with you. Do you get the message?"

I may have just scored two minor victories in court, but Peter had Dash and was using the court order to load his weapon. I knew now that the judge wouldn't enforce the access order, or the assessment order, and I held ten thousand dollars in useless court orders in my hand; Dash was over there in West Point Grey, distressed and frightened, with anger the only legitimate vehicle for its release. I imagined Peter and Dash talking legal strategy with their on-site family lawyer, Suzanne, or plotting how to get out of the psychologist's visit. I drove myself into an anguished frenzy going over and over the same question: *What do I do? Peter might be at home right now, skewing the day's proceedings, lifting sentences from my affidavits out of context to drive my betrayals into Dash's heart.* I couldn't say, "I know this doesn't look good, but believe me, I am trying to help." I couldn't say, "Now, don't let all this affect your self-esteem. You're a wonderful boy, and I'm saying these things about you only because I care." I was Exxon in Prince William Sound, Union Carbide in Bhopal. I was the global bad guy whose explanations were dismissed as so much self-protective spin.

I wandered around the house late at night, because it was quiet then and I could think. I felt heavy and trapped, in checkmate again. *What do I do?* The momentum was with me. I was finally, if haltingly, being heard in court. It could go all the way. But at what cost? During my wanderings, I'd tiptoe into the boys' rooms and kiss their warm baby-soft cheeks, and smell their sleepy smells, and sit in the rocking chair I had nursed all three of them in, and think of Dash, drowning in anger that wasn't even his. As I drove around the West Side, picking up groceries or having lunch with girlfriends or taking Colby to and from gymnastics, I heard in my mind Peter telling Dash that they had to *Stick together through this.* Or *You're going to be forced to see your mother. Don't you want to be with me for the summer, Dashy?* Or that he was going to have to see Dr. Joy, someone he didn't know and not the "trusted" Elterman. *Remember we don't believe in psychologists, Dashy. Dr. Joy's on your mother's side. She's trying to take your dad away, and you know how much you love your dad, don't you, kid?* As much as I tried to keep my eyes on the prize — getting Dash assessed, getting my access enforced, or getting custody and starting to heal Dash — I saw now that it would take a miracle to get that prize, because Peter would stop at nothing. *She says you're a dummy, Dash. She thinks you're nuts. She says I don't feed you properly.* Whatever it took to keep Dash primed and ready for battle. Dash's "I won't see you until you stop" was just Peter's "You'll never see Dash again if you keep going."

I couldn't bear it. I was exhausted. *I'm hurting my son and I'm not guaranteed a result. All I want is Dash on my doorstep at four o'clock on Wednesdays and Fridays or, better yet, safely installed in his room upstairs.*

Dave and I always found the money to go to court, but couldn't seem to do anything real with it. I had two minor court orders, but Peter held all the cards. He had Dash, a boy with no bruises on him, a boy who usually acted like an *ordinary* kid. His extreme loyalty to his father looked a lot like love, and Peter's obsession with Dash looked like devotion. Peter was presumed to be the best person for the job because the *last* judge had thought so, and he had thought so because the judge before him had thought so, and he had thought so because the court-ordered psychologist had taken a stab in the dark. Peter had layers and layers of credibility, where I had none. Justice Brenner had shown that he wouldn't confront Peter. He couldn't even threaten Peter with consequences for immersing a nine-year-old boy in his own custody case. I was pushing a rock uphill, without a guarantee that I would wind up with even a psychological assessment, let alone a strong access order or custody. I was prepared for an ugly, expensive trial, a big win, and many months of pain and adjustment for Dash, but as I sat numbly one morning staring at my desk, fingering the handle of a rapidly cooling mug of coffee, I realized, although I was ready to face all that, it was vitally important to Dash that we win this case. Overwhelmingly, though, I felt we were going to lose. Dash would be sent back to that house, with me not just scorned and dismissed this time but *excommunicated* for having taken "them" to court and lost. Dash would see for the third time that his dad was right. I *was* the wicked one. The courts would order Dash to stay with his dad, who was so powerful that not even his mother and "all her millions" could get Dash out of that house. *That will be it for his damaged soul.* The risk of continuing in court and failing was too great, and I lost my nerve. I wouldn't bet Dash's life on a crapshoot. I called my lawyer, John Fiddes.

"Stop everything. I can't do it."


Unmoored and utterly dejected, I sat at my desk after the call, casting about for some hope to appear, something to cling to. I had a two-year-old banging away on blocks next to me and a husband who would be home in a few hours. I had to find something in this mess that would give me hope and allow me to survive my decision. Dash's wild reaction to my going to court for him had shocked me and allowed me insight into just how entwined he and Peter really were. Their personalities had melded. Peter's needs became Dash's duty. Dash's "happiness" became Peter's *raison d'être*. This was much more complicated than any of us had thought. A court case was a cataclysmic event for them. It wouldn't get us where I needed to get us. I couldn't remove Dash from his father by court order. It would never work. I saw it clearly as I sat at my desk. Pulling us all out of the court system would ease the pressure on Dash at home. If Peter wasn't threatened by the prospect of me getting custody, he might let Dash visit. I would use those visits to bolster my relationship with Dash and help moor him that way. I'd still be outside the gates, but I'd be there. I had to get them *both* to trust me. I had to work with them *both* and recalibrate my expectations. I would bide my time and watch and learn. There would be no court again unless I was guaranteed a win. I wouldn't need court if I could pull off my plan: I would take my beautiful son's pain in my hands and replace it with love. I would rely on Dash to keep his promise that he would visit if I stopped "the court stuff." I would go on his word.

# Chapter 4
# Armed and Dangerous

"**M**om! Look at me!" It was Dash, running down the boards, about to leap off the end of the dock. He didn't have to tell me to watch. I hadn't taken my eyes off that wonderful creature for days. He crashed into the water in a perfectly executed dive-bomb and came up spluttering and laughing, a boy on holiday. He could have been anyone. Because it was Dash, though, it was a miracle. A year had passed since I pulled out of the court process upon Dash's promise to visit. He hadn't come more than a handful of times and then would go months without coming back. The only thing that had changed was my capacity — and that of my family — to cope with the disappointment.

"Did you see that?" he called, bobbing up and down in the lake. I waved from my deck chair, called, "Loved it, Dash! Do another!" and drank him in, each moment a pleasure, each of his shouts a tangible, almost shocking, reminder that he was actually with us.

"Dash!" I called, "if I pass Quin to you from the ladder, can you take him while I get into the lake?"

"Sure," Dash said, swimming closer. "Quinner, look at me! It's great in here!"

It was August 1994. Dash was ten. I couldn't remember the last holiday he had taken with us. But now we were all at Lake of the Woods, Dave's parents' summer camp. Dash had last come here when he was six and had loved it so much. Maybe that's why he was able to come this time, because it had been so special to him before. I had tried to keep Dash's first Lake of the Woods trip alive in him as a wonderful holiday memory and that might have been enough. Who knows? Maybe Peter was throwing me a bone or he wanted to go away with Suzanne. I didn't know. I didn't care. Dash was with us. And look at him! How he'd grown. Dash stuck close to me, as ever, and he really seemed happy, squealing with delight whenever he fell off his water skis into the clear, bracing lake. He was demanding of my love, and I gave him whatever he needed. I had to be in the boat whenever he water-skied, and I had to be there to praise him whenever he swam out into the lake. He hugged me all the time and wanted me to rub his back every night. I recognized the subtle desperation in his constant demands for love and attention, but there, on that beautiful island, when I closed my eyes tight and drew a protective barrier around our history, it was as if our bond had never been broken and I could forget we had seen each other so little. Dash was the funny, thoughtful, and charming boy I had thought lost, and it felt like the most natural thing in the world to swim and fish and sail with him. When we started to prepare the evening meal, I could almost see him look around the kitchen for his stuffed animal, Woofie, and the little pine stool he had sat on as a boy, chattering away, while I made dinner in our West Vancouver home so many years before. Dash took seriously his role as a double-digit big brother and was patient with his brothers, keeping a special eye out for toddler Quin and letting Colby hang off his shirttails day in and day out. Just that morning Dash had come running outside to me.

"Mom, can Colby and I go up to Gammie's" — that's Dave's mom — "house? She wants to show us an eagles' nest."

"Wow, a bald eagle?"

"I think so, yeah."

"Of course, go, go! But," I dropped my voice to be serious, "can you please make sure you hold Colby's hand tight as you go up all those steps? They are in the shade most of the day and can get very slippery."

"Okay, Mom." I heard them chatting as they walked up the stairs. "Colby, you better hold my hand all the way up, okay?"

"I like holding your hand!" He slid his hand into Dash's.

"Mom, I'll see you later." Dash turned back quickly and said, "And Big D said he'd take me wake-boarding later."

"Wonderful." Dash was being so kind to the boys. I mouthed "Thank you," and pointed at Colby, who was transfixed by the steepness of the stairs and was looking away. I made my heart shape with both my hands, and Dash eased himself out of Colby's hand for just a second and did the same back. My heart sang.

There were no tantrums. There was no running and hiding behind the couch when I needed the table set for dinner. Dash was loving and sweet the entire holiday. Dave's parents fell in love with him anew, as they had the first time he had come to the lake. We listened to the crickets sing as we ate our evening meals, and after dinner Dash and Colby jumped into their jammies and raced each other to brush their teeth before piling onto our bed to snuggle in for stories. They were both careful to give two-year-old Quin room. Dave held the book in his hands, like a talisman, a grin on his face, the sorcerer. The two older boys scattered themselves on the bed, smoothing the covers beneath them and grabbing pillows then discarding them for being in the way. Dash finally lay stretched out on his tummy with elbows sinking into the covers and his hands propping up his chin. Colby copied him, lying in exactly the same position, changing only when he did.

"Now — are we ready?" Dave would ask mischievously.

"Yes, we are!" they chimed in, and into the magic of the story we would fly.

The holiday was a shot in the arm for me: Dash was still himself. Away from Vancouver, he could relax and be the wonderful *him* that he was. Those six nights in Ontario were heaven. But as we flew over the prairies toward home, I watched Dash shut down, something I had seen him do so many times. He was preparing himself to go back to his father. He sank down and put his head in my lap. I could feel his warmth through my light summer clothes, and, as I stroked his sun-streaked hair, out of the blue he said quietly, with just the slightest edge of defiance in his voice, "You know, boys should live with their dads, because of the sports they do."

I paused. This was something he had been taught. Sport isn't parenting. Moms do sports, anyway. I willed him to remember riding his bike next to me as I ran at Jericho Beach when he was little and skiing with me at Whistler all those years. I had been to nearly every one of his soccer games, but I didn't prod him.

"Well," I said gently, careful not to dispute his opinion and invoke his loyalty to his dad, "I think I understand what you mean, but, you know, there's much more to raising children than their sports."

One of the frustrations of being a parent to a child who had absorbed such bizarre messages was that I couldn't take advantage of these moments of closeness to show him that he had been taught some really unhealthy ideas. Their loyalty to each other was so strong that he would be obliged to leap to his father's defence. That would ruin the spell we had cast over each other at the lake. I had practised the art of letting go for nearly five years, and I did it now, biting my tongue and skimming over the surface instead of trying to turn his head. There's nothing like parenthood to teach you to be patient, particularly having to be as peculiar a parent as I was now to Dash. Honest conversations would have to wait until he got older and grew independent of his father. So I looked down at that beautiful golden-brown boy, staring up at me with eyes that dimmed with every mile we flew closer to Vancouver, and said, "Well, to me, Dash, the important thing is not which parent you live with but that you have strong, happy relationships with both of them and you are happy."

Dash looked hard at me. Then he blinked, and the moment was gone. He put his heavy head back into my lap, yawned like a puppy, and settled himself for a nap.

"Mom," he said.

"Yes?"

"That was the best holiday I've ever had."


Dash didn't visit again for another three months, but he did join us for our Christmas-tree-trimming night in mid-December. After he had finally agreed to come, I had looked forward to the visit for days and called just before leaving home to pick him up to make sure he was ready. I flew down Trimble Street to get him and, as I pulled up, the door opened. A longer, leaner Dash ambled up to the car.

"Hi, Mom," he said.

"Hello! Hello!" I said as he climbed in. "Can I give you a big hug?" I held him for a long moment, then drew back and smiled. "You're not shaving yet are you, Dash?"

"Mom!" Dash smiled back.

"You're not in college yet?"

"No!" he smiled even wider.

"I'm teasing. It is just that we haven't seen each other for so long."

"I know."

"Have you got your seatbelt on?"

"Yup," he said.

"Good. Then we're off. The boys are waiting and there's a lot of work to do tonight. You should see the tree — it touches the ceiling! Have you eaten?"

"Yeah, a bit. But I'm hungry. Can I have a snack before we start the tree?"

"You got it. How about honey-bear toast? It used to be one of your favourites, remember?"

"Kind of."

"You used to love a snack before bedtime, so I would make toast with honey and we called it honey-bear toast!"

"Well, that or grilled cheese — whatever."

It was tough when Dash didn't respond with joy to little memories like that, but I rolled with it these days. "Okay," I said, trying to sound nonchalant. "Do you still drink lots of milk like you used to?"

Later I lined up my three boys in front of the bare Christmas tree the way I did every year. They shut their eyes and held out their hands; little Quin held out both, in case one wasn't big enough to hold his prize. Every year at Christmas I bought each boy a special tree ornament — all three the same — and when we took the tree down in January, I packaged them up carefully and put them away in boxes. In time there would be dozens of boxes, filled with three identical sets of miniature skis, toy trees, snowboards, snowmen, little pairs of skates, rustic canoes, log houses, Santas on snowboards. I loved the idea of my children growing up and taking their ornaments with them for their own trees, each ornament representing a childhood Christmas and the repository of a special memory. My parents had always made Christmas special, and I remember as if it were yesterday, that feeling of being a child on Christmas morning, opening my eyes wide and seeing our tree surrounded by presents left after Santa's midnight visit, checking if the cookies had all been eaten, if the tea had been drunk. I wanted that same magic to exist for my boys.

After my separation from Peter, I had wanted desperately to continue a sense of family togetherness at Christmas, but instead of coming in for a Christmas-morning tea, so that Dash could be with all four of us for an hour or two, Peter and Suzanne simply dropped Dash off on Christmas Day. Still, Christmases had worked reasonably well, because Peter's family tradition was to celebrate on Christmas Eve and mine was to celebrate on Christmas Day, so Dash stayed with his dad each twenty-fourth and came to us on the twenty-fifth each year. But on Dash's ninth Christmas we hadn't seen him at all, despite lengthy negotiations with both Peter and Dash, and I wondered now — *will he come this year?* Tree-trimming was one thing, as it wasn't a threat to Peter the way Christmas Day clearly was, but the signs were impossible to read. When Dash and I talked on the phone, he told me he was excited to be coming over for Christmas and was looking forward to eating "shortbread cookies, turkey with tons of gravy, and Christmas pudding!" and seeing Colby, Quin, and Big D. He took seriously my suggestion that he make a list, so that Santa wouldn't have to come up with everything off the top of his head.

Dash had missed so many of our special occasions, and so much of our lives, but he *always* came for the tree-trimming. So there he was with his favourite baseball cap on — turned backward — standing in front of the naked tree, all set to trim it with past years' ornaments and brightly coloured baubles and gifts.

"Hurry, Mommy!" said Colby, now four years old. His body wiggled in anticipation.

Quin, two, and a solid little boy, tucked in next to his big brother Dash and cried, "Now, Mommy! Now, Mommy."

"Hey, Quinner! You almost knocked me over!" Dash said, opening his eyes briefly and nudging him back, sending Quinten into gales of laughter.

Dash went quiet again, but his fingers jittered and his scrunched-up face was smiling as he waited for his gift. I gently placed the three little tissue parcels in their outstretched hands and said, "Okay, you can look now." They opened their eyes in unison and ripped open their parcels. They threw the tissue to the ground and held up their special ornaments. In each of my boys' hands was a furry brown teddy bear with a shiny gold string coming out of its head. It was supersoft and had a red-and-white striped scarf, along with a happy smile made of pink felt. The boys ran to the tree to put them up. Quin took a low branch, and I helped him wrap the string over the pine needles. Colby dragged a little stool across the floor and, with Dave holding him steady, put his ornament high up on a branch so his teddy bear was visible from every corner of the room. Dash reached up on his tippytoes and pulled the teddy's string carefully over a branch in the middle of the tree. When they were done, the boys all stood back to look. There were three bears for my three boys. We spent the next hour putting a riot of other sparkly, colourful trinkets on the tree; their bears were still in perfect spots.

I made our favourite tree-trimming meal of beef stew and whipped potatoes, and when Dave took the little boys off to bath and bed, Dash and I sat at the kitchen table with big mugs of hot chocolate and did the planning for another tradition I treasured. Dash and I had made a gingerbread house together every year since he was five. When he was six, we had made a barn and filled it with animals. The following year we had made an ornate church, the next year a log house, its roof covered in snowy white frosting. No design was too complicated — we were up for anything! We would flip through the magazine pages, and Dash would point to one, grin, with his eyes sparkling, and say, "We can do that, Mom! Come on, it'll be easy!" On the day, we would chat happily as we worked, both of us in aprons, our heads pressed together gently as we tested the icing to see if it was stiff enough to glue our pieces together. As hard as we tried, our gingerbread creations never looked anything like the glossy step-by-step pictures we tried to emulate, but to Dash and me, they were flawless pieces of art. We took pictures from all angles, and I always got shots of Dash with a wide smile and an apron that was plastered, by the end of the evening, with vibrant swirls of hardened icing. The finished product held a place of high honour in the centre of our dining-room table. The year before I had decided to do the baking of the gingerbread alone the day before Dash was due, knowing we would only have a few hours to put it together and decorate it before he went home.

While sipping hot chocolate, Dash and I decided this year we'd make a winter ski cabin, and we planned it meticulously, constructing a long list of ingredients I had to go and buy and deciding what kinds of finery the cabin needed to really come to life. I cherished every minute of the planning. The gingerbread nights were something I did only with Dash and, no matter what, our gingerbread night was the only other thing that Dash *always* came for.

But a week later the phone rang, and when I heard Dash say "Hi, Mom," my heart broke. He only ever called to cancel something with me. He was matter-of-fact, almost cold. "I can't come tomorrow night." I was devastated but went straight into emergency-mode — my window of opportunity was always so short on the phone. I knew from long experience that I had to leap straight ahead to make sure he didn't hang up without booking another time to see me.

"How about Thursday, Dash?"

"Um, I don't know."

"Friday?"

Nothing. I paused. "Oh, Dash, I'm so disappointed," I said.

"Yeah."

"Well, let's think of another night? Not Thursday, not Friday, what about—?"

"I don't really know, Mom." He wanted to get off the phone and, with a silent sigh, I closed my eyes and stopped pushing. I'd gone as far as I was willing, so I let it go.

"Let's say I call you tomorrow and you can tell me then what day works?" I said. "I love you so much, Dash."

"Yeah. Okay, Mom," he said noncommittally.

I put down the phone and the disappointment hit me. This was going to be the first gingerbread night he'd ever missed. *But it's not his fault,* I reminded myself. *If his home were healthy, he'd be able to come.* We'd had the tree-trimming, but now I felt suffocated and cheated. Black clouds were swallowing our Christmas traditions. What chance was there that Dash would come for Christmas if he had lost the courage to come for our gingerbread night? I called Dash the next day and every day that week, but got only the answering machine or Peter, who told me each time that Dash was "out." I kept trying. I couldn't let Christmas slip by. On Christmas Eve, I got through, and Dash sounded bright. Maybe he had found a private place to talk or maybe he was just happy, because he told me boisterously that he was excited he would be opening his presents with us the next day. My heart soared. Dash was going to do it.

"Well, we have big plans for Christmas Day, you know, Dash. We've got piles of presents here, and then we'll all drive over to Uncle Dave's and have Christmas dinner with him and Aunt Bev and Mikey. They haven't seen you for a year and are so excited!"

"Me, too, Mom."

"Think of all those extra presents you'll get," I teased.

"Will I be able to open my presents first?" Dash's voice rose an octave.

"Of course! Then breakfast. As many pancakes as you can eat!"

"All right!"

"Now what time did you say your dad would drop you here tomorrow?"

"He said ten o'clock."

"Well, then, that's exactly when I'll see you. I love you."

"I love you, too, Mom."

The next day Colby woke up early, ran in to get Dave and me, then raced downstairs to the mantel to unhook his stocking. He handed Quin his stocking, and they sat down together and turned them upside down, squealing as little wrapped toys and colourful candy flowed onto the floor. They were impatient to open the pile of presents, but Dash was coming at ten o'clock, and they knew they had to wait. Mommy and Daddy would make themselves coffee when he arrived, and then they'd get to open their presents. The boys were just as excited to see Dash as they were about their gifts, but ten o'clock came and went. Colby perched himself on a seat with a wide view of the street outside and waited, but no car arrived. We waited and waited, but an hour later we made our coffees and let the boys open the rest of their presents. They spread their gift wrap all over the floor and I knelt between them, explaining who the gifts were from and reading instructions, while Dave installed various sizes of batteries. I knew Dash wasn't coming and I couldn't talk about it yet, so Dave just let me be. We acted as though everything was normal, but my heartache filled the room. This was not normal. *Where is my son?*

Dash finally called at lunchtime, and I knew exactly what he would say. His tone was defensive and unapologetic. "I'm not coming," he said. He gave no explanation; his statement was a challenge. Dave had followed me to the phone and, as my shoulders sagged, I saw anger flash across his face, anger for the disappointment this wild child had brought to his wife and children, anger at Peter for creating this mess. And impotence. Dave couldn't do anything to protect me from all this, and he couldn't do anything to make Dash's life any different than it was. All he could do — and it brought him little comfort — was support me, and all I could do was try and stay in Dash's life. Dave had spent three hours the night before, on Christmas Eve, walking around the stores after work, aimless and helpless. He finally came home at nine o'clock, worn out, with a Krups waffle iron under his arm. "I think Dash would really like this, don't you?" he said softly.

I saw right through him. "Dave . . ." *It's okay.*

Dave shook his head and I saw his face drop as tears came to his eyes. "Pam, I'm so frustrated about our situation with Dash. I have no idea how to fix this. You know, I'm used to being able to fix . . . to solve . . . things—"

This gentle man's heartbreak was so hard to watch. He had been so steady for so long. Mad, not sad. Tall, not bent. And all I could do to solve *him*, in that moment, was to hold him and love him and for just one solitary instant be just *his* wife, not Dash's mother, not the mother of our boys, but the woman he married, the one who had promised to cherish and protect him. I was acutely aware of how much stress I had brought to Dave's life, and every day I saw how this man loved me and how he cherished Dash and wanted him in our lives — it was a testament to the sort of person Dave was. He had so much to give.

"It's because of you and the boys that I have the strength to keep going, Dave, and don't ever forget that," I said, while this courageous man slumped in my arms. "It's your love, Dave. It's you. I'll never forget it and I'll never take it for granted."

The following year, the year in which Dash turned eleven, I could count on my fingers the number of times I saw him. I wrote them all down, so extraordinary and fleeting were my encounters with him. I would find myself sitting at my desk writing a note or planning my week and wondering numbly what he was doing. Days and weeks passed when nothing dramatic happened, when no new salvo came from Peter, when he and I even had halfway pleasant conversations, but it only underscored how far I had fallen out of Dash's life, how irrelevant and harmless I had become to Peter. I saw Dash for a total of twenty-four hours the whole year: ten minutes on his doorstep in March, when I gave him a conch shell I had found for him on a beach in the Caribbean; a few hours in April, when Dash came over for Quin's third birthday; five minutes, later that month, when I took over an armful of Easter eggs and we hugged happily on his doorstep and chatted for a few minutes. When he made a love heart out of his fingers and thumbs as I was leaving, I was overcome with as much joy as unbearable grief — he had remembered our old goodbye, and I struggled not to cry right there in front of him. With breathtaking presence Dash released his fingers and took hold of my hand, saying gently, "It's okay, Mom."

I called him the day before Mother's Day, and he sounded flat. His voice registered no emotion at all at the sound of my voice. He answered my "How are you?" with an apathetic grunt. I had been planning the call for hours, and had hoped to catch him in a good mood. I shifted into a higher gear.

"Dash, do you know what day it is tomorrow?"

"No," he answered, suddenly wary.

"It's Mother's Day!"

"Oh, yeah!" he shouted, instantly brightening. I could *hear* him smiling. "Mom, I forgot."

"You know, we're having a special dinner tomorrow night. I'd love to see you."

I heard him take a breath, and he didn't speak for a long moment. "Maybe," he answered quietly. He sounded frightened, *frightened*, at the prospect of seeing me. I could hear the cogs turning in his mind, perhaps calculating the risk. "No, no. I can't, Mom. I've got to go now, okay?" I closed my eyes and said quietly, "I understand," and those two words brought the sound of my son's audible relief.

Throughout the year, Dash continued to agree to all manner of visits and trips and weekends and days out and dinners and special shows — *Aladdin on Ice* came to Vancouver that year — and then morosely cancelled on me. Dash's eleventh birthday in August came and went with just a parcel and a long-distance phone call from me from France. I had asked him to come with us, we had rented a house in Provence, and while he had been enthusiastic about coming, I could never get him to commit to the dates, or ask his father if he could go (we needed Peter's permission as the custodial parent to take Dash out of the country), or even to admit, "Yes, Mom, I want to come." He kept saying, "We'll have to see."

Everything Dash had ever enjoyed with me, with us all, was finally relegated to the past: our gingerbread houses, Christmas, our ski weekends, Canucks home games, family holidays. Trick-or-treating had long gone, but every Halloween we still went through the pretence that I would be involved. In the weeks leading up to that year's Halloween, Dash and I talked often about him coming with me to the shop and picking out a costume and all the makeup and accessories. Dash wasn't a little boy any more, so I had to create in him a bit of excitement about Halloween, but to his credit, perhaps to humour me, perhaps because he missed it, he talked happily with me on the phone about the kind of monster he wanted to be, whether or not he should wear black nail polish or would that be too weird? I had gone to the drugstore, the dollar store, and the costume shop, and had picked out all the stuff the three boys needed. I had everything for Dash's costume in bags ready to drop off at his house when, the night before Halloween, Dash called. *Here we go.*

"My dad's going to take me to the costume shop instead, Mom," he said matter-of-factly, but there was the slightest hint of a "Sorry, Mom" in there, a whisper of empathy from which I took hope: sometimes he acted as if he didn't care how his refusals and cancellations would be received. This time he did. I called the next night.

"Good luck! Are you all ready to go?" I asked brightly.

"Oh," Dash sounded slumped. "No, not really, Mom."

"Why not?"

"We didn't end up going to the store," he said. "It's no big deal though, Mom." *He has no costume. But it's no big deal.* No disappointment seemed to be a "big deal" any more.

Given how bizarre our life together was, part of the responsibility I felt as Dash's mom was to not do to him the things his father had done. So, no pressure. No manipulation. No lies. I piled on understanding and love and gave him, each day, a commitment I believed he privately relied on: that I would always keep trying to see him and I would love him no matter what had happened in the past or would happen in the future. Whenever Dash cancelled, he saved it until the last minute, as though waiting until the last possible moment to face the disappointment. His cancellations were as hard on our household as they were on me, because all four of us would have geared up to see him, the boys would save up their stories for him, but have only a couple of hours or a night's warning that he wouldn't be coming. The weeks became months; months became a year, and by the time Dash was eleven, I had stopped telling the boys he was coming at all, because he invariably didn't, and I couldn't bear their disappointment on top of mine. Whenever I did get Dash, it felt like a military coup. I would call Dave and Mimi from the car, and all I needed to say was, "I've got Dash with me." I kept it casual, because Dash was sitting right next to me, but it was code, and they knew what it meant. Other plans were summarily cancelled, Mimi would stay longer, and Dave would come home early to occupy the boys. When Dash and I walked through the door, for the entire time — a couple of hours usually — the household revolved around him.

My fury at the way Dash lived had been kept so deeply buried that it was hard to access. I was too sad and deflated most of the time to raise the energy for an outburst, and I kept myself too focused on the next day, the next visit, the next moment, to wallow for long. I never slammed drawers or threw things. When I replaced the phone in the cradle, I did it gently and breathed out a whispered, "Fuck!" but the pain of knowing that Dash missed so many things and endured so many disappointments cut through my life like a knife. Everyone lost in this war — Dash, Dave, the boys, Mimi, me, my parents, my brother Dave, Sandy, Terry — saw Dash once a year at best. We were all casualties.

Dash, of course, was the biggest casualty. As Christmas 1995 approached, so did our end-of-year trip to Maui. As I did every year, I invited Dash to come with us. And as he did every year, when we talked on the phone, Dash said how excited he was about coming with us.

"Mom, I can't wait to see the whales when they come out of the water!"

"Oh, it's so beautiful, Dash. They call it 'breaching.' To see them lift their whole weight out of the water like that is a real thrill. It takes my breath away and reminds me of how we humans are just one part of the universe, pretty insignificant and small."

"You mean kind of like ants?"

"Physically, yes, like ants. But I was thinking more on the cosmic level, too."

"Cosmic? You mean like 'Nanoo nanoo'?" he asked, breaking into laughter at this reference to *Mork and Mindy*.

"Yeah, nanoo nanoo! Hey, is that a Hawaiian word?"

"Sure, Mom. Right." Oops, I was at risk of looking like a dork. "Can I snorkel, too?" Dash asked.

"And boogie board. So we're on for Maui, nanoo nanoo?" I laughed.

"Yes! And nanoo nanoo to you, too!"

When the time came for me to book the tickets, Dash and I came close to talking about how he had to manage his life.

"Dash, you know that we need to get permission from your dad for me to take you out of the country?"

"Oh," he said quietly. Then he spoke with a resolution to his voice I had never heard before. "Then how should I tell my dad I want to come?"

Astonished, I had to collect my thoughts for a second. It's not like I'd ever had any success with Peter either. "I think it would be best done in a letter, from me. What do you think?"

"Okay, Mom," he said, conscious, surely, that he had just let me glimpse the way he had to live his life. I faxed off a letter as soon as I had hung up the phone. It was mid-November and, with the busy travel season approaching, I didn't have much time to buy his ticket, so I was anxious to hear from Peter. Days passed with no response. A week later I faxed another letter, but got nothing. I called the airline daily, checking that there was still space for Dash on our flights. Miraculously, they kept telling me there was, but when two weeks passed, I put the idea away. It wasn't going to happen. To my surprise, Dash came to trim the tree with us again that year and, as we sat that night, again, at the kitchen table, the time felt right for me to raise the issue. I was tense. It had been years since I had asked how things were at home, but now that I had him in the house, I was just about out of time to get him a ticket and I wanted to give it one more try.

"Has your dad said anything about the trip to Maui yet, Dash?" I asked. "I have to buy your ticket really soon."

"Dad? No. He hasn't said anything." From his look of total confusion, I assumed that he thought his dad had worked it out with me and that the trip was booked.

*Oh, no.* I scrambled to not say the wrong thing. "Well, um, did he mention the two letters I sent, trying to set it up?" I asked, not knowing what I should and shouldn't say. *Have I already said too much?*

"No," Dash said, looking blankly at me.

Peter was just waiting it out, letting the trip drift into oblivion like everything else. Damn him! I was furious. If Dash and I hadn't talked about it, Peter would have been able to blame me, as I'm sure he always had. *She never said anything to me about it, Dashy. Come on, I'm not a mind reader. Guess she doesn't really want you to go with them after all.* Years of fury scorched my blood, and I squeezed my eyes shut for a second. When I opened them, I looked over at Dash and my rage evaporated. What was the right thing to do for this boy with the miserable life? What could I do? I had never before involved Dash in my dealings with his father, but just then I decided to show him that at least I had followed through on my promise to organize the trip. I wanted to salvage something from the debacle. For the first time, I wanted to offer Dash some proof that I wasn't an unreliable or treacherous person. I gently took Dash's hand and led him into my den and pulled the two letters out of my desk drawer. Dash glanced at them, then at the floor.

I had in my hands confirmation that his father had deceived him, and that his needs and wishes and happiness had been ignored. I watched Dash carefully. I kept holding his hand.

"Dash, I need your father's permission, and I don't think I'm going to get it."

"I still really want to come though," he said quietly, a whisper of desperation entering his voice.

I had wanted Dash to understand that I had held up my end here. I had wanted him to see the truth, to feel and acknowledge his pain, but his loyalty to his father did not allow him to compute what had happened. He couldn't express normal feelings of anger and frustration toward his father, even when it was crystal clear that, instead of answering my letters and allowing Dash to go on a holiday he desperately wanted, his father had chosen to ignore them. Instead of saying, "Mom, can you call Dad right now and get this sorted out," or bursting into tears and shouting, "I'm mad at him for forgetting about this!" the look on Dash's face showed me that he knew his needs and wishes were unimportant, that he wasn't good enough for his desires to be met. Dash should have been a mess, but he choked it back as he always did. He kept his head down, and the quiet acceptance in his body showed me how much he had been through.

I gently pulled him to me. "Let's see what we can do to sort this out, shall we? I wanted you to see those letters so you would know that they were sent and that I have tried to work it out with your dad. But I'm so sorry, Dash." I pressed my lips into his tangled hair and kissed him quietly on the head. I hated myself for showing him the letters, for making it so clear that his father hadn't cared about his happiness. *How much more can he take? He doesn't have the capacity to deal with this.*

"I don't want you to think this is your fault. I wish I knew a way to make this holiday come true. Dasharoo, you mustn't think that you have caused any of this."

"I won't." His voice was muffled in my shirt.

"You're the most wonderful boy in the world. I want you to know that I feel that way about you. None of this is your fault. None of it."

"Okay," he said, but his voice was flat. There was no feeling in it at all.

"I wish I could squeeze all my love into you so it will always be there and whenever you need some you could just press a button!" I pulled back a little and smiled. "Let me look into those chocolate eyes of yours. Come on." He did, but there was nothing in them. Just blankness. I held him again and felt no melting, no softening. He did not pull away and he wasn't stiff, but nothing *gave*. In trying to help, I had hurt him — again.



How much time did Dash have? I kept hearing things from people about how Dash was faring in Grade Six. People knew I didn't see him and wasn't allowed contact with the school, so some friends looked out for him a little, through their own dealings with the school and reports from their children. They said Dash's school work was suffering; apparently his teachers were concerned. Though they all agreed that Dash was an intelligent child, and I know he had been an outstanding younger student, by Grade Five he was well below average. Dash had already dropped to the reading level of a Grade Four child, and by the following year he would be a C student across the board (with the sole exception of physical education, in which he excelled). By the end of the year he would have a bagful of "lates," many absences, and the first genuinely low grades of his school career. Though I wouldn't see the report card for another eighteen months, I knew Dash did very little work, showed no pride in what little he did, and was beginning to struggle to keep up with the rest of the class.

Dash's teachers felt that he wasn't as emotionally resilient as he should have been at eleven, which was reflected in a lack of self-esteem and an inability to concentrate. They worried that he was always tired — he told his teacher he "never" slept. The teacher told my friend Elizabeth MacKenzie, and she told me. When Dash was asked to draw a picture of his family, he drew himself doing a flip on his skateboard and his dad shooting a video of him. I wasn't there. Other parents said to me, "Dash has a hard life, doesn't he?" He hung out on the streets alone most afternoons and evenings. He looked uncared for. Suzanne and Peter had separated that summer and wouldn't reconcile, but Dash didn't mention it to me, not even once, even though Suzanne had been in his life for six years at this point, and it should have been a big deal. Another mother told me that children at school often told Dash he smelled bad, and "he just takes it," she said. "He says nothing. He never gets mad. It's like he's shutting down, emotionally." Dash's teachers wanted to speak to me, but the principal had told them they were not allowed to, even though they had spent months trying to get Peter to meet with them or take their concerns seriously. He didn't. I worried, but what could I *do* with information like that? I had to choose between living my life tied up in knots or just living my life. I put the information on the shelf and left it there.

My dad died that month. It was October 1995. I was forty-six years old and, although we knew Dad had pancreatic cancer, it was still a staggering loss. My brother, Dave, and I had taken turns visiting him every day, first in the hospital, then at Dave's house in June, then in the hospice where he died that fall. I felt overwhelming loss. Everyone had loved big, barrel-chested Jim. A Welshman through and through, he loved to sing and drink a pint, and had a wonderful, warm sense of humour. When he retired in Vancouver after a roving career as an engineer for the World Bank, based for years in Ankara, Turkey, he came home to be a grandfather, a father to me and Dave, and a good friend to my mother, even though they had divorced years ago. Every Tuesday when Dash was little, Dad had come over for lunch. He would fix things for me around the house, and after lunch Grandpa would settle into the wing-backed chair by the fireplace and Dash would run off to get his favourite books for Grandpa to read to him. They had read them together so many times that Dash would get excited when they were nearing the parts of the book they would repeat together.

"Run, run, as fast as you can. You can't catch me, I'm the gingerbread man!" Dash would shout. At other parts he would mimic Grandpa's deep timbre, and in that voice he would read with my dad all the story lines he knew. When Dash was older, he loved listening to Grandpa's stories about the ships Dad had been on during the war and the countries he had visited on duty with the British Royal Navy.

"Grandpa, tell me again about Egypt! What was it like to be on that big ship? Did you work there?"

"I worked in the engine room, which is the room that makes the whole ship go! It was hot and steamy and there were no windows and I couldn't see out."

"Ooh, so you didn't see the big waves going up and down?"

"No, which is lucky, because what if I was seasick, Dash?"

"Oh, that would have been bad."

"It certainly would have been."

"And then what did you do, Grandpa?"

"Well, after the war was over, your Gramma and I went to live in Montreal, and that was where we built our first house and your mommy and Uncle Davie were born!"

"It snows in Montreal, Mommy told me."

"It certainly does, Dash! It gets brrr cold and both your mommy and Uncle Dave would love to go skating outside and build big snowmen in our garden."

"Did they make snow angels, too, Grandpa?"

"They did, snow angels and lots of snowballs," said Grandpa with a chuckle.

And so it went. An exceptionally loving man, my father was excited by and engaged with world history and politics. A voracious reader, he spent his whole life learning. He never proselytized; he just loved to know things. It was through my mother that I learned discipline and endurance, but it was through Dad that I learned the great strengthening and healing power of laughter and the skill of remaining positive through hard times. My father had been on the high seas at war for seven years; my mother had lost her brother when his ship was torpedoed, and she had slept in bomb shelters and basements during the air raids that decimated Liverpool. My mother and father emigrated to Montreal with nothing but suitcases, and prospered, working as a team, starting an air-conditioning business and raising a family together. They remained close and my mother called my father at his Vancouver apartment every morning at nine o'clock until she died. They cherished their family and loved unconditionally. Dash had absorbed that love too, and responded as all children do, with trust and joy.

"Grandpa, Grandpa! Will you take me to Stanley Park to feed the ducks?"

"Of course! But do we have any bread for them?"

"Um! Yes, look! A whole loaf over there on the bench!"

"Then let's go, Dash! Come on, before your mommy sees we've taken her fresh bread!"

"'Bye, Mommy!"

And off they would go. They often went to the Vancouver Aquarium to watch the dolphin and killer-whale show, seating themselves in the front row where everyone got wet. They wised up quickly, and wore their outdoor gear whenever they went, coming home wet on the outside but dry on the inside, with Dash giggling and pretending for the rest of the afternoon to splash into the water like Bjossa the whale.

Dad had a free and loving relationship with Dash, but once the estrangement from me took hold, Dad stopped making impromptu visits for lunch and he stopped asking, "When will Dash be with you next? I want to take him to the Jungle Gym at the park." For a long while I tried to make up for or explain Dash's strange new behaviour — and then, as time passed, his absences — but Mom had taken me aside one day and said, "Pam, you have done a wonderful job raising Dash and he is a credit to you. Dad and I know Peter is using Dash to hurt you, and our relationship with him is drifting because of that. We love Dash with all our hearts and don't blame Dash for not wanting to see us. This is not Dash. It's Peter." A year before she died, Mom developed a serious heart condition. One Saturday morning she planned to come for coffee and a visit with Dave and me, and Dash, who she hadn't seen for a number of months. Sadly she died of a heart attack the evening before her visit and Dash never did see her again.

My parents must have talked about it often, and jointly they did the one thing that helped most: they never pushed and they didn't complain. When Dash was difficult to be around and distant or rude to them, Mom and Dad understood. When seven- and eight-year-old Dash dropped out of their lives, they understood that, too, and kept loving him. Gramma kept sending little cards and notes in the mail as she always had. My parents were hurt, but, like me, they didn't take it personally and they didn't question that Dash still loved them; they knew that he was just trying to deal with the pressure coming from his father's house, and this was the result. Still, they were angry about it, angry with Peter, and helpless. Though they were old now, these two dynamic, strong people, survivors of war and émigré poverty, couldn't do anything about their grandson's troubled world. And they couldn't do anything about mine.

By the time my father was diagnosed with cancer in the spring of 1995, Dash had seen so little of his grandfather that it was a struggle to decide whether or not I should take Dash to see him in hospital. Grandpa wouldn't be with us much longer and they *should* see each other and say goodbye, but their connection had been severed years earlier. I wrestled with it for weeks, while my father declined. Would seeing Grandpa provide Dash with solace, or just more trauma in the form of seeing someone he once loved and knew as a vibrant individual lying in a hospital bed? Dash had already suffered in so many ways. Would it be too much?

I remembered my mother's funeral three years earlier, which Dash had attended and to which he had responded well. Peter had refused to allow Dash to go on the grounds that he was "too young" (even though at an even younger age he had attended the Winnipeg funeral of *Peter's* father, a man with whom Dash had virtually no relationship). Then, my lawyer John Fiddes had called Dr. Elterman in hope that he could convince Peter that attending his Gramma's funeral was important for Dash. John said Dash was not too young and that going to his grandmother's funeral should help provide Dash with some closure. Eight-year-old Dash had gone, and he had grieved. Even though he hadn't seen her for more than six months before she died, Dash had cried when I told him, and he had sat quietly, between Big D and me, at the service. With all of us he sang her favourite hymns, including "All Things Bright and Beautiful," his high voice tiny and sweet. At the reception afterward, he chatted easily with the people he knew, which were many. He was open and interested and sad that Gramma had gone, but he responded well to our celebration of her life. After the reception we went outside.

"The minister is going to sprinkle Gramma's ashes in the garden."

"Does that mean we can come and visit her here, Mommy?"

"Yes it does," I told him, tears in my eyes, so grateful for his sweetness, and so sad to have lost my mom.

"Don't worry, Mommy. It's okay. I'll give you a big hug."

I crouched down for his hug and told him how kind he was to think of me. "You must be sad, too, Dash."

Dash looked up at me with his big brown eyes all serious. "I'll miss Gramma, but she was your mom, too."

"She was a really good mom, Dash."

"She was a really good gramma."

Now, with my father's approaching death, dealing with Dash was like communicating with someone who was in a semi-coma: I never knew what would reach him and when or if he would ever release some — or all — of his burden. It had been years since I'd seen him cry, since he'd let me into that part of his world. What I did know was that underneath Dash's self-preserving attitude of distance was a young boy who cared very much for this old man. It was important to me that he respond to his grandpa's death, painful though it might be. Bottling it up would be worse. I already feared that his heart was closing over. I had raised him to care about others, especially those less fortunate than himself. Until he distanced himself from my family, he had carried with him a healthy respect for others, especially the elderly and the infirm — which my dad now was. But as the years had rolled on I had found this empathy noticeably diminishing in Dash, as he put more and more of himself and his pain in inaccessible places. I didn't want him to forget the importance of loving other people and caring for them, and I looked for opportunities to remind him. With Grandpa in hospital, it might ignite some feeling in Dash and dust off the images he had in his darkened memory of the family he once loved. And so I decided that, even though it was going to be painful for Dash, I didn't want his grandfather to die without Dash feeling anything, or *facing* it in some way. He had buried so much. He needed to let something out.

I called Dash that morning. "Hi! You're up early for a Saturday."

"Hi, Mom."

"I'm glad I caught you."

"Why? What's happened?" Dash asked curiously.

"Dash, Grandpa's been taken to hospital."

"Oh —"

"Now, don't worry. But he is very sick, and I don't think he's going to get better."

"What do you mean, Mom?"

"Well, Grandpa has cancer, and because of his age they can't operate and get rid of it, so he probably won't get better."

"Mom, are you saying Grandpa is really, really sick?"

"Yes, Sweetheart, I am. So I was thinking that you should come soon and visit him."

"Okay."

"It may be a bit hard for you, but I think you should see him. And of course it would mean the world to him."

"Okay, Mom. When shall I come?" This was easier than I had reckoned.

"Well, how about this afternoon?"

"Okay."

"We'll only stay a few minutes, because Grandpa gets tired quickly, but seeing you will make him feel a lot better."

I bundled Dash into the car a few hours later. We talked about skateboarding. He needed a new board, and we planned to go and get him one after we saw Grandpa. He was open and chatty on the drive, and then listened carefully when our conversation turned serious. I told him what to expect when we saw Grandpa, and explained that his illness had progressed, and that he didn't look all that good. When we got there, Dad held Dash's hands gently and they talked.

"Come a little closer, Dash. I won't bite. Let me take a good look at you. My, you're getting more and more handsome every day. Come here, let me tell you something secret." He smiled. Dash smiled too, and leaned into him. "You get all your looks from me," he whispered.

Dash grinned and stood up straight again. "Oh, Grandpa, you haven't changed!"

"I wouldn't dare! Who'd recognize me?"

"Hey, what's that tube for anyway?" Dash pointed to Dad's intravenous tube.

"That? Oh, that's just for looks. No, it's because — so they say — I'm not eating enough. But you should try the food here! No wonder!"

"You'll be home soon, and you can have burgers maybe."

The two of them chatted lightly and easily until I stood up and went over to fluff Dad's pillows. "We should probably go now," I said quietly to Dash. "I think your grandpa might be a bit tired."

"I am, Pam. But boy it was good to see you, Dash." Dad looked over at me, and his eyes were flooded with gratitude that Dash had come. *Thank you,* he mouthed to me as Dash walked away and stood by the door.

"I'll see you tomorrow, Dad."

"I hope you feel better soon, Grandpa." And we quietly left the room. I thanked Dash for coming with me and for being so thoughtful and kind with Grandpa, and from the look on his face I thought that Dash was glad he had come, too.

Dash had dealt so well with the hospital visit a month earlier that I felt confident he was prepared to attend Dad's funeral. I felt it was important, in part to provide Dash with another forum for goodbye and closure, but also because I was relying on him backing away, at some point, from the pressures that had governed his childhood. I had to make sure that when he did he would not feel that he had been excluded from important events in my family's lives. I didn't want Dash to call me from his college dorm at nineteen and say, "Mom, why did you leave me out of family things, if you cared about me so much? Wasn't I family, too?" I had taken that approach for years, and Dad's funeral was another place to include Dash and show him that he had family.

Peter at first refused to let Dash attend the service, saying again how inappropriate it was for a child Dash's age to go to a funeral. I assured Peter that it wouldn't be a depressing funeral but a beautiful and loving memorial. "Peter, it won't be heavy-handed. The service will be lovely, and celebratory." Still Peter refused, and as with my mother's funeral, it was only after my lawyer intervened and talked to Peter's lawyer that, for whatever reason, he finally decided Dash could come.

St. Francis-in-the-Wood in West Vancouver is a cedar-shake-roofed stone church so quaint and pretty it could have been plucked straight from a village in Devon, England. My brother and I had attended Sunday school and were confirmed there. My mother and father had been lifelong members. My mother was in the altar guild, and my father, with his strong tenor, had raised the roof on Sundays. This was where my mother's ashes had been scattered. My dad's would be, too. With a catch in his throat, my brother joked that scattering dad's ashes on top of mom's would drive her crazy all over again, this time from the grave.

On the day of Dad's funeral, Dave and I walked up the path to the church together, into a crowd of about fifty friends and family. Dash was at my side. Dave stood quietly talking with my brother's wife, Bev, and I hugged my brother and greeted some arriving friends. I looked around for Dash and saw that he had run off and climbed a tree. I walked over and asked him to come down, but he ignored me and clambered onto the roof of a six-foot trellis archway. The guests had filtered into the church and would soon be waiting for us. I couldn't get Dash to come down. The more I begged him, the more he ignored me. He didn't appear to be angry; he was off in his own world, where he didn't listen to me, and the more I asked of him the more he drew away. The minister had come out and was looking at me, waiting to start the service. I sized up this child of mine, scrambling around on the archway, and my heart started to pound. The minister did not know the details of our lives. He did not know all that had passed. All he saw was a child doing something beyond inappropriate at his grandfather's funeral, and he saw that I couldn't get him down. My face grew redder as I imagined him thinking, "What kind of parent would allow this to happen at a funeral and what sort of a parent must she be if her child behaves this way. What's wrong with *her?*"

Of course the minister probably didn't think any such thing, but I felt it, and I had felt it many times before — on the soccer field, or when I bumped into parents of children from Dash's school in the supermarket, or at social events around town.

"Please, Dash," I said softly, mindful of the people inside the church, wanting to keep my business private from them. "Please, we have to go in now, the minister is waiting for us. Everyone is inside already. Big D is inside, waiting for us."

It took a few minutes, but Dash did come down; then he ambled along, idly kicking at grass tussocks and dirt mounds as he walked painfully slowly up the church steps, defying me to make him go any faster. Part of me wanted to scream at him like I never had before. I had just lost my father. I wanted to say, "Dash, stop it! This is Grandpa's day. Just behave will you? Shape up! He loved you so much," but the first word would not have even passed my lips because I saw what was happening. Dash was acting like a five-year-old not to be naughty or rebellious but because he couldn't cope. Instead of internalizing his grief he was externalizing it the way a much younger child would. What he was doing was the equivalent of Dash stomping his feet and shouting, "No!" at the top of his voice.

I was furious at Peter for damaging our son so badly, furious that Dash was a broken child. I grieved for my father and the collapse of my family. I lashed at myself, too. Dash was not equipped to be there. Peter had crippled him, and now he was right: *Dash shouldn't have come.* I didn't scold or discipline Dash, I just took his hand and guided him to our seats next to Big D. I looked around at Sandy and her eyes were wide looking back at me. *He's worse than any of us thought. He's so damaged.* She nodded, mouthed *I love you,* and turned her gaze back to the minister. While he spoke of the contributions my father had made to his community and family, Dash squirmed in his seat, whistling, humming, and burping, lolling his head from side to side, staring out the window with great animation. He didn't once look at the minister. The weight of the day was already so heavy, and here was my lost son, who had removed himself so far from his world that he couldn't even *act* as if he cared about what had happened to his grandpa. He had locked his feelings away for so long that he couldn't even respond to the quiet, reflective mood of the family that surrounded him. I held his hand tight as he burped and grumbled and tried to keep him as quiet as I could, keep him in his seat, at least, and focused on me, if not the ceremony. I had no time to think about my wonderful father.

Dash had shown me, for the first time, the full effects of his childhood, the trauma of his separation from me, and the dysfunction in his home. I hadn't seen it clearly before, in our two-hour visits every month or so. I hadn't heard it during the sporadic phone calls. I hadn't seen it at Lake of the Woods. It had taken a death for Dash to show us his damage, his inability to sit quietly and monitor his own behaviour. The funeral marked a watershed in our lives: Dave, Sandy, Terry, my brother, and his wife — we all knew that sitting in church that day was an abused child. Like a slap to the face, I realized that I had been kidding myself for a long time that I was still a parent to Dash. I hadn't protected him, and look what he had become.

We struggled through the service and then repaired with my brother and his wife to a seaside restaurant to celebrate my father with a farewell dinner. There, Dash clattered the cutlery, balanced a knife on his forehead, sprinkled the salt and pepper all over the tablecloth. He played with the flame of the candles and flicked wax, squirmed in his seat, and shouted at the waiters to bring his food. My brother Dave's patience was wearing thin. It had been a stressful time, and a long afternoon, and I couldn't ask him to take any more. Even though my brother had been there with me through everything that had happened with Peter during our marriage and then the six years of our separation, he was burying his *father*. He may have loved Dash dearly, but he had his limits. *Don't*, I pleaded to him silently across the table. *Don't. You know what he's been through. This is an eleven-year-old boy who's stuck at age five. This is pain. This is not him.* My brother checked himself. *I'm sorry*, his face read. Dash had been horrible on the day of our father's funeral. He had been disruptive and rude. But it was how *dysfunctional* he was, how *ill*, that finally made me burst into tears, apologize for leaving early, gather Dash's hand in mine, and ask Dave to take us home.

I called Dr. Norman Goodwell's office and made an appointment. I went in the following Monday with a renewed sense of urgency. Dr. Goodwell and I talked about Dash in the way we always did, not in highbrow psychological terms, but instead focusing on practical things I could do to try and turn the situation around.

"In detachment, what is vital is that the parent who has been removed from the relationship breaks through as often as possible to try and regain the childhood bond that has been severed," Norman said. "Your phone calls, your caring and loving conversations, trying to see him, and the all-important thing, contact, are all crucial here, particularly as the detachment appears to have progressed even further. You have to get more time, not these little bits. You need time with Dash to reconstruct your bond, to mend the break, if you like."

"I feel like I'm living with a ticking time bomb, Norman, and there isn't a day goes past when I don't reach out to Dash in some way or think of some new way to try and reconnect. I just don't get the time."

"Time is crucial."

"The system seems stacked against me, Norman. I don't really know where to go from here in court. I don't know what argument to make."

Offhandedly Norman said, almost by the by, "You know, in family-law circles, what has happened to Dash is called something different. It's not called detachment, it's called Parental Alienation Syndrome." *This has a name?* After our appointment ended, I rushed to Chapters bookstore, but couldn't find any books on Parental Alienation Syndrome. I wheeled my way into a parking spot on harried West Fourth Avenue and tried Duthie Books. Nothing. Nothing even on file. I called Norman Goodwell for a reference and found out that the only book that existed on Parental Alienation Syndrome was a dense, cold text for clinicians and legal professionals, written by an American child psychiatrist named Dr. Richard Gardner. He had self-published the book, and I immediately called the phone number of the distributor listed on the copyright page. The book took weeks to arrive, but when it did I slogged through it from cover to cover. Peter fit the profile of an alienator to a T. Dash fit the profile of an alienated child to a T. Custody of the child was a precondition for inducing Parental Alienation Syndrome, and Peter had it. I was the stereotypical targeted parent: a passive, pleaser personality, a peacemaker — ripe for exploitation.

Now I could name what had happened and not sound like an obsessive paranoiac psychobabbler. I didn't have to speak in euphemisms any more — "I don't see Dash. It's because of his father's anger" — and I was no longer forced to make loose and clumsy comparisons (Peter to a cult leader, Dash to a programmed child). I could use real words: indoctrination; campaign of denigration; alienation. *My son has been indoctrinated. Peter Hart has alienated his own child from his mother.* I had always had bits and pieces, gleaned from instinct and desperate reading (Peter Hare's *Without Conscience*, a foundational work on psychopathy, and various books on attachment theory, Dr. Goodwell's specialty and an emergent field of child psychology), but suddenly the whole picture added up: Peter's continuous need to control me, his inability to let go of his anger (ostensibly about the trial, but probably far more generalized than that. This man hated *me* — and everything I represented in Dash's life), the unmistakable contribution made by his abuse of alcohol and drugs, the relentlessly negative messages ("indoctrinations") about me and my family with which Dash had been bombarded since he was five years old, the critical role of Peter's family and associates — those who encouraged and never questioned the exclusive way he parented Dash. All that coupled with Dash's fierce loyalty to his father and his sharp psychological decline confirmed the thesis. My family was living with Parental Alienation Syndrome.

With the alienation left to run as rampant as it had been in Dash's case, my disappearance from his life was utterly predictable, because my banishment was the *point* of all that Dash had gone through. It was the point of Peter's custody petition and the subsequent trial. It was the point of getting and keeping Dr. Elterman onside and involved. It was the point of my being kept away from the school, the neighbourhood, the doctor, the dentist, and the point of all the missed access and screened and deleted phone messages. Peter was sick, but he wasn't unique. Parents all over the world have done this to children. Some do it because of their personality disorders (psychopathy and clinical hysteria are often actors in these larger-than-life dramas), but others consciously, deliberately, seek to destroy their ex-spouse and know that alienation is as good a way as any to do it. Some are so mired in their anger and hurt from a breakup that they actually think they are doing the right thing — a delusional and irrational version of a parental kidnapping, which is supposed to protect the child from the other parent. The one constant in the case studies that Dr. Richard Gardner's book presented was that the parent who has been made to disappear has *not* done anything to deserve it. It is often allowed to happen because of the personality types involved, but the parent has not *done anything* — been annoying, been cloying, been abusive, over-protective, or unnurturing. As I had protested all the way along: *I'm a good mom, and Dash's reasons aren't reasons at all, they're excuses, and they come from Peter.* Dash's excuses had always been trivial — like Dave always giving Dash the smaller piece of pie; that my house was "over-regimented" and "no fun." So this was what it was about, I thought as I read. *Peter hates me so much he will use our child to ensure my destruction.* He wants my marriage to fail; he wants me ruined. I realized the full force that day of what it is to be hated by someone you once loved. My pain was a source of satisfaction to Peter, and my child had become a weapon of my destruction. I felt so preyed upon that I picked up the phone and called Dave to hear his reassuring words of love and acceptance.

Dr. Gardner's book also told me something that I hoped would change the course of Dash's life: that the only solution to severe, entrenched alienation is court. Parents that alienate are, if not *bona fide* pathological, at least convinced in an absolute and paranoid way that they are right. In other words: they won't stop. I finally had the information I had been sliding inexorably toward for six years. *Court.* I had thought that Dash would be able to see me if I dropped the custody proceedings a year and a half earlier, but he wasn't. I had thought that if I stopped going to his soccer games, which I did for a whole season, it would help our relationship, but it didn't. It couldn't have, because Dash wasn't in charge of whether he had me in his life or not. He wasn't the one who decided whether he saw me or not. What I didn't know, although somehow my poor, frustrated husband instinctively did, was that hardball was the only way to make a differ-ence. I had to go and get the legal standing to say "No" to Peter's power plays and to re-establish my relationship with Dash. Only then would the syndrome begin to turn around. My passive legal strategy had been wrong. I had made the *wrong* choice, believing that I had *no* choice, and I knew now that I had to go back. I felt panicked. The "system" might still be the biggest gamble around, but I needed it. I had to go to court and not stop till I got Dash out of his father's care.

Finally I had something I could use.

I was overcome by a need to tell my story to someone who had gone through what I had gone through, who could help me see the path ahead and give me some feedback on what I had learned. I was desperate to talk and listen, and now my therapist Bob Armstrong wasn't enough. I didn't want to vent, or air my distress. I was gripped by a need to connect with someone who was in the same boat as I was. I wanted to see how other people coped, to see how they had fared in their own struggles. I looked in the Yellow Pages, asked Bob, phoned the Ministry of Child and Family Services for a referral, and finally located a custody-and-access parents' group on the west side of Vancouver that met once a week. It was a group of six women, but all of them had custody of their children, all of them lived with their children, at least half-time, most had more. They had problems with deadbeat dads or had suffered through horribly abusive marriages — but they saw their children. I automatically felt my difference, the leper who didn't even have joint custody, but the women were immediately accepting, inviting, and inclusive. They drew me in, as women have forever provided a haven and community for other women, looking after their own. None of the women could believe how rarely I saw Dash, given how close we lived and the specificity of the court order that had given me half his time. No one had experienced the withheld and manipulated access I did; no one's child looked quite like mine did now. Everyone there was dealing with really difficult issues, but no one was in the same boat as I was. Yet they saw me, and they saw my pain, and they heard what had happened to Dash's heart, and they saw that it was not right. As I told my story, I cried hard and long, years of trauma coming out, seas of tears. I said, "Thank you, ladies," several times and tried to give the floor to another mother who needed the group's support, but they wouldn't let me stop.

"Keep going," they said. "Let it out."

I talked for nearly an hour. By the end I was exhausted, and all the other moms were crying, reaching out to touch my arm, smiling at me through their tears, accepting and supporting me. Despite their own problems, they gave me their time and love. These women were strangers, but they could see I wasn't a bad mom. They saw I cared about my son and felt my pain at his loss. All these years I had listened to the judges and Dr. Elterman and my own lawyers telling me not to argue, not to fight, not to disturb anyone's precious peace, because Dash would come around in the end. Well, *my* peace was disturbed. My son's *life* was disturbed. All these women were much worse off than me — one of them lived in a shelter, and they all worked around the clock trying to get by and raise their children. Meanwhile, I had the luxury of a nanny to help with the house while I raised my boys, a supportive husband, and for the first time in my life, the ability to be a full-time mom. Yet these women had to tell me, "You have rights here! You deserve better than this. So does your son. Go back to court because your child needs you." They all expressed, in the space of an hour, what I utterly lacked, because I had repressed it for so long: *rage*. Rage at what had happened to my son. Rage at my ruined relationship with the beautiful boy I had carried in my own body for nine months. Rage at the court system for letting him fall out of my life. Those women showed me exactly how angry I should be, and how much I was worth: I deserved to see my child. I *didn't* deserve this treatment, this dismissal, this callous obliteration from my son's life at the hands of a man who hated me, and I *deserved* the courts' support. They showed me that I had to put on the armour of war, because this *was* a war, and I had to wake up and see it for what it was. I had to fight. I was not going to get to see Dash by backing off and being nice and compliant and going back to my lovely home in Kerrisdale and closing the door on my son's troubles. I had played by the rules and sucked down everything that had been done to me for the sake of Dash, but it hadn't worked. It was worse. Dad's funeral had shown us all. In the room with those beaten but endlessly courageous women, I saw that fighting for something I believed in, something I had instinctively done but in too quiet a way, was *right*. I *believed* in being able to love my son and I believed in him being able to love me, and I changed after that meeting. My worth had been measured by people who cared about me without even knowing me. They didn't see me as a second-string parent, so why *was* I one? I went home cold, in shock, but those six women had restored my faith in myself. Dr. Richard Gardner had given me the underpinnings of a case. I was now prepared for a long and bloody battle for my child.


I called my lawyer, John Fiddes, and told him that he had done great work, but that I had to find someone new, someone who really understood what Dash had gone through and was prepared to argue PAS and child abuse. I interviewed half a dozen lawyers, asking, "Have you heard of Parental Alienation Syndrome?" and only one had, a family lawyer with a busy practice: Jamie Martin. He was about my age and had five children. He had been a child advocate for years before entering private practice.

He had heard about Parental Alienation Syndrome, believed it was real, and listened intently as I talked to him about Dash. I warned him that my second-to-last lawyers' offices had been fire-bombed and that John Fiddes's home had been burgled. Jamie didn't flinch. Jo-Anne Bogue, his assistant, would, in time, become so emotionally connected to my case that she would be with me at every hearing.

Jamie was willing to go into court with a psychological syndrome that was all but unknown, and I told him about the very base of my conviction.

"I don't want to present this as some weird little syndrome, Jamie, because it's not," I said. "What happened to Dash is the syndrome, through and through. But at its core this is simply a specific set of tactics used by someone who wants a particular result — the destruction of a child's relationship with his mother. It doesn't matter whether Peter consciously intended this to happen or whether his emotional problems made it inevitable. I don't care. I care about the result and I care about making Dash's life better. Indoctrination is psychological abuse. The forced separation from me is psychological abuse. And Peter has filled the gap in this child's life with *neglect*. That's not okay. I'll go in and argue whatever we have to argue — alcohol, Dash's difficulties in school, whatever — but that's the base of my conviction here, Jamie. This is abuse."

"Dash has no bruises on him and emotional abuse is almost impossible to prove," Jamie said, "but your case is serious, and I believe you when you say Dash is in trouble." Jamie said he was prepared to use the words "child abuse" about my case and not let a judge's uncomprehending stare back us down. I gave Jamie Dr. Richard Gardner's book, covered in yellow sticky notes, finished the coffee Jo-Anne had brought, wrote out the first cheque, and asked him to start work immediately. I told him to draw up an application to have Dash psychologically assessed and my access time restated. I wanted the 50 percent of Dash's out-of-school hours I was originally given but had never received. I wanted Peter forced by a court to facilitate my access to Dash. I knew he would never *encourage* visitation, but I wanted him forced to at least get Dash out the door. If Peter made it happen, if Peter gave his permission, I knew Dash would come. I knew he wanted to.

Dash was a trained monkey and just as free as one, so I wasn't surprised when he phoned immediately after my lawyer's courier had served our notice of motion on Peter.

"I won't see you until you stop doing this to my dad," he said.

"I'm not seeing you anyway, and I haven't for two years," I replied gently, to no response. "I'm a parent, Dash. I'm *your* parent, and you should be seeing me like the judge said years ago. I don't have a choice anymore." Dash stayed silent. "I'm doing this because I believe it's the right thing to do. You have a right to your mother. I have a right to *you*, and you're going to have to trust me that this will work out, Dash. I love you and I'm doing this for you."

I was the direct cause of a new round of pain and pressure for him, a new round of action-stations at home, but this time I was determined I would stay the course.

"I understand how you feel," I said gently, "and I understand that you won't see me. But I will still call you, Dash, and keep trying to see you, because you're my son and I love you with all my heart."

Dash remained true to his word. I didn't see him for the next six months as our trial date crawled closer. My faith in the system was at rock-bottom, but my faith in *myself* was solid and strong for the first time since this had begun. What had happened to my family was not right. We all — especially Dash — deserved more than this. Now I needed to protect him, and I was going to do it in the one place in which I had three times already been put at a disadvantage and tainted: Peter's turf — the courts. Being a pleaser hadn't fixed a single thing. I was armed and dangerous, and I had been thwarted too long. I was going over the gunwales for Dash.

# Chapter 5
## In the Belly of the Beast

On December 13, 1995, we sat before Justice Mary Ellen Boyd, the judge who had ordered my removal from Dash's school in Grade One. Back then, she had described my intentions as "honourable," but she had decided that, because my being there had so agitated Peter, the custodial parent, I should not be allowed to stay. I wondered if she remembered our case now. I wondered if she reflected on the wisdom of removing a caring and engaged school parent or whether she asked herself why, six years later, we were still in front of judges, still having problems, still "battling" over Dash. We were in front of her now because I wanted a court order that would make sure I saw Dash at Christmas. As we did in each of the half-dozen pretrial hearings, we went with a case based on issues the judge was most likely to understand. I wanted to go in with PAS and child abuse; I *had* to go in with Peter's deviations from the court order. Jamie talked about the 50 percent of Dash's time I was supposed to have and didn't get, about my 1993 decision to instruct John Fiddes to stop court proceedings and rely on Dash to set up visits with me regardless of what the court order said, and how that had failed, about my struggle to reach Dash by phone and my lack of basic information about Dash's education and health. Only then did Jamie tell Justice Boyd that the community around Dash was concerned about him, and that we believed that Dash was a PAS child. I had heard that Justice Boyd had been touched by PAS, too, when she married a man whose child had been alienated from him. I wouldn't have wished this on anyone, but that day in the courtroom I hoped it was true. I hoped she had seen what I had lived, and had the insight to see what was happening here.

Mary Ellen Boyd was the first judge who dared to speak directly of Peter's role in the broken relationship between my son and me. She said, "For the past few years this child, rightly or wrongly, has had the impression that it would be in his best interests to defeat his mother's attempts to exercise access. The boy appears to have just decided he doesn't want to do it. He has unfortunately been given the impression that the matter is in his control and he has exercised that control. That is inappropriate." My heart beat faster. *Does she get it?* "The custodial parent," she continued, "has the duty and the obligation to do everything possible to encourage and foster a healthy relationship between the boy and the non-custodial parent." *Yes, keep going.* "I think that the possibility of this child, who is literally pre-pubescent, not being encouraged to have a healthy relationship with his mother is inviting disaster. I haven't heard anything said today that would come even remotely close to suggesting that the mother, exercising access as any other parent would be entitled to, would somehow harm or damage this child."

I got a weekend of access starting the next evening, December 15, and a whole week of access close enough to Christmas to count. Peter was to drop Dash to me on December 30 — which indulgently allowed for a Christmas Day departure to Mexico that Peter had booked as soon as he received my notice of motion asking for Christmas access.

I knew Dash would withdraw from me now that I had a court-ordered access weekend lined up, so I called him right away to nail down the weekend and pump him up about coming. Our routine was well-established by now. I generated a desire in him that was strong enough to withstand his father's sidelong glances, comments, or obstructions. Dash and I spoke happily for half an hour about the whole range of things we were going to do on our weekend, but the next night, Dash wasn't delivered. No one phoned, no one explained, and no child came. Our court order was useless. I left a message every day for Dash to please call me, but heard nothing. *Oh, well. We still have our week,* I told myself. On Christmas Eve I selected two presents, his Christmas card, and a little chocolate Santa, and drove over to give them to him. Though it was nearly lunchtime, all the blinds were still drawn. I knocked, expecting nothing, but out of the corner of my eye I saw Dash lift a blind to see who was there. He broke into a wide grin, disappeared, then flung open the door and hugged me hard. He came outside and closed the door quietly behind him, all smiles. I told him I had brought only two presents, because I wanted us to open the rest together. He looked quizzically at me. "When you come and stay next week," I said. He still looked confused, and then I got it. *He hasn't been told.* I had to be careful. This was Maui all over again. "You know, Dash, the judge has said that you're going to be with me for a *whole week* at the end of December? After your trip to Mexico!"

"Really?" His eyes were bright.

"Yep. The thirtieth to the seventh of January. A good long time."

He repeated the times and dates so he wouldn't forget. "The thirtieth to the seventh. The thirtieth to the seventh." He unwrapped his chocolate Santa and bit into it with a big smile, chocolate smearing across his front teeth. He pushed the mush into his mouth with his finger.

"Now, Dash, what happened last weekend? Why didn't you come over? You know, your dad agreed to it, so I really thought I would see you."

Dash looked up at me, bewildered. "Mom, I didn't know I was supposed to be seeing you last weekend. I didn't." Agreeing in court to the weekend had simply been a public-relations exercise. *Goddamned Peter.* But I only had another minute with Dash.

"Oh, don't worry, we'll get it sorted out, Dash. Just give me a hug." He smiled and I squeezed him hard. "The important thing is you're seeing me at the end of next week. I miss you so much, you know," I said.

"I know."

"I've been trying so hard to see you, but just hang in there, we'll work it out." Dash looked at me, squinted his eyes, murmured quietly, "I know," and it wasn't until I was nearly home again that I realized that we had whispered our entire conversation.


Peter and Dash flew to Cabo San Lucas the next day. Dash ran off to find his school friend, Stephen Frosch, and his family, who were holidaying there too, and spent the day with them. The next morning, Peter took him back to their hotel. Despite the gum Peter was chewing furiously, Stephen's mother, Melody Frosch, smelled the alcohol. The next day Stephen saw Dash walking down the beach toward their hotel. He was carrying a plastic bag full of clothes. Stephen took him to their condo, and Melody asked Dash where his father was.

"He's gone to his property."

"Oh?"

"He said to stay with you."

Alarmed, Melody called Peter's hotel, but he had checked out, leaving no forwarding number. Two days passed before Peter phoned and announced that he would be back later that day. He and his son, Greg, had driven upcountry to view a piece of land Peter had bought. When Peter arrived back at the hotel, he didn't go to see Dash, who was swimming in the hotel pool. Instead, he dithered around, talking about returning the rental car and doing a variety of other things. Peter was halfway out the door again when Melody said, "What about Dashiell?" Peter shrugged and said, "Oh, I'll be back later. If Dash wants to he can walk back along the beach to the hotel and meet me there." Melody was shocked at Peter's cavalier attitude to the safety of an eleven-year-old, but it confirmed her long-held suspicions that things were not right in the Hart residence. Whenever Dash was over for dinner, he ate huge meals and always asked for more. "He never seems to want to go home," she told me. "And never has a set time he's expected." Melody would often say, "Shouldn't you be getting home soon, Dash?" Dash would shrug. "No." Once he said, "I wouldn't want to go home and be alone anyway. There's nothing to do."

When Melody told me about her experiences in Mexico I urged her to write an affidavit for me. She gave powerful backup to my own concerns: Peter's drinking, a laissez-faire attitude toward Dash's welfare, Dash's lack of supervision. When her affidavit was circulated to Peter's lawyer, Peter called her in a rage, but she replied coolly. "I've only said what's true." She added, "And you were in Mexico on days Dash should have been with his mom." Dash and Peter had flown back from Mexico four days into the week of access I had been given.

"Well, that's not really true," Peter said, and then told Melody, "I'm a great Dad, and I know everyone down there at the courthouse. They won't do anything."

Melody refused to allow Stephen to play at Dash's house after that Christmas in Mexico — something Dash would blame on me. It had happened before, he said. Or so his memory said. "In preschool I think there was this kid named Brett," Dash would say later on the witness stand, "and cuz my mom told his mom that my dad was a bad parent, I stopped seeing him. And there's another kid called Brian, and the same thing happened." *In preschool?*


In early January 1996, we asked another judge for joint guardianship and a restatement of the half-time access order decided by the divorce trial judge, Justice MacDonald, in 1990. "The history of this matter is disturbing," Justice R. Bruce Harvey said. The order had not been complied with, Dash was "unwilling" to see me and there was "no current or even reasonably current independent expert assessment of the child" available to the court. Justice Harvey wondered aloud what he could do to bring the access I was getting more in line with the original access order and said he wanted to find some way "to attempt to get this young boy to have the opportunity not only to have a father but a mother, too." But the judge seemed crushed by the weight of responsibility. He dithered. After assuring us that our case would be rushed to the trial list, he adjourned the joint-guardianship decision. I had asked for a contempt-of-court charge to be brought against Peter, because he had ignored the Christmas access order, but Justice Harvey didn't rule on that either. He only ruled on the issue of costs which, as usual, went to me — tangible evidence that Peter's conduct was the reason we were in court, but not what we were after.

Because Justice Harvey had lamented that "A child cannot be forced to comply with access requirements," I was relieved for him to pass us on to yet another judge. *Maybe the next one will get it. Maybe the next one won't be timorous.* I needed a judge who could make visitation happen. Children don't like cleaning their teeth, but a good parent makes them do it. Children don't like going to school every weekday morning, either, but a good parent makes them do it. I wanted Peter to be told that, if Dash wasn't bundled in a car and brought over to me, or put on the doorstep at four o'clock on Wednesdays and Fridays, he would be *made* to comply. That meant contempt of court. That meant fines, jail time, losing custody. Dash had to know the courts were serious. But this judge wasn't up for it, and I needed one who was willing to be a *super parent.*

Justice Harvey listed our case for April, a long three months hence, and Peter dusted off his weapons immediately. He once again tried to sue Dave and me for invasion of privacy. He accused us of having instructed our "agents" to "harass and annoy" him. Peter's lawyer, Russell Tretiak, began issuing galling parenting instructions to me:

> I suggest that the best way for your client to have a decent and fulfilling relationship with her son is to gradually build up to that. To demand the impossible will simply exacerbate the problem. I believe your client is at a watershed in her relationship. If she continues the practice she has followed in the past, she will regrettably not have a relationship with this child. I have taken that view for some time now and it certainly seems to have been vindicated by the events.

And, devastatingly, but unsurprisingly, Peter deployed Dash. That year I received flowers on Mother's Day — a first — with an attached card from Dash, containing a carefully crafted message: "For you on Mother's Day. I would have delivered these personally except for... Hope you do the right thing. Dash."

What was the "right thing" as far as they were concerned? Two days later Dash faxed a typed note, adding: "it is not right to treat me this way. please <u>do not call</u>, you may call when you stop this stuff. Any way happy mothers day. p.s. this is a follow up note. Love Dash." We were back to where we had been two years ago. *Oh, it would be so easy to believe Dash would come if I drop out. I would give anything for this to have such a simple solution.* But I knew PAS now. I had read Dr. Richard Warshak's *Divorce Poison*, written following the publication of Dr. Richard Gardner's book. It confirmed what I had lived. "Some PAS children claim that they will renew contact with the alienated parent 'when the time is right' but I have learned that often the time is never 'right.'" No, I couldn't wait till Dash got older and left home or Peter

Dash.

Peter Hart and me with newborn Dash, August 1984.

Three-month-old Dash with me in front of our house in Point Grey.

Best friends Sandy and me with our new babies: Dash at three months and newly born Warren, October 1984.

Dash and me in Florence the year Peter and I lived in Italy.

My mother, Doris,
with two-year-old Dash
in our garden.

Dash with Big D
looking at a world
map at my house in
West Vancouver.

Dash and me sitting in the tree house Big D built for Dash in West Vancouver.

My father, James, David Richardson, Dash, and me at our wedding in the garden of our home. A week later David and I had our first son, Colby, born September 29, 1990.

Best friends Warren and Dash on a fishing trip we took them on to April Point, spring 1991.

Big D helping Dash clean a fish at the cottage in Lake of the Woods, Ontario.

A "ham sandwich" hug with Dave's mother, Tannis,
Dave, and Dash at Lake of the Woods.

Dash and I making our
Christmas gingerbread
carousel, 1991.

Milkshakes all around! Quinten, Dash, and Colby
in our kitchen, Kerrisdale, 1994.

The year Dash joined us for Christmas, 1995.

Quinten, Colby, and Dash climbing on our
"climbing tree" in the back garden.

Dash, so proud in all of
his new clothes, 1997.

Dash looking distressed after telling me to leave the soccer field because he does not want me at his game. Quinten, not understanding, tries to pull him back but Dash continues to walk away after this shot is taken and goes home with another boy.

Dash, Quinten, and Colby on our heartbreaking and heartfelt trip to Maui. He had agreed that Lord Byng was not working for him and that he needed the attention that Glen Eden could give him.

Our final Christmas photo together in December 1999. Dash was
antsy and unsettled that Christmas morning in Whistler, so we
quickly got everyone together and went snowmobiling as I was so
afraid that he would not last the day with us and would hop on a
bus home to Vancouver. It worked out and we had a wonderful
Christmas dinner together, just the five of us.

A week after Dash died his friends painted this huge graffiti near
Granville Street Bridge, a powerful and beautiful tribute.

Recovery: dealing with my anger by running a half marathon in May 2001.

Quinten, me, Dave, and Colby at our house in
Mougins, France, in summer 2005.

sobered up or hell froze over. Dash had a right to a happy childhood. I couldn't watch him eke out this existence any more.

The weeks passed and Dash's continued absence and brutal messages to leave them alone, lay off, stop the court proceedings jangled more and more in my mind. When Dash raged on the phone about the "court stuff," I listened with my heartbeat suspended, frightened to breathe in case it blew him farther away. I was panicked by the extent of his immersion and, during one phone call, I came to a crystal-clear realization: *guardianship isn't going to be enough.* Being able to make decisions for Dash and get him tutors won't get him to my house. It won't rebuild our relationship. Peter was going to direct this child forever. I needed custody.

When Jamie added "custody" to our application Peter's household must have gone on red alert. Peter wanted my claim dismissed, but the judge wouldn't do it. He tried to have my entire case dismissed as "abuses of process," but the judge wouldn't do it. Peter instructed his lawyer to keep ignoring our letters about court dates, access days, and report cards that still never came. (Peter would write, a month before the trial, "There is no reluctance at all from me that these school reports be provided. There never has been. If your client has not been sent a school report, by me, on a particular occasion, all she has to do is remind me." By then I had yet to receive Dash's report cards for Grades Two, Three, Four, and Five.) Peter accepted work on a case that conflicted with our upcoming trial dates, and then insisted that *our* trial be adjourned. Jamie was incensed and told the judge so. "This trial is about his son." Peter tried to have a judge remove Jamie as my counsel on some trumped-up legal technicality, and, when that didn't work, attacked him personally. "Money isn't everything, Jamie. You appear to have no professional responsibility or morals. You start messing around with the day-to-day happiness of a youngster because of the lure of money that has been dangled before you. You will eventually pay the price of the disrespect of everybody. You, Mr. Jamie Martin, are irrelevant."

We pressed on. Peter predicted grandly that the trial would not only be a waste of time, but would further alienate Dash from me. "There is a certain point when even a balanced, strong, well adjusted, popular, untroubled, young, approaching-12-year-old boy, will put his foot down and draw the line." His reason as to why Dash wouldn't visit morphed again. Perhaps because the notion of Dash being so "angry" at his mother when she had done nothing wrong had become publicly unpalatable, Peter now made Dash a normal kid who wanted flexibility — he wanted to be with his friends rather than his parents. From what I knew of Dash's life, this was nonsense. Dash had been inveigling himself into his friends' homes for a long time now, to be away from his father's drinking, to get some attention, who knows, but Dash already wasn't home. He already wasn't with me. He *had* the flexibility he wanted.


As difficult as it always was to reach Dash by phone, make plans, and then actually see them carried through, I never stopped trying. Sometimes I would have to give myself a break, take a few days, dust myself off, and then pick up the phone again. Other times the frustration of trying to make a simple plan a reality would send me to my lawyer. I would ask him to send a letter to Peter or his lawyer, asking for confirmation of an agreed-upon arrangement. It was that way on January 22, 1996, when I had arranged with Dash to take him to a Canucks hockey game. I would use anything and everything to try to get him to spend time with me, and I hoped his beloved Canucks were the ticket this time. Dash was wearing his parka and watching out the window when I pulled up. My heart surged as he ran to the car. I never knew, I never could really be sure, even when I called en route from the car, that he would want to come, that he hadn't changed his mind. *Thank you, Canucks, for getting him out the door.* I reached for his hand automatically as we walked across the street to the stadium and was thrilled that he didn't pull back, or slide out of it once we were across. Dash was eleven years old, and I was impressed that holding his mother's hand didn't make him feel weird. I was proud that in some ways he was still his own man. Though I longed to brush his hand across my cheek as I would have with a younger Dash, I instead talked lightly about the game. We joked with and nudged each other as we stood in line for food, then juggled our hamburgers, fries, and cold drinks back to our seats. My leg touched his, our arms brushed, and as we passed the cold drinks back and forth, we analyzed the game, the referees' penalty calls, and the relative talents of the players on the ice. I looked at him constantly, just to take in his eyes, his smile, the freckles that sprinkled across his nose regardless of the season, his skin and cropped hair. I didn't waste time worrying or feeling sad or thinking of what was coming up in court. I just sat happily with him as if we saw each other all the time, as if our lives were normal. After the game we followed the crowd out of the stadium and got into the car, disappointed that the Canucks had lost, but happy because our evening had been so much fun.

"How are things going at school? Grade Seven is a big year, isn't it?"

"I guess. Yeah, it is!"

"Well, enjoy it while it lasts — you're the seniors now, but next year you'll all be juniors again!"

He laughed at that. "Yeah, Mom, I'm the big senior . . . actually, you're right! We *are* this year!"

"So, how about it? Do you like your teachers? Have you got any projects or tests coming up? If there's anything I can help you with, I'm always here to help with your homework — even if you just need help by phone."

"I'm fine, Mom," he said. "But I wish you wouldn't go to court against my dad."

I looked straight ahead. *God, how do I handle this?* I had to be honest. I had been accused for so long of "lying" to Dash. How much would he accept or even understand? "Dash, do you know something? Court is the last place on earth I ever want to be. But I don't believe I have a choice now. I worry about you; you know I do. And I don't see you nearly enough. It's important for children to spend time with both parents and, when that doesn't happen, they have to go to a judge who can help. Your father and I don't seem to be able to work this out ourselves. Sometimes court is the only solution to the problem; that's why it exists. It's like, at school sometimes, when you have a problem with your friends and you try really hard but you just can't sort it out yourself — well, then what do you do? You ask a grown-up to help you, right?" Dash nodded and looked at me. "Well, it's like that."

"But it doesn't matter who raises me, Mom."

"Well, Dash, to me it does matter. It should matter to you, too. Parents are the most important people in a child's life. Your father and I are the people who should raise you unless we are somehow unable to." I reached for his hand across the car, keeping my eyes on the road. I wanted to pull over and look into his eyes, but I didn't dare break the moment. "I love you with all my heart, and I need you to understand me: I'm not going back to court to hurt you, or to hurt anyone. I'm *not* trying to hurt your father. I'm in court to get them to help us. Do you understand?

"Kind of."

"I'm not trying to make matters worse. I'm doing this so they get better. Please trust me. I only want things to get better."

I stopped the car at a red light and finally turned to look at Dash. I spoke softly and carefully. We were nearly at his house. "When it comes to my children, Dash, I'll do anything in the world to love and protect you. I do it with Colby and Quinten. I do it with you." From a look that flashed sylph-like across his face, he seemed to swell a little at that. "I'll never go away, you know, Dash. I'll never disappear from your life." I drove on, and as we pulled up in front of his house, I stopped the car. Dash immediately looked down at his lap. "Can you look at me, Dash? This is important." He did. "I want us to try really hard to keep our lines of communication open. If you're upset by what you hear or read, please call me. There are always two sides to every story and I want you to call me and talk to me if you're troubled. Okay? Can you do that?" I looked into his eyes for a long time and we shared a short silence. "We'll get through this, Dash. We all will — your dad, me, you. You'll see."

I still have hundreds of vignettes, little treasures, that I can call up from those days. The boy who wouldn't visit made it so clear, when he did come, that he was glad to be with me. We sat in the kitchen and talked about what he wanted to be when he grew up ("a lawyer, like my dad") and how he was worried about going to a big high school soon. We discussed books he wanted to read and movies he wanted to see, and we made plans for the summer. He wanted to come with us to Lake of the Woods again, and asked me to get him a new wetsuit so he could stay in the water longer with Big D. He talked about how he'd been falling out with some of his friends at school. We didn't just live in the present, as many estranged parents and children do. I made sure we always, *always* discussed the future and made plans. When I drove Dash home he said,

"You know, Mom, I could take a bus to your house, couldn't I?" and my heart leapt and broke at exactly the same time. Both of us were trying to find ways to defy his father.

But the reality was that we were heading into a trial over his custody. Dash was kept right up to date with all the grisly details. According to Peter, Dash had known everything "from day one." He wrote that, "Dash has been always, without exception, fully aware of what has been transpiring, and said and written, etc, throughout these past 7 years." And, "Dash is going to hear about this this afternoon, as soon as he gets home." Dash said later that he read everything that came to the house as he was given ongoing proof about how imperilled he was. Peter faxed me a note in April 1996, a couple of weeks before the trial, after yet more missed visits had forced me to try and have him cited for contempt of court again:

> Dash becomes disturbed by process servers on our home doorstep, presenting documents of accusation against his father, of Contempt. But not for long is Dash upset. Very brief indeed is that. He quickly graduates to a thoughtful analysis, and a resulting displeasure with, and resentment of, his mother and her lawyer . . . for this invasive conduct, and for the making of these accusations, which he sees not only as false, but also, even worse, as offensive, small and mean.

In court, Dash would say he sometimes sat down and read the affidavits himself, and other times he read them with his dad. "Take a look at this!" Peter said they exclaimed to one another. When I found out later that Dash had a reading level that roughly followed his emotional level — suspended at a Grade Four — I knew that Dash wasn't reading those documents alone. I read an article written by Dr. Peggie Ward of the Children and Law Program at Massachusetts General Hospital, who wrote that, "The willingness of a parent to directly involve a child in the litigation should be a red flag that the parent may well be using the child to further his own agenda, even if the child is apparently acquiescent." All I could do was hope the judge would see it, too.

Days before the trial began, I had a call from Elizabeth MacKenzie. Peter had called her the night before.

"He said, 'I understand that you've been talking to Dash's teachers,'" Elizabeth told me. "He also said, 'You know that's against the law. Dash is an okay guy. He may get into fights and smell a bit,'" Elizabeth said.

"Oh, my God, Elizabeth. I'm so sorry."

"I said, 'I'm not interested in talking to you about this, Peter,' but he cut me off and said, 'You've involved yourself in my family, so I will involve myself in yours.'" I cringed. Elizabeth continued. "'You wouldn't want anything to happen to that beautiful daughter of yours now, would you? If you consider that a threat, it is.' So of course I hung up — I mean, what do you say to that? He called straight back and left a long message asking why I would want him as an enemy when I had such a nice family, that he'd charge me with violation of privacy. He shouted, 'Coward, coward!' and hung up."

For as long as I had had problems with Peter, Elizabeth had been around. I had carpooled with her when Dash was a little boy at preschool. Her daughter had been in Dash's class since Grade One. When I was forced out of Dash's school, Elizabeth filled some of the void for me — and continued to do so over the years. Peter called her my "agent," but to Elizabeth it just didn't seem right that she would know things about my son's life that I didn't. Elizabeth would tell me sometimes when Dash was sick or report that her daughter had told her that Dash was in Mexico on school time.

Three years earlier, when Dash was nine, Elizabeth had been engaged in a conversation with her daughter's teacher, when talk shifted to Dash. He was having serious problems at school, the teacher confided. His attendance was poor, he wasn't happy, and the teacher very much wanted to speak to me, but when she had asked the principal, he told her she couldn't. Alarmed, Elizabeth had gone to the principal herself and asked him to intervene, but he had said his hands were tied. "In all my years as a school principal, and I'm three years from retirement," he had told Elizabeth, "Dash's is the saddest case I have seen."

A month before the trial, Elizabeth spoke with Murray Stephenson, the new principal of Queen Mary Elementary. "Dash does almost no work in class," he told Elizabeth. "He's bright enough but he's unhappy." Murray had spoken to Peter many times about Dash's troubles, but when Peter had defended his son "as though he was in a courtroom," instead of recognizing his difficulties, Murray worried. The fights Dash had been starting at school and his increasingly bizarre playground behaviour should have worried any parent, but when Dash dropped his pants at a teacher in the playground, Peter first dismissed it as something that couldn't have happened, then claimed that the playground supervisor was "out to get him." Murray told Elizabeth, "Dash is the kind of child who will be suspended from high school." Elizabeth asked that I be brought in, but Stephenson reiterated the school's long-term position: legally he couldn't tell me. I already knew that. When he had first taken over the job of principal at Queen Mary Elementary, I had written and introduced myself, asking him to send me report cards, attendance records, and anything I needed to know, but Stephenson had written back that he could not. As a non-custodial parent I was not entitled to information directly from the school. *I am a pariah*, I thought.

I had tried earlier in the year to meet up with a mother whose son, Ben, was a friend of Dash's. Dash had mentioned this friend now and then when we talked on the phone, and after thinking about it for a few weeks, I managed to get Ben's phone number and called his mother. I wanted to get to know her. Perhaps she was someone who would call me sometimes when Dash was playing there and invite me to drop in. I didn't tell her that, and she probably thought my calling her was a little unusual, but she agreed quite happily to meet up with me for coffee the following week. I sat in the Starbucks on West Tenth and waited for her. When the first hour passed I called her from my cell. I got the machine. "Hello, Trina, it's Pam Richardson. Maybe I've made a mistake! Am I in the wrong Starbucks? Did I get the wrong day?" I went home after two hours without hearing a word. I called again but got no answer. When I finally reached her a few days later, she was angry and agitated. "Don't call here again!" she said. "I've spoken to Dash's father and I don't want to get involved. I don't want to meet with you. Not now or ever."

I was so grateful that Elizabeth cared enough to risk speaking out. "You're so brave. Thank you, Elizabeth. You can show the court my argument is real, that I'm not ranting about my ex-husband. You're independent and you know what's happening at the school because you have talked to the teachers yourself."

"MacKenzie is nothing more than a predator at the school," Peter wrote in a venomous note to Jamie. He charged Jamie with inventing Elizabeth's affidavit: "By crafting and causing to be sworn and filed Elizabeth MacKenzie's affidavit, you have caused this litigation to become so foul, and full of misrepresentations and so unpleasant for Dashiell, that you have *summa cum laude* succeeded in the alienation of Dashiell from his mother." Dash had been shown the affidavit. Smelly. Ripped clothes. Nowhere to go. Failure. Worried teachers. Drunk father. *Where will this man stop?*

All the judges in the pretrial months had expressed concern over the absence of an up-to-date psychological assessment of Dash. Jamie had written letter after letter to Russell Tretiak, requesting Peter's consent to the appointment of one of the three new and unknown psychologists he had found, but we were told Dash would see no one but Dr. Elterman. In early February 1996, a hearing was held to decide the issue and, despite our protests, Justice Janet Sinclair Prowse ordered that Dr. Elterman be our assessing psychologist again. He knows the case. *Blah blah blah.* The reasons bored me to tears. Having dragged his heels, once Dr. Elterman was appointed, Peter leapt into action. Within days he trotted Dash off for a chat with the psychologist, who dutifully wrote a letter to Peter's lawyer (but not mine), applauding Dash's "surprising insight and mature attitude." He reported that now Dash couldn't name any specific reasons why he didn't want to visit me, except that the overstructured nature of the access schedule bothered him. Dash just wanted to be with his friends. He wanted to hang out. It sounded perfectly reasonable. But why would a schedule that he had ignored for years so bother Dash?

To my surprise, Dash had come skiing with us at spring break, just before Peter arranged that February session with the psychologist, and while I had cherished every second of it, I couldn't help wondering if

Dash had been enormously brave to come or whether he had been sent. Two weeks after that trip — a week before the trial began — Dash went again to Dr. Elterman. In court when my lawyer asked Dr. Elterman why he thought Dash had come to Whistler, he said, "Dash felt that there was a certain need to see his mother at that point."

"Why at that point?" Jamie asked him.

"I don't know. He, I mean, I could only say that he felt that with an assessment coming up, that this was an important thing to do."

"Would an eleven-year-old child think like that or would his father think like that?"

"Well, I don't know, but clearly Dash knew that an assessment had been ordered and then he went to visit his mother."

I didn't want Elterman on our case, but a court had ordered it and we had to live with it. So I asked Jamie to call him. "Mrs. Richardson has serious misgivings about your work on our case and believes you dealt with her negatively and prejudicially," he told Dr. Elterman. "She doesn't trust you to assess her accurately and professionally, but for Dash's sake, naturally she agrees to see you. I hope that you are able to look at this material with the fresh eyes it clearly needs."

I was anxious awaiting my interview. "Surely it's so clear by now that even he will see it," I said to Dave the night before the meeting. But in the back of my mind I heard Dr. Elterman speak glowingly of Dash's "surprising insight." He saw insight, I saw indoctrination. Could Elterman shift and acknowledge what we saw happening? At the custody and divorce trial, when Dash was six, my lawyer, Gerald Reid, had asked Dr. Elterman if Dash was an honest boy.

"Yes," Elterman replied, "he's an honest boy."

"And is what Dash says the truth?"

"I would hope so," Dr. Elterman replied.

The worst thing you can do is rely on the testimony of a PAS child. A PAS child is the abusive parent's closest ally and the court's least reliable witness. In their assessment interview leading to the second custody trial in May 1996, Elterman reminded Dash that there were long periods when we were not in court but he still wasn't visiting me. Dash had said, "That's because she never called. I'm the one that checks the answering machine. She never called." Elterman was shocked to learn that I had called Dash four times a day during the specific period he referred to, and every second day in general. Elterman said defensively, "Well, that's not what Dash told me."

I prepared for the interview for days, fretting over it and checking and rechecking my documentation, organizing the same tapes I had given Dr. Beyerstein and testing the batteries on my portable tape player. I wrote out a bullet-point list itemizing everything I needed to tell him and copied all the affidavits, court orders, report cards, and my handwritten notes, and put them neatly in a folder with section dividers and labelled tabs. I listed all the people I wanted him to speak to: Elizabeth, Melody, Myrna, Dash's teachers. I was determined to make Dr. Elterman understand that this was not a case of teenage angst or a parent with a laissez-faire lifestyle, but bona fide neglect and abuse.

As a mother, knowing that my child was being abused and neglected and being able to do so little about anything, ripped my heart out. To have been told for years that I had to just suck it in and wait for Dash to come around had been like asking a stampeding bull to stop and smell the pretty roses of Pamplona — I had wanted to scream and scream, but I had to stay calm instead. Couldn't look emotional. Had to simply document it all. With anxiety rising in my stomach, I opened Dr. Elterman's office door, smiled brightly, and sat down on the edge of the nearest chair with my folder of material on my lap. I was eager to begin, and because Jamie had already told Dr. Elterman that I didn't trust him and did not believe he was impartial, I wasted no time on pleasantries.

"Dr. Elterman, if I can, I'd like to start by having you listen to some answering-machine messages that Peter left, over a number of weeks. I believe them to be representative of his drinking habits, and they appear not to have changed to this date. Some of the messages were left in the morning, some in the early afternoon, some in the evening." I explained as we listened to the tapes that I wasn't criticizing Peter or his lifestyle or avenging myself. I had had the same concerns during our marriage, and they had only become worse, "as it would," I said, "if left untreated." I wanted Elterman to understand that I believed alcoholism was a disease, not a personality flaw. I wasn't attacking Peter. "So far as his drinking and drug use *affect our son*, I think I am right to be concerned," I said. I watched Elterman for a response but got nothing. "Peter has said I am out to ruin his career or harm him professionally — well, I ask you not to believe that. I care only about Dash here." As I was leaning forward to change tapes to the last one, Elterman spoke for the first time.

"Look," he said impatiently, "how many more of these do you have? I get the drift." (Weeks later when we were in court, when asked if he had noticed slurring on those tapes, Dr. Elterman said calmly, "I don't recall.") "I think Peter does have a drinking problem. I have actually thought that for some time."

I looked up, quick as a whip. "*How* do you know this? And why didn't you call me and talk to me?" As I watched his nonchalant expression, a shrill voice came to my head: *He doesn't think this is a big deal.*

"Yeah, he would call sometimes with the same voice, and it sounded like he had been drinking. So?" *So?!*

"Umm. Well, Dr. Elterman, I *am* concerned that he calls me when he has been drinking and that he does it so regularly."

"Perhaps he has something to discuss with you at the time? He admits to being 'inebriated,' as he says."

But I had to drop the issue. Dr. Elterman was beginning to defend Peter. I just hoped that the implications of Dash living with a single parent who could be intoxicated from midday on would be clear once I left.

"Dr. Elterman, I have seen so little of Dash over the past three or four years. The structured access you recommended only happened for the first year. Then I tried to make access work by Dash and me deciding between ourselves when we saw each other. I thought that removing the court's schedule would encourage Dash to make plans with me, and he did — visits, lunches, holidays, games, and outings of every kind — but our arrangements cratered once he returned home. I have a list of the times I have seen Dash in two years. It would often take me two weeks of calling and leaving messages to even reach him by phone. He never said he hated me or my family or that he was bored with me. He would say he couldn't come over because he was busy, or doing something with his dad, but he was often just home alone. This is not a child who does not want to spend time with his mother. I believe this is a child whose loyalty to his father does not allow him to."

Dr. Elterman shifted in his seat.

"It's difficult for me to get a clear picture of what's happening in Dash's life because I don't see him much, and I have no access to the school, so I can't meet with Dash's teachers. I hear negative things about my son and I can't understand why I would if he is in such good hands with Peter. I have parents who tell me that Peter was drunk at the school choir night or the school play or on the soccer field. I hear that the teachers want to talk to me but aren't allowed to. I hear that other parents won't let their children play at Dash's house because it is not supervised and the father drinks."

"Do you have the names and phone numbers of any of these parents who won't let their children play at the Hart house?" Elterman asked.

"Yes, I do. The head of Dash's soccer division said to another mother, 'Dash is skateboarding alone late at night, at one o'clock in the morning. He's adrift in the community. His father doesn't see it. He says, "Stay out of my business. Dash is fine. He's happy." Well, he's not. Where is this boy's mother?' The mother he was talking to told him, 'Dash's mother has been in court for —'"

"Mrs. Richardson," Dr. Elterman interrupted. "I'll have to talk to Suzanne MacGregor about all this."

I sat, stunned. *Why?* "Suzanne doesn't live there any more; she's been gone six months, even more. Why would you need to speak to her?" I was struck violently once again by the contrast between Elterman's treatment of information that damned Peter and information that damned me. In previous years, when Dash went marching into his office saying "I hate Dave" or "They question me non-stop" Dr. Elterman *never* called us. Now he wanted to rush me out of his office so he could call Suzanne MacGregor. Suzanne appeared in Elterman's report saying that, in all the years she and Peter lived together, there had been only "a few" occasions when Peter had consumed an "unreasonable" amount of alcohol, but that Peter "might have addressed this through counselling if it did not have ramifications for the custody case." A few months later, during the second custody trial, Dr. Elterman told the judge that, when his report was released to Peter and me, Suzanne had called him right away. She had not meant to say that. Elterman had got it wrong. Flustered and probably panicking, she must have realized her injudicious comment about treatment had substantiated an issue Peter had successfully denied for years — the very existence of his drinking — and flagged that it was a problem so substantial that he should have been in counselling.

"Is there anything else you want to tell me?" Elterman sounded bored and irritated, and it flustered me. There was *so* much more I wanted to say.

"Dr. Elterman, have you heard of Parental Alienation Syndrome?"

"Yes, I have."

"Do you believe in it?" I asked. "Do you believe that a parent is capable of alienating a child from the other parent?"

"Do you mean, do I think this is a bogus syndrome? No, I don't. I have been involved in about twenty cases." It was like drawing blood to get anything even close to a dialogue going. I felt as though we were in parallel universes.

"Then you know of Dr. Richard Gardner? Have you read his book?"

"Yes, I read his book."

"Well, I have, too. Dr. Norman Goodwell and the therapist I've been seeing for years, Dr. Bob Armstrong, believe like I do that Dash is a PAS child. I believe Dr. Gardner when he says PAS is child abuse and that children are profoundly affected by it." I was desperate to add something that would shake him out of his complacency. I had one shot and I didn't want him to go off and talk to Suzanne only about alcohol; that was just one of the factors. *PAS is emotional abuse.* I wanted him to understand that dramatic PAS interventions were needed here: the alienation had to be reversed. In order to do that, Dash had to see me or Dash had to be moved. But I was getting nothing from Elterman. I felt as if I had to beg for his time, but I couldn't get impatient. I needed him.

"I believe that what is behind all this is that Dash has not been given permission to have a relationship with me, his mother, whom he loves. I see it destroying him. I have looked at my own contributions to this situation, but Dr. Elterman, in my mind there is only one possible conclusion — that my son has been programmed, that it has gone unchecked for years, and Dash is now entirely capable of taking on the campaign against me himself, with minimal help from his father. That *is* Parental Alienation Syndrome."

"Well, obviously I have to talk to Peter. I will also be seeing Dash. Is there anything else?" *Is there anything else!*

"Well. I have a folder here with all the documents, affidavits, letters, and reports I have referred to and a list of people I would like you to contact." It was on the tip of my tongue to add "if you don't mind" and I wanted to kick myself.

"I really do need to call Ms. MacGregor now," Elterman repeated.

*Great.* "Dr. Elterman, with all due respect, I believe Suzanne is one of Peter's enablers. I don't believe she is capable of giving honest information about Dash or Peter, because she is entrenched. You have to be either with Peter or you're against him, and for her own reasons she chose to protect him and let all this happen while she was living there." *Oh, no. I've blown it by talking about "enablers." He said six years ago that I "overpsychologize."* Labelling others wasn't going to convince Elterman that what I was saying had merit. I had said too much. I got no sense that Elterman had shifted at all, or was able to shift, or that he was even concerned. I had a lot more to say, but thought I had probably talked about enough of the wrong things to warrant my leaving it where it stood. My time was clearly up anyway. I stood and without shaking hands we parted.

Elterman's new report hardly deviated from his earlier two. He admitted no errors and stuck to his original story. Yes, Dash and I were alienated from each other, but he used the word in a general sense — implying that we had become detached from each other. He must not have believed my story, because his recommendation was not to "get the child out of Peter's house and get Peter into substance abuse and psychiatric counselling" but that *Dash and I* should go to "counselling together for perhaps ten or twelve sessions in order to become re-aligned better as mother and son." Peter's behaviour was more of an omission than commission. "I do not believe that the responsibility for this can be placed entirely on Mr. Hart although perhaps he could have been more vocal and insistent that Dash go on access visits. It is not good enough to simply say that it is entirely the child's choice. Mr. Hart possibly could have insisted at times and said that it was important to him that Dash have a relationship with his mother. There are, however, other sources of this apparent alienation, which emerges in Dash as a distance and a mistrust of his mother" — our "questioning" of Dash, Dash's troubles with Dave, and on and on. In Dr.

Elterman's opinion, our alienation was something that had just happened, an incompatibility of sorts, not something that had been done to us.

Although Dr. Elterman believed Peter needed to address his alcohol use or it would "increasingly affect his professional and personal life," he didn't appear to think Dash was already in an unhealthy environment. Dash, Elterman said, was still Peter's first priority. He asserted that Peter had Adult Attention Deficit Disorder, which even Peter said he didn't have, but which apparently explained what to the rest of us looked like intoxication. He devoted just half a line to Dash's threat to jump out a window. He didn't mention Peter's verbal abuse of me or his bullying of Dash.

Still, some of Dash's responses to his questions in their interview must have struck Elterman as odd. When Elterman asked eleven-year-old Dash what he liked about living with his father, Dash said, among other things, "He gives me respect." What did Dash mean by respect, Elterman wanted to know. "He says 'You can have the bigger half' or 'I'll get some later for myself.'" Dash's inability to see anything negative in his father or their relationship was textbook PAS, but Elterman didn't label it or interpret it as alarming, even though it was peppered throughout the report. About Dave: "He's the opposite of my dad." About whether or not Dash missed me in 1995, when he saw me for only a handful of hours all year: "I didn't miss her because I associated her with the back and forth. I sort of miss my mom now, but because of how she's been acting, I don't feel that right now." And what Dash didn't like about being with his father: "Nothing." Still my shoulders sagged as I read. Despite the curiosities, there was nothing in here that would help Dash, and when Dr. Elterman took the stand, he began his court testimony with assurances that Dash was a capable and mature boy. "Is he a child who is in any trouble emotionally?" Elterman asked the court grandly. "I don't believe so." Dash was "a reasonably happy boy made unhappy only by the court proceedings." "He is self-confident, with good self-esteem."

But Dr. Elterman knew little of the situation in which he was embroiled. He said on the stand that he knew Peter had banned me from Dash's school, but that the impression Peter had given him, as recently as a couple of months before the trial, was that my ban was a recent phenomenon, a fresh issue. He was shocked to learn that I had been excluded from my child's educational welfare since his first day of Grade One. He had been similarly surprised when I told him, during my interview that day in his office, that I had not been allowed to speak with Dash's doctor for the past six years. He admitted, when Jamie asked, that he didn't know that blocking a parent from the child's school and physicians was a nearly universal tactic of an alienating parent in PAS. He said that Peter often called him out of the blue to apprise him of the latest developments. He sent Dash along for appointments out of the blue. Those dates coincided with hearing dates, and I wondered, sitting there in the courtroom, *did your reputation just creak a little, Dr. Elterman?*

If Elterman hadn't seen Dash's alienation in 1989, I would have understood. It's hard to see. But not to see it the following year when permanent custody was decided was incredible. By 1996 I was shaken that he still ignored it. Sitting with Jamie before the trial, in a hushed voice, I listed the PAS indicators on nervous fingers.

"One, a previously loved parent is rejected by the child upon the family's split or shortly thereafter. Two, one parent is preoccupied with winning the child or defeating the other parent. Three, one parent shows a great lack of respect for the other parent and does not facilitate or respect that relationship. Four, in the child's eyes one parent can do, in Elterman's own words, 'no right and the other no wrong.' It becomes as black and white to the child as it is to the parent. Five, the rejection occurs over trivial matters. All these factors are crystal clear in my case and have been for years."

"The judge will see it now, Pam. Even if he doesn't understand the syndrome or believe it exists, he'll see that Dash isn't thriving where he is," Jo-Anne Bogue said.

"This is a textbook PAS case," Jamie added.

"Jamie, I would have given anything for it not to be. For this to be a figment of my overwrought, overprotective imagination. But —"

"But it's not. This is happening. And we're going to get Dash out of there."

We had been before six judges in the seven months that led up to the trial. The judges had all been concerned. We had been added to the trial list speedily and we were once again before Justice Donald Brenner, who had heard our application to vary access in 1993. We had been told that the 1990 access order still applied, and that Peter was expected to comply with it. Peter had been ordered and then reordered to give me Dash's report cards and access to his doctor and dentist. Peter had requested adjournments and dismissals, but, for the most part, they had been rejected. And on day three of the custody trial the judge gave me a big win. Beginning right away, Justice Brenner said, Peter and I were to be joint guardians of Dash. That order allowed me direct access to Dash's school life, an ability to meet his teachers, something I had not been able to do since he was five and a half years old. But when I called Principal Murray Stephenson the day after the decision and tried to make an appointment with him and Dash's teachers, he replied that I could not. On a challenge from Peter, a lawyer for the Vancouver School Board had advised Stephenson that, because the order hadn't *specifically* allowed me "ad-hoc" visits, I could only attend the school for the thrice-yearly parent-teacher nights, the next one of which was months away. My first real win disappeared right before my eyes. *I have rights but not the right rights.* Jamie and I went immediately to Justice Brenner for clarification. He confirmed that he had intended for me to be able to meet with the teachers and principal whenever I wanted to and that I had *full rights* to communicate with the school from now on. It was a dazzling victory. Peter could no longer control what I knew and what I didn't. The veil was lifting.

As the trial continued, Peter took the stand for six days and did what I had seen him do so many times before. He obfuscated when Jamie asked hard questions, he changed the subject, went off on tangents, altered his story, and irritated even the judge. Peter had spent years telling me on the stand that "Dash has decided" not to visit; it's "Dash's decision"; "Dash is making choices. I respect that." After Elterman's testimony, which was lightly critical of Peter's empowerment of a child Dash's age, Peter changed his story. "I didn't say it's up to Dash's choice until Dash got upset. So, okay, okay, I said, you don't have to go. That's all I did. It wasn't as if I said you decide, son. I didn't say anything near that. I never, I never put it on Dash to make his own decisions." Peter's testimony was also filled with paranoia that read like something from a psychology text:

"This all started off as a plot for custody. She wanted custody all along and it's so blatantly apparent how this thing started off, they knew they were going for custody when they started off with the equal guardianship. The whole thing was a set up."

"I am under siege."

"Mr. and Mrs. Richardson are my only enemies."

"I was basically being vilified as I am now."

"I'll be looking over my shoulder all the time."

Dash must have believed I was forever waiting to storm the castle, as his father assured him that he spent every conscious hour guarding the gates. At the same time Peter blurred the lines between himself and Dash, and they became one person. Peter would complain that "we" were dragged into court. "We" are being persecuted. "We" are being vilified. Dash had taken on Peter's views because he was rewarded for them, and Peter defended Dash's views because they were his own. In time they were no longer emotionally separate people. It was frightening to watch.

Peter called in a slew of criminal lawyers who swore to Peter's good character and fine parenting. One said that he had never met me but had "heard all about" me through another lawyer. The evidence of half a dozen of them consisted entirely of things Peter had told them. Stoked by Peter's stories, en masse they gave the impression that Peter was a persecuted single parent of chirping, happy Dash. One lawyer, Ken Westlake, a close personal friend of Peter's, testified to my selfishness over Dash, although we rarely socialized and had spent no time together with Dash. He claimed to be close to Dash, but conceded that he had not even seen him for two years. Ken Westlake testified about seeing my husband, Dave, snorting coke and drinking heavily at a party in 1989 at his sister-in-law's house, but under cross-examination admitted that Dave had not been at the party at all and that he had never met him or seen him before. In a desperate attempt to explain away the drinking problem that even Dr. Elterman now believed existed, Suzanne — separated from Peter now for a year — brought to court various alcohol-based homeopathic medicines and tinctures that were meant to explain Peter's alcohol-infused breath. She was persuasive, a senior family-court lawyer, and soon to be a provincial court judge. Greg Hart got up and said that Peter was the "best parent I have ever seen." Dash was "blissful." Greg, now in medical school, never saw his dad drunk, he said, and "everyone in the household hated the topic" of visitation, access, and my relationship with Dash. I wanted to shout out, *If you hated dealing with me so much why didn't you just deal with it like millions of other people do and let Dash see me? When I didn't get access for weeks and weeks and weeks why didn't someone just facilitate it? When I called seven times in a week to try and speak to Dash, why didn't you give him the messages and the space to call me back?* Could Peter really be that persuasive a force? Was their guilt so strong that evidence which tarnished their carefully crafted stories was rejected as a matter of course?

"Dash deserves to live with healthy people," I cried that night with Dave. "At eight, ten, eleven, Dash doesn't need a father who is his best friend, he needs a *parent*. He doesn't need a house of fun, booze, and no boundaries, where he can come and go as he pleases." Dash needed to know that the world was a fair and good place, not a place where people were "out to get" him, "dig dirt" on him, and "vilify" him in court.

Our ten-day trial stretched to thirty days. Peter was spinning it out. I couldn't figure out if there was a reason behind it, but Jamie took me aside in his frustration at the time-wasting witnesses and explained, "The older a child is, the less likely a judge will move him without considering very carefully what he wants."

Dash's twelfth birthday was looming.

We didn't want to give Peter more opportunities to delay and get us off track. We didn't call doctors Beyerstein, Goodwell, or Armstrong, even though they had important things to add. We knew that Peter's lawyer would object to their testimony, because none of them had ever met Peter and we couldn't afford the time — as it was Peter had asked for and received twelve adjournments during our trial. Jamie and I focused on the tangible issues that demonstrated the PAS best: the total failure of my access, our superficially hostile estrangement, Dash's unhealthy behaviour, and the sharp dip in his progress at school to which my "agent" Elizabeth MacKenzie and Murray Stephenson testified. Melody Frosch spoke about the lack of supervision at Peter's home, Dash's general unkemptness, and Peter's aggressive phone manner. She spoke of the Mexico trip. Myrna Halpenny, who had told me privately that she feared a backlash from Peter for appearing in court, testified to seeing him drunk when she picked up her son, Myles, from their house, about the evening she was having a coffee at my house when Peter arrived disoriented and slurring to pick up Dash, and about the phone call *she* had received when she wrote her affidavit.

Peter had told the court Dash "couldn't wait" to testify; he had "so much to say," and he would "bring him down here anytime." And so my son was called to the stand halfway through Peter's case. We knew he was coming: he was on Peter's witness list. I held my fingers pressed to my lips when I saw him enter the room, trying not to cry. *Is your heart breaking today, too, Dasharoo? You're already so damaged. Your presence here is a given; your testimony coached. We know what you're going to say. So go home, dear one.* Jamie stood and objected vehemently to Dash's presence, but Justice Brenner waved him off. Jamie was as concerned for the case as he was for the child. Dash's evidence would undoubtedly be against me. Dash's position had already been made so clear, through his father's affidavits, through his messages to me, through his "do the right thing" notes. Why put him through it? All we could ask was that our objection be recorded. I touched Jamie's arm. "Ask him as little as you can," I whispered. A father of five, he nodded. He was as horrified as I was.

Dash climbed into the witness box wearing his father's clothes. He looked straight ahead as he was sworn in. When Justice Brenner welcomed him, said he hoped he was comfortable, and offered him some water, I wanted to get up and leave. I wanted to go out in the hallway and be sick. My job was to protect Dash from harm and I had not. I was helpless, incompetent. I had failed in my objections, I had failed in the first trial, I had failed in 1993 to see it through, I had failed forever, and my grief turned to agony when Dash turned to the judge and said that testifying was his "greatest wish." I had worked so hard for so long to not feel any hatred for Peter, but as I sat with Sandy, squeezing her hand, I started to shake. I could feel poison rising up in me. I *hated* Peter. I hated him more than I'll ever hate anything for the rest of my life. For using our child, for abusing him, for leaving him alone and *frightening* him. For all the years Dash had lived with anger. For creating the perverted loyalty that had frozen Dash's heart. For ignoring his son except when he needed him to punish me. For putting his needs before his son's at every turn and for giving Dash no limits or ability to grow into a healthy young man. But mostly I hated Peter for having killed the trust and joy that had flowed so freely in that child. The cruelty of it, the sheer perversity of it, struck me like a brick that day in court. I had to raise my hand to my face to hide sudden, angry tears.

Dash's testimony was as we expected. His convictions were strong but with details conspicuously absent. Peter's lawyer, Russell Tretiak, tried to engage Dash in his testimony, but Dash floundered. They took him off the stand and brought him back days later. Do you remember a time that you hadn't seen your mom and Dave for a while? *I'm not sure. I couldn't say I do and I couldn't say I don't. I'm not really sure.* Did you go to the Canucks game? Did you have a good time? *I guess so, I don't remember much about it.* I heard some stories about how you would have to get changed over at your mom's place or sometimes you would have to get changed over at your dad's place to go play soccer? Can you tell the judge anything about that? *I can't really remember anything.* When you were at your mom's house, would she take you right to the field? *I can't really remember.* You can't remember anything about it? *No.* If you went to your mom's on a Friday night, you would miss goofing around with your friends at home? *I can't really remember.* Do you remember the first time you saw Dr. Elterman? *No.* Do you remember who took you to Elterman's office? *No.* Do you remember if anyone was in the room with you? *No.* Dr. Elterman said this year that you don't have any specific reason for not going to see your mom except for that sometimes you don't feel like visiting your mom? You remember telling that to Dr. Elterman? *No.*

And so it went on. Dash answered "I can't remember" twenty-three times. He was a nightmare witness for Peter's lawyer, but he did remember some of his lines. He remembered not wanting to visit me and the "seven years of accusations." He had almost no memories of good experiences with me but crystal clear recollections of my "insults" toward his father, the relentless "questioning." Dash said angrily, "Dave asks me 'How's Suzanne?' and I think what's it his business how Suzanne is doing?"

When it was his time to speak Jamie asked, "Does your mom question you?"

"Yes."

"What did she question you about?"

"Regular stuff."

"Like what kind of regular stuff? I mean, you know, 'How's school?' or what?"

"Yeah, 'How's school?' like, 'What are you doing lately?', 'What are you up to?' that sort of stuff. Then she's like, so 'How are your sports doing?' That sort of thing."

Jamie had one more question. "Do you love your mom?"

Looking down at his feet, in a soft but clear voice, he answered, "Yes."


Two months into our never-ending trial, one sunny Sunday morning in late June, Melody Frosch called me. "The boys are swimming in the pool, Pamela. Do you want to come over and visit?" For a second I was confused. "Dash is here," she said.

Dash had told me he wouldn't see me because of the "court stuff," but the thought of sitting with Melody and watching Dash play in the pool was too tempting to refuse.

"Melody, thank you. How long have they been there? Have I got some time?"

"Yes, yes. Dash slept here last night and they just jumped into the pool now."

"Okay. I'm going to quickly whip up a batch of Rice Krispies squares and come right over. I'll be about twenty minutes." I hung up and called to Dave to help me get the boys organized: we were going to see Dash. I ran back into the kitchen with my heart hammering and pulled the Rice Krispies and marshmallows out of the pantry cupboard, melted the butter on the stovetop, poured it all over, stirred it a bit, spread it out in a tin, threw a tea towel over the top, got the boys in the car, and drove off.

As we walked through the Frosch's back gate and around to the pool, I could hear my son's laughter as he cannonballed into the water. Stephen

Frosch shrieked, "Watch it, Dash! Geez, you nearly got me!" A wet child clambered out of the pool. "Oh, yeah? Well watch this!" We heard another dive-bomb and more squeals. *God, I've missed this boy.* Colby ran ahead. Melody was sitting in a big straw hat and waved Quin and I over. Even though she know my situation, I wondered what Melody thought about this mother who had to be called over to see her son.

"Hello, Dash! Hello, Stephen!" I smiled my biggest smile and willed my nerves to be gone. I patted the tin under my arm. "I brought you boys some Rice Krispies squares." Dash was suspicious. He narrowed his eyes when he saw me, but called out a reticent hello and then a bigger one when he saw Colby and Quin. "Dash, would you swim with the little boys?" I asked, to break the ice.

"Sure, Mom." We helped them into the pool and the four boys splashed and swam. I didn't try and butt into their fun and went instead to kiss Melody on the cheek and visit with her. I moved my chair so that I could watch them, sipped my coffee slowly, pretending calm, and chatted lightly with Melody. I engaged with Dash little by little as I sat there. "Can you do your crawl, Colby? Great dive, Stephen! Dash, he nearly got you then! Show Stephen your forward somersault, Dash. You know, the way Big D taught you!" Dash took a deep breath and did his forward somersault. He smiled when he came up for air. I called, "How's your backstroke coming, Dash? Have you been practising? Show me!" Dash swam the length of the pool on his back. "Dash, I'm impressed!" I said, and we smiled at each other then. It was electric. We had plugged away and a spark had caught. Then Stephen jumped into the pool right next to Dash and they were gone. Quin, with his little floaties on, paddled around in the shallow end, and I watched the waves to make sure they weren't getting too big for him. He was immersed in his own world, smiling, flapping his arms, proud of himself for staying on top of the water. Time passed with everyone happy.

Later Dash asked me to drive him home. "I'm disappointed with you, Mom," he said as soon as we drove off. "You weren't supposed to see me."

"Well, I'm glad I did, Dash."

He had a hard edge to his voice. "I told you that I didn't want to see you until you stopped the court stuff."

I was used to this conversation and stuck quietly to my message. "I know what you said Dash, but I don't feel that I have a choice. I've tried everything else, and now only a judge can help us sort all this out."

"Yeah, but . . . " his voice trailed off.

"Every situation has two sides, Dash."

"But I've heard both sides."

"From whom?"

"My dad."

"Dash, both sides is when you hear from each person directly."

"You don't know how hard this is on me, Mom. Every day gets tougher. You don't know how hard it is to be at my house right now."

My throat tightened. "I think I *do* know how hard it is. I hope this will make a difference. I know it's been hard for you to trust me and believe what I'm saying, but from the bottom of my heart I need you to understand that I don't mean to hurt you by being in court. We're a family, your dad, you, me. And we're way off track and have to get back in line. You have the right to both your parents, Dash."

"Well, I could live without you." I smarted.

"But you don't have to. If I died you would live without me, for sure, but I'm alive and I live ten minutes away from you. That's weird, isn't it, Dash?" I looked straight ahead and focused on the road, but Dash was silent and I could see that he was listening. "Dash, I hate court. I hate it. I hate being there, I hate writing affidavits, I hate being in that building. If there was another way I could make a difference, believe me, I would do it. Remember what I told you when we spoke in January, that when parents are having problems and they can't resolve them, a judge has to come in and make a decision that helps?"

"Yeah," Dash said, but he was wilting. We had arrived in front of his house and I stopped the car.

"Please believe me Dash, I will keep trying to see you because I love you."

"Can't you just stop? I want it over."

"I know you do. We all do. But it's a bit like saying 'I want to be in Grade Twelve now' without going through the other grades first. We're in a process. Like when countries have problems and they go to the UN to sort it out. It's a process. We're almost there."

Dash shifted the tin of Rice Krispies squares from his lap. "I have to go, Mom."

"I know. But it was so good to see you today. I'll call you tomorrow. Maybe we could do something, next week?" I looked into his eyes and tried to read what he was feeling. There was nothing there. "Umm, I don't know. Maybe. I'll call you."

"I'll call *you*! I love you, Dash, with all my heart."

I put my hands together in our little heart, but he ignored it and clambered quickly out of the car. Two days later, from the stand, Dash asked angrily, "What was she doing showing up at my friend's house with a batch of Rice Krispies squares?"

I promised the judge that, if I was given custody, Dash would stay on at Queen Mary Elementary (with a tutor to help him enter high school), continue on his soccer team, and see as much of his friends in the neighbourhood as ever. Nothing would change for him, except that he would be installed in my house on a primary basis. Dash would have permission — indeed, the court's sanction — to begin rebuilding his relationship with me. My family was ready for it. I promised the court that I would ensure that Peter had lots of access to Dash, because he needed both his parents. It served no one to obliterate Peter in the way that I had been. I told the judge, "I'm not here to take away Dash's dad. I'm here to give him back his mom." At the end of August 1996, two weeks after Dash's twelfth birthday, the trial-division people called Jamie: Justice Brenner had made his decision. I was picking up groceries at Granville Market when Mimi called me on my cell.

"Pam. The judge has a verdict," she said. My stomach rose into my throat. "Come home. Jamie is on his way here."

"Has he said anything?"

"No. Just come home."

I ran out of the market toward my car, fumbling for my keys, breathless and excited. *I'm getting my son back.* I drove, vaguely mindful of traffic lights and cars, but able to register little else. I saw Jamie and Jo-Anne waiting on my doorstep as I flew down my street and parked at the gate. I leapt out of the car, but went only three steps before I took in the expressions on their faces. Jo-Anne looked stricken; Jamie, devastated. A former child advocate, he couldn't believe what he held in his hands. I knew, and convulsed into tears.

"No. Jamie. Please—"

"Pam, he's given Peter sole custody again."


Justice Brenner had seen so much, from our court appearances in 1993 — giving us the ultimately doomed order for an independent assessment of Dash by Dr. Leslie Joy — to the completion of twenty-nine days of evidence in 1996. He was troubled about Dash's disintegrating progress at school. Peter was a liar. Peter had a drinking problem. Peter had committed "custodial parental misconduct." He had sent astonishingly inappropriate messages to his son. I was a good mom and Peter's behaviour toward me was "appalling." Peter's refusal to send me school information, Justice Brenner said, was part of a "continuing wish to dominate" me "and to force" me to go to him "and ask for things such as report cards." It was "part of his ongoing efforts to control" me. Given his current state of mind, Brenner said, it was likely he will "continue to be a substantial impediment to the access relationship between Dash and his mother." Brenner believed that, if I was given custody, I'd have encouraged generous access to Dash's father, while Peter had "no interest in doing anything to assist in improving Dash's relationship with his mother." The judge handily rejected Peter's argument that I had caused my own estrangement from my son by bringing custody applications. The judge found the abuse and interrogation claims to be nonsense. The only blight against me was that Dash did not want to live with me.

After twenty-nine days in court, I had been successful in obtaining one thing — joint guardianship — but Peter had challenged even that order and we had to go back and ask for clarification in front of Brenner. Yes, I could now see the teachers, get report cards, and seek information from Dash's doctor and dentist, but because it was joint guardianship, any decision-making had to be agreed upon by the two of us.

Attempting to force Dash to leave the parent whom he loves and with whom he wants to remain would clearly be a draconian outcome, Brenner said. The clearly articulated wish of the just-turned-twelve-year-old child "outweighed the negative probability" that, if he remained with Peter "Dash's relationship with his mother will continue to suffer." Dash wanted to remain "where he has always been" and the court, "if satisfied as to the capacity of the custodial parent, should be wary of taking what would be the drastic step of ruling that a six-year-old custody order be reversed." Dash was believed, and Peter was seen as fit — or fit enough. My relationship with Dash could go down the toilet so long as Dash wasn't moved. *This is a nightmare. And it's never going to end.*

But there was still more, a pièce de résistance. Justice Brenner gave Peter a free hand and took away the only tool I still had — the threat to Peter of future proceedings if he didn't stop what he was doing to Dash. Justice Brenner declared that the question of Dash's custody was never to be brought to court again, and that he would continue to be the judge on record for any future matters. Like many in the judicial system, he hoped that Peter and Dash would settle down if the custody question was put away forever, but I knew it would just bring the iron curtain back down on Dash. As I sat on my steps I knew. *He is lost to me now.* I knew it in my bones. Would he be lost to himself? PAS children can suffer for the rest of their lives. As Dr. Richard Gardner says, being "programmed to believe things that don't coincide with their observations and experiences" can produce "a paranoid delusional system that . . . may last for years, if not throughout a child's life." Dash was not only going through a relationship breakdown, he was directly enmeshed in his own mental breakdown. I wanted to run inside my house, call Justice Brenner, and scream at him what my heart already knew. "You spineless man! This boy is going to die."

## Chapter 6
# Bringing in the Troops

Dave and I led the kind of life some people think glamorous and exciting, with our years filled not just with raising children but with dinners, business functions, "society" and charity events. I met new people all the time, and because women are women they always asked, "Do you have children?" or "I have two at home with the sitter. How many do you have?" I would always say "three" and hold my breath to see if the topic would just fade out. If it didn't, I would tell a truncated version of my story. "I have three children, but I am only raising two," I would say. "I don't see my first son, Dashiell." I'd explain what happened and then watch their faces.

Some looked at me like I was from another planet. *What do you mean you don't see your son? Have you been to court? How did you ever lose custody in the first place?* Some would narrow their eyes and wonder what I had done to make this happen. I learned to deal with it all and I never, ever lied. I never made up a more palatable story. I never disowned Dash and said, "Two boys." I never made it easier on Peter and the courts by pretending to understand what had happened. I made it political, telling anyone who asked that what had happened to me was happening to thousands of other parents around the world. "This can happen to anyone," I said. "The courts don't understand and they don't act until it's too late. But at least I haven't been alone. I have support. Some fight this as single parents or while working double-overtime to make ends meet. Fighting PAS is a full-time job."

It was so easy for other people to talk about their children and their families, and it always reminded me that something every other mother did with so much ease was so painful for me. I always knew what I had missed, because I didn't miss any of it with my other two children. I comforted myself with the knowledge that children are built out of both their parents, and Dash still had me. I hadn't gone anywhere. I was thankful that he still lived only ten minutes away from me. I was thankful for the wonderful things I had in my life. I had given birth, in my forties, to two healthy babies who had grown into happy, open, strong boys. I had in Dave a wonderful and supportive partner. I was grateful for what I had and I loved my life, and because of that I was able to move forward. It's amazing how little time there was to dwell, anyway. The "Dash" side of my life — trying to reach him by phone, arranging visits, baking treats, and writing letters to be dropped off, and constantly thinking about how to make things work — was a constant balancing act with looking after Colby and Quinten, looking after our home, and nurturing my marriage. I was mostly too busy surviving to dwell inside my pain. As long as I was still trying to make a difference for Dash, I felt that I was allowed to take-five on the misery and live fully in the part of my life that was emotionally sustaining.

I could put Dash and our struggles aside when my family sat down to dinner or when I lay down with Dave at night — because I *had* to. We all needed a break from my worry about him. I needed an oasis; we all did, and we found it in each other. Because Peter had done this to destroy me, if I didn't carve happiness out of the rubble he would win. So my family was my guardian, warding off the demons, repelling Peter's hatred while I slept. I stayed logical and sensible. I didn't reach for something destructive to ease my pain — drink, drugs, an affair, yelling at my kids when I was tired and frustrated. I turned instead to my children and laughed and taught and cared and dug up the best of me. I turned to my husband and thanked him for his love. I included Dash in our lives all the time, letting myself simply remember and cherish him. When we were on holiday or at the lake in Whistler, Dave and I would often flash a glance at each other and say, "Dash would love this" or "Remember when Dash . . ." and I encouraged the boys to do the same thing. We rarely spoke about how little we saw Dash. We spoke about how we were going to see him soon, and we looked to a future when things would be different, not to the past when there was only pain.

The reality was still there, though, each morning when I woke up, that Dash was truly gone now. The site inside my heart that since his birth had been Dash's permanent real estate was emptied and scraped clean that summer. He'd moved out. Now and then I would look around our dinner table or sit as a passenger in the car with Dave driving the four of us to a movie, and I would struggle sometimes to clearly picture what my family would look like with Dash *in* it. My family didn't look whole, but it didn't look flawed, incomplete, or wrong either. We were a unit and we all had lives, and Dash had, by now, after all this time, floated to the side of it. But I could still feel how Dash had melted into my arms and I could still see when I closed my eyes at night his beautiful, gentle brown eyes as they looked into mine, and hear his quiet voice when he told me, "I love you, too, Mom." Moving on didn't mean leaving Dash behind. It meant being able to get up every morning without paralyzing heartbreak.

Now and then I passed the house that had been so warm and beautiful when Dash, Peter, and I had all lived on Trimble Street — and where Dash and Peter still lived. It had become as neglected as Dash. The front door was peeling and scuffed; the windowpanes were cracked and repaired with tape. Six months after Christmas in 1997, the previous year's tree lay sprawled in the front yard, with tarnished strands of tinsel twisted in its bare branches and its metal stand still attached. Dash was alone at home with his father now, with Greg doing his residency and Suzanne long gone. When Dash wasn't at school, he spent his time by himself, on the streets with his skateboard or at home in his room. He was burning through his friends with his neediness and defensiveness, with his indifference to their needs. His long-term friends still loved and supported him. They saw the pain he was in but didn't know how to help.

A friend of Dash's told me recently that he became a hard person to be around after the 1996 trial. He had been left without hope, so of course he was difficult. Dash's good friends knew he was in trouble. Newer friends, more troubled friends, took advantage, as they pushed him for invitations to his house because it was fun and unsupervised. They could drink there. Even when Peter was home he was often drunk, and the children could do what they wanted. Dash was embarrassed about the way his father acted around his friends. He turned beet red.

Kids had been coming to the Hart house to drink, smoke, and hang out since Grade Six; the girls had been coming since Grade Seven. Peter called himself the Pied Piper. The children made fun of him, but Peter seemed unaware, and Dash never said a word against him.

I didn't know any of this for years. What I did know was what Dash told me. He said that he organized most of his own meals, making sandwiches for dinner or grabbing subs and pizzas out, so I got him a junior membership at the Jericho Tennis Club, somewhere he could go to eat healthy food and relax a bit. Though he never, ever, called me when he was there, I knew from the tab receipts I paid each month that he did go, and often. I would have given anything to be able to cook for Dash, to care for him, but I had to let these other people try and do it: the club, his peers, his friends' parents. Peter had long stopped picking up Dash and dropping him off at his friends' houses, leaving Dash to skateboard there and back or rely on the charity of other parents. Dash was drifting and unparented. It had been a year since the trial, and he was thirteen years old. Though not always successful, I still tried to pick up Dash at the specified time as all three of us had agreed in court.

One Wednesday afternoon Dash's teacher, Donna Andrews, saw me waiting for him on the front steps of the school and asked me into the classroom to talk. She cared a great deal about all her pupils and was well-loved by parents and students alike. She looked out for Dash and had flagged his troubles early on. She had been a teacher for a long time and knew intuitively which children had supportive home lives and which didn't. She knew within weeks of Dash's beginning Grade Seven that no one got him up and ready for school and no one helped him with his homework. As the year progressed and Dash slipped behind, she had tried to be there for him. She organized a morning tutor to help Dash work, and she called the house those mornings to make sure he was awake and on his way to school. Still, Dash did very little. He rarely handed in assignments and, when he did, the work was dreadful. His report cards showed consistently low marks. He was a long way behind the class, and there were only a couple of months until the end of the school year and the change and tumult of high school. Donna told me

Dash might not make it in high school. She believed that, if he went there as emotionally and academically unprepared as he was, he would drop out within a month. Dash had shut down. He was standoffish and evasive. He gave monosyllabic answers when asked questions. Sometimes he couldn't sit still and disrupted the other students so much that Donna had to isolate him in the classroom. Sometimes he was sent out of the room altogether. Dash told Donna that he went to bed "very late" every night but still couldn't sleep. He mumbled and slurred his words at school, and the vice-principal, Carol Andison, suspected him of going home at lunchtimes and getting drunk. Donna thought it more likely that Dash was just mimicking his father. He had done it all his life.

Donna had begun calling Peter every week, sometimes two or three times, with grave concerns. Donna told me that Carol Andison had begun calling, too, but it was neither effective nor pleasant. Peter was enraged. "You fucking people, just let him be. Haven't you ever had a bad year?" But Dash wasn't just having a bad year. He was having the "bad life" he had cried about in my arms when he was eight years old. "You people lay off, or I'll pull him out of the school," Peter told Carol.

When Donna told me what Peter had said, my heart seized. If he'd said the same thing to Dash, it would have terrified him. His school was his support network and the only link he had to a caring community. Dash's charisma had endeared him to his teachers long after he became a difficult pupil. He felt important at school, because he was a natural leader and still had good friends. He had a teacher, a vice-principal, and a principal all reaching out to him and trying to help and understand him. It was clear to the teachers that Dash wasn't fine, and they looked to his father to see why. Why wouldn't Peter involve himself in his child's life? He wore Vicks VapoRub on his clothes, which Donna believed was to disguise the smell of alcohol. She had heard stories from other parents about the state of Dash's household. She believed that Dash parented his father.

Donna paused after telling me all this. She looked at me hard. I had known for so long that Dash was in trouble, but at that instant, in that second between knowing and not knowing, I wanted desperately for her to say that everything was going to be fine, that Dash was a happy little daydreamer, and that my worries weren't real. What she said was: "We believe Dash is depressed. Pam, he might be suicidal."

Dash's situation had become urgent enough for Donna, Carol, and Murray Stephenson, the principal, to consider something radical. They thought about calling child services, but didn't have any confidence in the outcome. That was a crapshoot, too, and might make everything worse. They had used the phrases "depressed," "psychiatric problems," and "potential suicide," and they couldn't stand aside and watch a rapidly worsening situation. Still, they were teachers, not social workers, and it took a lot for them to stand up. Out of my conversation with Donna came a new forum: court. They offered me their standing as Dash's educators. They agreed to tell Justice Brenner what they knew. Despite his pronouncement that our custody issues could never go before the court again, I was sure that Dash's deterioration at school would be so alarming to Justice Brenner that it would finally force his hand to do something to help Dash.


Jamie gave Peter notice of the hearing, as he was obliged to, but didn't tell him we had the teachers coming. Peter would have got a restraining order, called the school board, threatened to sue, or raised a posse. He would intimidate the teachers — he had a reputation at the school for doing just that — and I couldn't risk scaring the teachers off. We deceived Peter and his lawyer, but I was beyond caring. Peter had had enough chances to help our son. The courts had only ever given me silk-thread connections to Dash, but the teachers gave me another chance. When I gathered them up and went to court, my back was straighter and my shoulders squarer than they had been in months. After all my years of trying to convince my lawyers, our judges, and Dr. Elterman, at last people outside my sphere of influence were saying that Dash was in a dangerous and neglectful environment. Now that I wasn't in this alone any more, neither was Dash. I wanted him in my home. I wanted an independent psychological and educational assessment to tell us what we were dealing with and the authority to get Dash the counselling and academic help he needed. The joint guardianship I had been given at the 1996 trial had amounted to nothing precisely because it was joint — I still had to get Peter's permission to do anything and Peter never gave it. I needed more. So I was asking for a psycho-educational assessment and *interim* custody of Dash (pending the outcome of the assessment). I wasn't asking for a complete custody reversal. I wanted to start the ball rolling without making anyone nervous.

The hearing was set for April 24, 1997. Peter had been served, and knew the date and time, but didn't show up in court, knowing that judges almost never allow *ex parte* hearings or decide matters of any importance without the other party being present in the courtroom. We begged Justice Brenner to listen to the teachers' evidence anyway. It had been difficult enough getting them to go to court in the first place. Were the rules of procedure more important than a child? Brenner dithered. Then sighed. And called Donna Andrews to the stand.

"Ha, ha, ha, ha!" Donna threw her head back and laughed maniacally from the witness box. "Do people do this very often? Is this normal behaviour?" The crazed laughter that Donna recreated on the stand was one of Dash's bizarre new behaviours: roaring out loud at totally inappropriate times. It really bothered her; there was madness in it. It bothered her as much as his chronic disruptiveness and day-long fidgeting. The way he mumbled, stumbled, and fell off chairs bothered her, too. Dash "walked crooked" and bumped into things, pretended he couldn't do basic tasks and couldn't give Donna a straight answer or look her in the eye. Dash was unmotivated and very, very low. A letter from the school months earlier had spelled out Dash's lack of progress: he had now fallen to two and a half years below his grade level in reading. The only math he completed was done with a tutor. On twelve assignments, Dash got zero on four, missed two altogether, and scored badly on three others. In language arts he'd handed in nothing. His home reading had not been completed or signed. In social studies, he had done none of the assignments given out in the previous weeks. Donna had asked the rest of the class to help Dash on a communal basis, and they did. The other kids encouraged him, making up "a little game with him to encourage him to work." "Come on Dash," they would say, "this one's easy. Let's do this one together." It did help, but not enough.

Donna found it strange that she knew almost nothing about Dash, and wondered why he was secretive and defensive. "Dash never, ever, talks about his father," she said. "He never talks about his mother. He does not give any information about his home life at all. I know a great deal about all the students in my class, but not Dash." She said that, when she became concerned enough to "do a bit of prying" during a talk with Dash, she quickly received an unpleasant phone call from Peter, reprimanding her "for butting into something that was not my business." Peter had made it clear that I was not to be involved in any way. Donna told Justice Brenner she had met with me at a parent-teacher night and, after mentioning it to Dash, she received — freakishly quickly — a phone call from Peter, despite the joint-guardianship order now in the school's files. "What do you mean she was there? How did she know to come? To come to parent night? She showed up?" he had said, aghast that I had been to the school, and furious that Donna had spoken with me.

Donna had never been so involved with a student as she was with Dash. She had phoned Peter twenty-five or thirty times to talk about Dash, for truancy, for missing homework, for late attendance, poor work, absent work, bad behaviour, general concerns. Peter told her what he told everyone: that "their" problems were my fault. "The trial his mother forced me into," he said, had devastated his law practice and he was busy rebuilding it. He said Dash was fine and just needed to be left alone.

"I would always let Peter talk," Donna told Justice Brenner, but "basically I'd end up saying, 'Well, Peter, I really don't think you're understanding what I'm trying to say, and I'm glad that you think that everything is fine and dandy, but what I'm telling you is what I see in the school. It's not fine and dandy. Dash is not all right.'"

When Carol Andison, the vice-principal, took the stand, she agreed that Peter was a big part of the problem. Just three weeks before the court hearing, Carol had called him to reschedule a meeting she and Donna had arranged with him to talk about Dash. "I said, 'Peter, I'm just phoning to reschedule the meeting that you missed last week,' and he said, 'What's this meeting about?' I said, 'Well, you know we're quite concerned about Dash. We need to do some problem solving about what we're going to do,' and he immediately became incredibly abusive, just incredibly, swearing at me, telling me, you know, 'You f'ing people don't know what you're doing,' just screaming at me. I said, 'Peter, I'm going to have to hang up. I don't understand why you're yelling at me. I'm just trying to schedule an appointment.' And he said, 'You'll have to forgive my manner.' I said, 'Well, no, I don't have to forgive your manner. I don't want you swearing at me.' Anyway, he did stop swearing, but he continued to scream at me, 'Let this child be, just let him be. You don't know anything about children.' So I said, 'Are you going to come to this meeting on Wednesday morning at 8:15 or not? Just give me a yes or a no.' He said, 'I'll be there,' and hung up on me. That was the end of it. And he never showed up."

The principal, Murray Stephenson, told the judge that Dash's behaviour had become so bad that he had been permanently removed from his French class. He started fights, but when he wasn't raising hell, Dash was "emotionally withdrawn." He had begun a strange new habit of lying down on the floor of the classroom like a corpse. Dash's eyes were almost permanently downcast and he had an over-quiet, solemn demeanour. A year earlier Dash had been a "relatively happy boy," Stephenson said, but he was no longer the same boy, and the rapidity and extent of the changes alarmed him. "I believe he needs some professional assistance — and what form that takes I don't know, perhaps psychiatric help — but he needs a professional to guide him in a very different direction," he said. Peter knew about Dash's troubles in the finest detail but there had been little response: no alarmed phone calls, no offers to do whatever he could to help his son, no visiting the school to meet with the teachers.

Surely, I could step into that vacuum?

We asked Justice Brenner for an immediate decision. The timing of Dash's transfer to my interim custody would be perfect: he was at a wilderness camp with his school on a small island off the Sunshine Coast. I could pick him up at the ferry on his return and take him straight to my home. I knew the plan would fail if we had to pick him up from his dad's. If Peter got to him first, or if he was allowed to be at the house watching Dash pack, Dash wouldn't be able to come with me. He wouldn't be able to defy his father like that. Still Brenner wavered. *Jesus Christ, will you just act?* I thought. But he adjourned us for a week to wait for Peter to come and give his side of the argument.

In a brutal blow, which belied all Justice Brenner knew about our case, he ordered a copy of the teachers' testimony to be sent to Peter so that he could prepare an answer to my claims. *No! Don't you dare send that transcript!* my mind screamed. *Dash will read it. You know he will. How many times can you hear Peter tell you Dash reads everything? That school is all Dash has. He will shut down there, too, if he thinks the teachers have aligned with me.* Jamie leapt to his feet to argue. But it was done. *Oh, my God, what have we done here?* I panicked. Dash would read not concern and care but betrayal in what the teachers had said about him and his father. Donna Andrews was the only mother figure Dash now had, and he would dump her over this. She was interested in Dash and she cared for him; she helped him. He turned to her, too, and one day he might have even talked to her about his life, or asked for help, but I knew the transcript would change all that.

Sure enough, Dash it was given the transcript to read as soon as he got back from the camp, and he hated Donna intensely after that. He never forgave her for testifying, according to his friends. She was a traitor, just like his mother, and that brought the count of Dash's healthy influences to exactly zero.

With sagging shoulders, Jamie and I went to court the following week. They sagged further when we saw Ken Westlake there with Peter. A senior criminal lawyer, he was, in his own words, one of Peter's best friends. Five years before the teachers took the stand, Ken Westlake had written, in one of many affidavits, that Peter, "makes Dash feel good about himself. . . . Dash idolizes Peter. Peter is Dash's hero. That is plain to see. . . . Peter is the best parent I have met." Six months before the teachers took the stand he had breezed into one of the hearings after our second custody trial, adjusted his glasses, and declared to Justice Brenner that he was now twelve-year-old Dash's lawyer.

Peter was outraged that we were in court again. He declared, "All of a sudden Mrs. Richardson has ingratiated herself with the teacher. That's exactly the same thing that happened before, and it's what's upsetting Dash at school. He told me, 'She's just going to gather up evidence, Dad.'"

*Don't believe him, Brenner.*

Yes, Dash "could probably shape up a little more in terms of doing his homework better," Peter said, but he was a "happy, happy kid" who was just distracted. "He's emotionally as sound as anybody can be. He just needs a little tuning up at school." *Don't believe him. Listen to the teachers. This man can't see past himself.*

"Do I have to call another twenty witnesses to say he's one of the happiest kids?" he asked. When Justice Brenner told him the teachers' evidence had certainly been damning, Peter fell on an old standard line — no one understood Dash like he did. "The picture painted here is totally inaccurate," he said, his air of bemusement crawling on my skin. "They don't even know Dash."

To my plea that Dash be ordered to undergo a psycho-educational assessment, Peter pulled Dash out of his hat. "I assure Your Lordship, Dash will not go to any psychological assessment," Peter said, and those twelve words sunk us. Dash was thirteen now. Of course he wouldn't be forced to go. Brenner shifted in his seat. *Then just move him,* I begged, as Jamie pleaded the same with the judge. *Move him and I will work with him. We can get an assessment later. Just give us time to start his healing. Let him live with a healthy family. Let him learn what unconditional love feels like. Don't let him lose this chance. Soon it will be too late. Give me custody. My family is committed to healing this damaged boy. I will hire any expert I have to, any counsellor, any tutor. I will take him anywhere. Please don't make me watch him simply fade away.*

But Peter knew his judge. He knew his system. He pulled out his reliable trump card: If you shift him, Judge, he will run away. *Oh, he won't. He won't. Don't believe them,* I willed. But it sealed the deal. It was over. Brenner wasn't going to write another failed order. He wouldn't be our super parent. Brenner said he wouldn't go against what he had found at the trial — that Dash was happy at his dad's home and wanted to stay there — and he wanted to talk personally with Dash before he decided what he should do. *Oh, God,* I put my head in my hands. *This is a child who lies like a corpse on the floor of his classroom! How much more can he take?* Though Jamie remained the gentleman he is, I saw a look of disgust cross his face and then a kind of sad, muted resignation. *How can this be happening, after those teachers sat there and said "potential suicide"?*

I wanted to finally, after all these years, dissolve into a fit of screaming. I wanted to be mad and bad and to express the disbelief, outrage, and hysteria that I had so often felt sitting in these rooms, to break down for having to colour within the lines all these years and get nowhere. For having sat in front of a dozen judges who did nothing. For having to think of every solution and hand it to them on a silver platter for them to ignore. I wanted to let it all out and show them all what battling this maniac for my son in this hamstrung institution had done to me. I was in court when I should have been home with Mimi, the boys, and the husband I was neglecting. Instead I was here again, banging my head against this brick wall. *How many chances have you people had to do something that helps this child?* I wanted to shout. "I'm not the only one Dash is slipping away from. Peter is going to lose him, too!" But as I watched Peter grandstand, Justice Brenner demur and murmur, and Jamie struggle, I said nothing. I stayed in my seat, my face reddening from the effort of keeping my frustration inside. Neither Jamie nor I did any shouting. I looked down at my palms, which showed red half-moons where my fingernails had pressed into them. I crumpled into my seat. Unable to vent my rage, I simply went numb.

Jamie stood up. We had prepared for this. If, after all this time, Justice Brenner couldn't see how damaged Dash was, how far in denial Peter was, how worried the teachers were, then we had to get away from him. We needed a judge who didn't suddenly go inert every time he saw us. I wasn't going to walk away from my son, and I wouldn't let all these adults fail him yet again.

"I'd like to ask Your Lordship to dismiss our entire application," Jamie said in a strong voice, filled with hope.

There were smirks all round from Ken Westlake and Peter, but I hardly noticed. I was too busy rushing up to talk with Jamie. My adrenalin had spiked. We had only this one last shot. We were going to appeal Brenner's decision from the 1996 custody trial the year before. Though we were out of time by a month or two (appeals have to be lodged within twelve months), we were desperate, a child was involved, and late appeals were by no means unprecedented. I was still so overwrought from the hearing that I couldn't handle being there on the day of our appeal. So for the first time in seven years of hearings, I sent my lawyer in alone.

Jamie was alone, then, and so was I, when the appellate judge threw our case out.

Neither the "interests of justice" nor Dash himself would be served by allowing it, Justice Ian Donald said. "Too much water has passed under the bridge." The kick to the stomach came at the end of a short hearing. Justice Donald, who had the teachers' entire transcript in front of him, told Jamie, almost casually, that I could go right ahead and apply for a new trial if at some point "a dramatic change of circumstances" occurred. Dash was a depressed insomniac who almost never saw his mother and was unsupervised at his drunken father's home, failing elementary school, possibly abusing drugs and alcohol, and potentially suicidal. How much more "dramatic" did Justice Donald want it to get? Jamie had stood in court, broken, as the judge stood up, fluttered his robes, and left the room.

By June, the end of Dash's Grade Seven year, the teachers were exhausted from trying to manage him. I asked Jamie to get Justice Brenner to agree to host a mediation session with Carol Andison, Peter, Ken Westlake, and me. For now, Justice Brenner was all we had. We had to work with him. Maybe the mediation format would produce something positive. But my hopes were dashed as soon as we sat down. Peter and Ken Westlake were as loud and aggressive as they had been in court. They talked over everybody, and Justice Brenner just sat there in his sharp suit, looking down at his splendidly polished shoes, uncomfortable without his robes, high bench, and gavel. When I handed around Dash's latest awful report card, all he managed to say was that the grades were a concern, and that Peter "should watch Dash's academics." Carol told them Dash was totally out of control. He wasn't in class at all any more, because Donna, openly distraught about his rapid deterioration, could no longer handle him. It was Dash's last month of elementary school and he was spending every day of it sitting at a little desk outside the principal's office. The two lawyers pooh-poohed all that, but suddenly Ken Westlake volunteered to act as a go-between for Dash and me; he wanted to facilitate access visits, he said. Justice Brenner breathed a sign of relief. *Why don't you just get Jack the Ripper*, I thought, but I had to make it into something. I choked down my rage, got out my little pocket calendar, smiled sweetly, and negotiated a visit with the lost son I now hadn't seen for nearly four months.

It was to take place at a picnic table in a park near my house, and turned out to be a chaperoned visit. Ken Westlake picked up Dash and brought him to the park. To my surprise, Ken didn't leave. He didn't even go off and pretend to make some calls on his cell phone or stretch his legs on a short walk. He sat shoulder to shoulder with Dash, and the three of us bumped through awkward conversation and stilted silences that I felt driving deeper wedges between Dash and me. Ken Westlake had a predictable chilling effect on Dash, who sat there pale and unkempt, unhappy and hardened. Ken hovered over him and said, "Tell her, Dash. Tell her how it makes you feel when she goes to court all the time. Tell her how you feel when she badmouths your father," but Dash could hardly say anything, let alone his lines. My heart broke for him as we struggled to connect. Following Ken's cues, knowing I had to address them, I said, "I understand that the court process was horrible for you. I do. But I only went because I love you. I believe with all my heart that you deserve to have your mother in your life." Dash gave me nothing. I didn't dare try to hold his hand. I was terrified of what would happen to each of us if he recoiled. I just continued, talking soft and low. I told him I was worried about him at school and at his home, and that I worried for him because he seemed so unhappy. He managed to get out, "You badmouthed my dad and you called him a drunk," but his heart wasn't in it.

"No, Sweetheart, I didn't. I don't badmouth your dad, and I think you know this. And I will always be concerned for your welfare and I will always look out for you. I worry about you and I love you. You are my son."

Dash drew in a breath but couldn't meet my eyes. "I won't be visiting you this summer."

*No! Not again. Not another summer missed.* I had to think fast. I was losing him. I stood up. "Would you come with me a minute?" I didn't wait for him to look up at Ken for permission; I just took his hand and led him away. A soft, yielding little boy again, for just a second, he came.

I slowed then stopped, and we stood under a big maple tree. We were two brutalized human beings who had once shared an unbreakable bond, and suddenly Peter's success seemed absolute. Dash couldn't speak. He looked sick, scared, and *tired* . . . so unbelievably tired, but by ourselves, among the whispering trees, with the sun dappling his face through the leaves, I took his other hand lightly in mine. He wouldn't look at me and stared hard at his beaten sneakers.

"Dash," I whispered, "brown eyes to brown eyes." His hardness softened and slowly, agonizingly slowly, he looked up at me. It was the first time he had looked me in the eye in months, and the sliver of a connection we made in that moment, under such inhumane and humiliating circumstances, gave me more hope than any court ever had.

Dash was about to start at Lord Byng Secondary. I knew that if I did not prepare the school in advance, Dash could be viewed as just another messed-up, neglected kid. I needed their engagement and understanding. I needed them to care for an nourish Dash. Visiting the school a month before Dash was to start there, I spoke with the school counsellor, Bob Lewis (and later the vice-principal and Dash's eight new teachers). I said that I wanted Dash's new school to be a haven, as Queen Mary Elementary had been. "Dash has had a really tough childhood," I told Bob, "and he might be aggressive, unpleasant, uncooperative sometimes, but there are reasons for it, and they come from a deep and traumatized place." I wanted to prepare him, when he met Dash the following month, to look beyond Dash's misfit behaviour. His poor academics, inability to concentrate, and bad work habits were behavioural not academic; even the minor learning glitch that Queen Mary had identified was most likely tied directly to his trauma. I explained to Bob about PAS and got him to understand what it was to be a programmed child, what Dash's loyalty forced him to do and think, what losing his mother so brutally had done to him, and what his home life was like. Dash and his father now lived worlds apart. It had been bad enough on West Fifth Avenue but now, in a new place on West Tenth, Dash had his own entrance and nearly complete separation from his father. Peter lived on the top level and Dash on the ground level. I told Bob that Peter drank, but that he seemed to be drinking less than usual right now, which was a positive thing. I told Bob about the other parts of Dash: his sense of humour, how naturally curious and intelligent he was, how popular he had always been with his peers.

"He doesn't think he is particularly good-looking, Bob, but he really is. And he loves animals and gardens and peaceful places and he lives to skateboard. His dream is to be a professional boarder, and I encourage that as much as I can. As long as he has goals he will make it through, I think. I supply anything that will help him, a big mat for his breakdancing, new trucks for his skateboarding. But he's been through a lot. He needs a basic education —" I paused for a second. "Look, Dash has to get through high school. I'm afraid he'll end up on the streets if he doesn't have support in his life, someone looking out for him, keeping him on the rails. Bob, he's so *angry*. I worry about what it will do to him. It's poison. His dad doesn't know any different any more, but here at school Dash is surrounded by people who can care about what happens to him, try and turn him a different way, show him some peace." I mentioned that Donna Andrews and Murray Stephenson of Queen Mary had talked about depression and possible suicidal feelings in Dash.

"It sounds like he shouldn't be here," Bob said.

"I know, but he is here," I replied. "Queen Mary really wanted Dash to go into a bridge program, you know, one-on-one instruction in a small group setting away from school, a program that would work to improve Dash's academic skills until he could meet the demands of high school? But Peter refused to sign the papers. Dash said he is nervous about going to a big high school, and I am worried he will get lost in the system if no one is watching. I would love it if you would be my eyes and ears, here, Bob. Dash will not come to me. He needs someone he can talk to and *I* need someone who sees him regularly and can keep me in touch with how he is and whether or not we can do anything more for him, or something different."

Once school started, Bob Lewis saw quickly that Dash's formal education truly was going to be of secondary concern until Dash started to heal. Dash would not excel, but between Bob and his teachers he might be kept from falling off the rails completely. Over the course of time, Bob arranged for Peter to come in and talk about "Dash's academics." If the meetings had been about Dash's "emotional health," Peter would have walked out or defended Dash, blamed me, and stopped listening to what Bob was saying. Above all we needed Peter to stay open to Bob. So running beneath the casual chats with Peter about Dash's marks and classroom behaviour was an agenda — that of getting Peter to trust him. The goal was keeping Dash in school and his self-esteem as high as possible, and Peter was instrumental to that. Bob checked in with Dash and his teachers often to see how he was doing and looked over his report cards, checking his attendance and tardiness and spending an inordinate amount of time on him. By the time I met with the teachers, most had already figured out that Dash didn't have a home environment that encouraged his schoolwork or helped with his homework. Some of them gave him less to do than anyone else; other teachers let him complete his homework in class. He attended the "skills centre" instead of French, which allowed him to catch up on some of his work in a supervised environment. Dash was so well supported that first term that he did well. He passed. By the second term he was floundering, though, languishing behind his classmates and losing interest by the day. He led his peers astray in the classroom, which made him popular with the kids but not his teachers. He was time-consuming and disruptive. The teachers were amazingly tolerant, but they only had so much patience for a student who did not want to be there.

Dash was angry at everybody and everything. Kids started to pity him. Some thought him a loser. All of them knew he was different. He was the only kid they knew whose house was open at all hours of the day and night for slacking and boozing. He was, as always, frequently absent and late, and the teachers, the vice-principal, Terry Howe, and Bob Lewis fought to deal with his confrontational behaviour. He was aggressive toward any adult who didn't "respect" him or who slighted him or his father, and the cynicism and lack of trust or good guidance left Dash without any idea how to act in the adult world.

Bob Lewis told me after Christmas that he believed Dash's acting out, his class performances, were all poses. "Dash covers up his troubles. It's a mask, and it hides a huge amount of pain and grief. He's not sleeping. He's not in good shape at all." Some thought Dash was on drugs, but I think it was exhaustion. Bob Lewis agreed when I suggested that

Dash's insomnia was probably a manifestation of his inability to find peace. Dash, thirteen and a half, may have had so much noise in his head that he couldn't sleep. Or maybe there was no noise at all. Like his expression now, maybe his head was just dead flat, silent.

Bob went quiet for a moment then looked at me with solemnity. "Dash is hanging by a thread, Pam. I don't want him to become another statistic."

I went cold. *Don't tell me things my heart already knows.*


In May, Bob Lewis met, as he did from time to time, with his in-house team of counsellors to brainstorm the school's troubled children and work on strategies to help each one. They discussed Dash and agreed that nothing that had been attempted at the classroom level had stemmed Dash's "failure or near failure in all subjects." Bob Lewis had phoned Peter over and over, but Peter now refused to meet with him. He said, "My private life is to be respected." Bob Lewis told me he thought Peter did care very much for Dash — and might even have loved him. "But his love for him is unhealthy. He cannot deal with what is happening with Dash." Peter had idealized his son for years and dealt with Dash's pain as he did his own — with denial and aggression. And I was still nowhere to be seen. By mid-1998, the end of Dash's first year at high school, I had seen him only six or seven times since September 1996. We'd had dribs and drabs: a golf morning, a shopping trip a couple of months later, skiing at Whistler during spring break, the hour in the park, but basically nothing.

By June, Bob decided that Dash's case needed to be raised to a higher level. Dash was the only subject of discussion at the Jericho Area Central Screening Committee meeting, a program under the auspices of the Vancouver School Board that existed to provide support, resources, and interventions for children considered to be "at risk." I went along and, as I had done many times, told the panel Dash's background story. I was positive and hopeful. I knew they could only do so much for Dash while he remained in his home environment, but the intervention might help or lead to something else, which might lead to something that actually helped him. Step by step. That's how I had to do this.

The committee decided that Dash should enter Lord Byng's Urgent Intervention Program immediately to get a short-term burst of extra help. Dash would not only be assigned a tutor who would work one-on-one with Dash at school, he would get a social worker, the school psychologist, and more intense time with Bob Lewis, all of which was designed to support and help him. I only had joint guardianship; we still needed Dash's father's permission, so the case manager wrote to Peter, who had failed to attend. She practically begged him for his support for Dash to join the program. Although he had "declined any special support for Dash" in the past, she wrote, she hoped he would "reconsider." Rage flooded through me. Peter couldn't put his pen to a piece of paper authorizing an intervention for Dash that might keep him in school, but he had spent months in court hearings, in making phone calls to the principal and the school board, and in writing a sixteen-page affidavit to keep me out of Dash's primary school all those years ago.

Some fifteen months before the intervention meeting, I had started a process that had produced something I now decided to use. In April 1997, around the same time the Queen Mary educators had come to me with their concerns, I had decided to file a complaint with the B.C. College of Psychologists about Dr. Elterman's conduct on my case. While it had been Peter who had induced the PAS with which we all lived, it was Dr. Elterman who had failed to provide a check against Peter's abuse of his son. Dr. Elterman had recommended the sole custody that had provided the environment within which Dash's alienation from me could flourish. Over the years Bob Armstrong's mood had gone from simple disbelief to outrage that a five-year-old had even been the subject of a sole custody order in the first place, because the rule of thumb was that one is issued only when one parent is assessed as extremely unfit. From the first Dr. Elterman had said I was a good parent. None of the dozen judges we went before ever said I was anything *but* a good parent. Dr. Goodwell told me that he had seen many custodial assessments he disagreed with but could still respect on a professional and scientific level. But of the reports Dr. Elterman had written in Dash's case, Dr. Goodwell wrote in his letter to the College of Psychologists, "I am afraid that this is not the case in this matter. It may be that this is quite uncharacteristic of Dr. Elterman's work, but I am unable to turn the other way and ignore something that has such serious and unnecessary ramifications for a son and his mother." Goodwell wrote, "I could not follow the logic of Dr. Elterman's arguments and could only deduct that either he was aware of information he was failing to report, or that his conclusions were coloured by prejudice or bias. I could not see how his conclusions were warranted by his reported observations or findings." As an example of bias, Goodwell reported that, in 1990, when Dash was six, Elterman had quoted me saying that "Peter and Dash have a wonderful, warm relationship. He adores Dash and Dash adores him," but didn't quote any of my very real concerns about Peter's physical violence toward me, his drinking, lies, secrets, and controlling, aggressive, and manipulative behaviour.

My therapist, Bob Armstrong, had for years watched, through my many, many sessions, my lack of access and dwindling relationship with Dash with growing anxiety for the child. Dr. Armstrong was appalled by Elterman's weak suggestion — seven years into Peter's sole custody — that Peter "could possibly have insisted" that Dash visit me more. Dr. Armstrong said, "in the absence of abuse or neglect, the custodial parent must insist that the child be with the non-custodial parent as per the court order." Pointing to my stay-at-home-mom status, my stable and supportive marriage, and Colby and Quinten, two thriving, happy children, Dr. Armstrong told the college, "This is not the profile of a mother who would be so rejected by a child." He was astonished by my repeated rebuffs from the courts and appalled that Dr. Elterman remained connected to our case. As Dr. Armstrong put it, the result Dr. Elterman had hoped for at the beginning of the whole process — that giving Peter sole custody would end the "war" and bring peace and normality to Dash's life — had failed. Dr. Armstrong believed Dr. Elterman was trying to minimize the extent of Peter's alcoholism when he suddenly diagnosed him with AADD in his third report. Elterman neglected to report Peter's lies during their interviews about how often and how much he drank. Peter said he'd been drunk three times in thirty years. Denial is a definitively established red flag for alcoholism. Dr. Goodwell told the college that Elterman had failed "to deal with serious concerns of neglect and the failure of the father to facilitate the relationship between the mother and son. He appears to blatantly excuse these serious shortcomings by diag-nosing the father with Adult Attention Deficit Disorder." Bolstering my claim was the fact that Dr. Elterman saw Dash in ad-hoc sessions at his office. In a letter to Peter's lawyer (but not to mine) in 1993, Dr. Elterman had said, "I believe that I have a very good relationship with Dash and he is very familiar with me and my office." According to the college by-laws, it is a clear conflict of interest to produce assessments in court for a party one is also counselling, and to me it was a solid ground for complaint. It was a conflict of interest that had long alarmed me.

When I told Drs. Goodwell and Armstrong in early 1997 that I wanted Dr. Elterman's reports investigated, they encouraged me to go for it and said they would support me. If I could bring a case of negli-gence against Dr. Elterman, an independent assessor might be appoint-ed to investigate our case. If that happened I was sure that the PAS would come out. No judge would leave Dash in that home if that hap-pened. So, in April 1997, both Goodwell and Armstrong had written to the Professional Standards Committee of the B.C. College of Psychologists and asked that my case be investigated for evidence of professional misconduct and breaches of ethics — extraordinary and brave acts in a closed professional community such as theirs.

A month passed with no reply, so I called and asked the registrar of the college, Dr. Ed Kramer, if he had received my complaint. He told me brusquely that he had sixty complaints on his desk. Yes, he had mine, but wouldn't get to it until July or August.

So I waited. And waited.

Then I called. And called. And called again.

At the end of August 1997, the college had written and asked for more documentation, including release forms that would allow them to interview Drs. Goodwell and Armstrong. I organized all the documenta-tion in a binder, sent it by courier, and waited again. Another month passed with no word. I called and Dr. Kramer told me he had not received my package. "That's curious," I said. "I sent it by courier. I received a delivery confirmation. Why don't I call you back after I speak with the courier company." I called the company and they confirmed that the package had been delivered a month earlier. I called Kramer back and in the meantime my package had miraculously been found. It had been "put away in a confidential file." By then six months had passed since the complaint had been filed.

I waited five more months. I called Drs. Armstrong and Goodwell occasionally to see if they had been contacted, but they had not. Two months later again, in mid-March 1998, three months before I sat in the intervention meeting thinking of my next step, the college wrote and told me that an investigator had been hired after a long delay caused by a "lack of funds." The investigator had presented an initial report to the college. Dr. Elterman had been asked to respond. I waited for more news while another month ticked by. Then another two. Eight more months would pass until I reached the end of my rope. In November 1998, I wrote to the college and told Dr. Kramer I was prepared to pursue legal action against the college for its inaction on my complaint. That got their attention.

In January 1999, twenty months after I had filed my complaint, I received a definitive response from the college. My complaint did not "in any respect" "constitute grounds under which the board of the college could act." It dismissed my argument. It dismissed Dash. It never did interview Drs. Goodwell and Armstrong. I had known them in a therapeutic capacity, the college said, prior to making my complaint, and neither of them had had any contact with Dash or Peter. *But! But!* I wanted to protest. *Just talk to them! Conduct an inquiry! That's all I want!* I had sent four hundred pages of documents, given them two well-respected psychologists, and nearly two years to investigate. I had given them strong prima facie evidence and believed it would have been enough to pry open my case.

My allegation that Dr. Elterman had made an improper diagnosis by attributing Peter's erratic and unstable behaviour to AADD the college dismissed by downgrading Elterman's strongly worded reported opinion to a mere "belief." It said, "There is no evidence . . . that Dr. Elterman did expressly diagnose Mr. Hart as having AADD, nor indeed did Dr. Elterman systematically set out to assess whether or not Mr. Hart suffers from AADD, but rather Dr. Elterman just stated his belief in that regard." When is a court-ordered psychologist's belief a belief and when is it an opinion? Dr. Elterman *believed* Peter was Dash's "psychological parent," and that belief saw the custody of a five-year-old go to an erratic, occasionally violent, uncommunicative, non-negotiating alcoholic. Why wasn't Dr. Elterman's *belief* that Peter had AADD considered similarly solid? In a field where so little is actually "provable" these definitions seemed utterly situational. Did they shift to suit the circumstances?

Not only had the college not talked to Goodwell or Armstrong, it had not called me, Peter, Dash, or any of my listed corollaries. Its members spoke to only one person before throwing out my claim: Dr. Michael Elterman. The college didn't send me a copy of his responses, even though I asked for it and it was within the college's by-laws to do so. "You will note the operative word," I was told rather tersely, is "may, not must." Like Emperor penguins huddling through the Antarctic winter, the members closed ranks around Elterman. The committee went a step further and decided that, because I had eventually threatened legal action, I was "adversarial and litigious" and would therefore never be satisfied with "any result other than the one you want." It was Peter's old argument and the same argument that has suppressed women for centuries. What then was termed "uppity" and "unfeminine" now was described as "litigious," and they believed it of me without asking me a single question. The college's letter also suggested that I had sought an investigation in order to help my custodial position, and I wrote back in disgust. "My child is the victim of extreme parental alienation at the hands of his father. Whatever the outcome of the investigation, it will have no bearing on my situation, and I did not start this process with that objective in mind. I have no expectation that a change of custody would even function, so bad is the situation. The psychological damage done to my child by a man described by Dr. Elterman as a "perfect parent" is probably irreparable, and I hold no hope of reconciliation."

Out of the ashes of disaster, though, came a phoenix.

To apply some pressure to the college during the many months of its stalled or non-existent investigation, I had sent a copy of my complaint to then–attorney general, Ujjal Dosanjh. Twelve months before the college finally threw out my claim, the office of the attorney general offered to appoint Allison Burnet, a senior child advocate, to our case, to "act in the interest of the child." I had been so crushed by my experiences with clueless bureaucracies, that I had simply filled out the form requesting an advocate, sent it in, and forgot about it, expecting nothing to happen. What I got was a powerhouse who knocked the system, like a roach, onto its back. The child-advocate program was not designed with neutrality or impartiality in mind. Instead, the advocates can take strong partisan positions on behalf of the child. The child advocate is allowed to take sides, favour one parent over another, oppose both parents, or even oppose the child if he is acting against his own best interests. Here finally was the super parent I had been searching for in the courts for so long. I wouldn't have cared if she decided against me as well as Peter, or if too much water really had passed under the bridge for Dash to accept it. If she wanted to send Dash to a residential school or an intervention program out of the province to get him away from Peter or to slap us both in jail and raise him herself, I didn't care. *Whatever works. I just wanted Dash safe.*

At the beginning of March, three months, before the intervention meeting, Allison Burnet strode into my house in a tailored suit and high heels. I was struck by how feminine, or more to the point, how *female*, she looked. Where I had been intimidated and tried not to be noticed or hit with the stereotypes women in court are hit with, she projected an air of utter invincibility. *Just try it*, she seemed to say. *Just try and get to me.*

We settled in at the kitchen table with hot coffee and I told her my story. I knew Allison was going to see Peter right after me, and I knew how persuasive he was. My worry was borne out when she called me that afternoon.

"Pam, have you ever thought of just taking a break from trying to see Dash? Just wait for him to come to you?" she asked.

I flew into action. I couldn't watch another professional miss this. I begged her to grant me another interview. I had not hit my mark the first time, so I gathered more documentation, including Dr. Richard Gardner's book with all its sticky notes. I took with me to her office the manipulative faxes Peter had sent, his scrawled ravings to my lawyer, the transcripts of the teachers' evidence from the year before, Dr. Beyerstein's report, and the letters from Drs. Goodwell and Armstrong. I walked Allison carefully through the history of the case from the first trial onward; how I was convinced beyond a shadow of a doubt that my son was a programmed child and that the last thing in the world he needed was for me to fall out of his life in the hope that he would come to me.

"He won't ever come. The time will never be right, Allison. There will always be something, because his father hates me so much that he has never given Dash permission to have a relationship with me. This goes very deep and goes back nearly ten years."

Allison looked at me and nodded. "You know, I saw this," she said. "I saw Peter denigrate you in front of Dash during our visit, many times. If he can't control himself even when he is with me, someone whose reason for being in his house is, to a certain extent, to judge his parenting, God knows what he must do when they are alone."

What I had said had meshed with what she had seen with her own eyes, and from that moment she became my strongest ally and Dash's lifeline.

Peter said Dash didn't want an advocate and already had "a lawyer of his choice, whom he is very satisfied with." Dash was "adamant" that he did not want to be "questioned" or have his teachers "questioned." Dash, Peter's affidavit said, "has had it. His last two years of primary school were made miserable by his mother's actions, and during the last half of grade seven when Pamela started to attend the school, he became alienated from his teacher and the vice-principal, both of whom he got along well with before she began attending." I knew Peter's story by heart by now. If only we could all just chill out, cool off, take a break, Dash would be fine, etcetera, etcetera, etcetera. Citing respect for Dash's wishes to be left alone, Peter refused to let Allison talk to Dash, and refused her access to Dash's files at Lord Byng.

Allison Burnet wouldn't have a bit of it. She went straight to court and demanded that Justice Brenner force Peter to "provide the child for an interview" and sign the file-release form. Brenner ordered it, and I was shocked at his total lack of resistance to Allison. Someone had finally pushed Peter onto his back. I cried with relief when I called Dave and told him. I knew now that she was going to get us what we needed. She could help Dash. Allison Burnet talked more with me, and spoke to Dash's educators and other parents in the community. She came firmly to the view that Dash was a full-blown PAS child and that his best interests were patently ill-served by both his father and himself. She was going to support me.

A month later, with the iron-clad support of the family advocate, Jamie served on Peter a notice of motion: we wanted interim custody of Dash. In the alternative we wanted three months of unbroken access over the coming summer. We had to have *time* together, to "break the back of the alienation," as Allison Burnet said. It's what I had told a dozen judges for over seven years.

Dash phoned me and left a message that he wanted to see me. *Of course you do*, I thought, weight hanging like a saddle across my shoulders. Dash's first visit in two years was no more than Peter sending Dash, armed and loaded, to shut me down. Though Peter's story for years had been "I just can't get the kid to go," he *could* get Dash to visit me, and he could do it whenever he needed to. As I drove to pick up Dash the next day, my stomach had been clenched for twenty-four hours.

Still, the fact was that Dash had finally been given permission to see me. He held my hand all the way home. I made a big lunch, with fat sandwiches, cookies, milk, fruit, and chocolate, which we ate out in the back garden with Quin, now six years old, and Mimi as we planned our day. Dash wanted to go shopping for clothes, so off we went, just the two of us. Colby and Dave were fishing with Dave's dad in Saskatchewan, and Mimi and Quin waved us off as though we, too, were going on holiday. That day he was telling jokes and acting silly. Nearly fourteen years old, he held my hand happily, which surprised and delighted me. His body had changed. His face was growing up. In the skate store he caught me looking at him and smiled broadly. I hadn't seen him for so long that it was surreal being with him. It was still so easy. Every minute had a dreamlike quality, and even the most mundane events were punctuated with intense feeling. Renting the evening's movie took on the significance of viewing a Fabergé egg collection. I had my son back — if only for the day, I had him.

We drove home. When I asked Dash to call his dad and let him know he was staying for dinner, he answered, "He knows. He told me to visit you today." *Okay, here it comes.* But still he said nothing. I prepared burgers and homemade fries for dinner, and the three of us hung out. Quin was beside himself that his big brother was there, and Dash was as calm and peaceful as I'd seen him in years. He visited his room and looked around at all his stuff. He picked up the framed photographs and looked at them with real interest and flipped through the photo albums I had left out for him. The three of us curled up and watched the movie, Dash's legs lying over mine, Quin tucked under my arm. It was impossible to believe anything had ever happened between us. It was heaven. I waited patiently for him to say what he had to say, but he said nothing. He was stretching out his time with me. We made sundaes. Dash's serving was huge and he ate the whole thing, hamming it up for Quin, who shrieked with laughter. Dash giggled; I held my stomach and howled. We cleaned up the kitchen and I told Dash I should probably be getting him home. He nodded, the smile wiped immediately off his face, and he started to gather up his shopping bags. Our day had been so wonderful, but I was beginning to feel sick. I dreaded the drive. Quin jumped in the back seat, Dash in the front, and a few blocks from his home he let go of my hand. I gripped the wheel and forced myself to be calm.

"You like me visiting, don't you, Mom?" he said.

"Yes, Dash, I love it."

"Well you could see me more if you stopped the court stuff."

"I don't see you, Dash. And I haven't for nearly three years."

"I've read some papers," he said. "About more court stuff."

I turned briefly and looked at him. He was composed, emotionless. I smiled. It may have come out as a grimace, but it was dark and I tried. "Dash," I said gently, "you've been sent on a mission today, and now that you've delivered the message, we don't need to discuss it any further. Let's just get you home."

"I'll never see you again if you don't stop."

*Oh, Dash. How can you possibly bear this?* I wanted to keep driving. Over the border. To Mexico. *Get this boy away from his life.*

"Dash, I don't see you now," I said again. "I don't see you." My voice was low. I wanted to soothe him. I knew he melted when I spoke to him with such love; he was melting now. He didn't want what he was saying. He didn't speak. "I don't think it's fair for your father to send you as a messenger, do you?" I said. He nodded quietly. He knew. "Your father should call me when he wants to tell me something. He should discuss these things with me directly." Dash nodded again. Surely what I said made more sense than what he had been told to say.

"If I have to come and see you, I'll just get on a bus and go home," he said, but it sounded hollow and childish, put on.

"Dash, the courts have been very patient with your dad. You know they have been. But they are losing their patience."

At that Dash shut down. "I don't want to discuss this now," he said. He stared out the window and hauled his bag full of new clothes up onto his lap as if preparing to make a break for it. Stopped in front of his house, my heart was hammering. *When will I see you again? Will I see you again?* I wanted to ask. "I love you," I said. I knew what was coming. Dash got out and stared at the ground for a long time. Then he spoke.

"This is goodbye."

Peter's lawyer called the interim-custody hearing "frivolous," "vexatious," and an "abuse of process," but Allison Burnet wasn't scared of those guys. She had the power in this courtroom. She didn't mind insulting the judge; his order had been a bad one. "I think this is a sorry state of affairs — when a court can listen to twenty-nine days of evidence, determine that this child should be seeing his mother, and still the child never gets to see his mother — and something has to be done to protect this child's emotional well-being," she said.

Brenner sighed. "So this long, sad saga simply continues," he said. "Nothing has changed." The last six years' worth of access orders weren't worth the paper they were printed on because they contained no consequences for Peter if he continued — as he would — harbouring Dash in breach of court orders.

"There is no doubt in my mind that this access would have occurred with the father's support," Allison continued. "If the child is now told that, if he doesn't go with his mother then his dad is going to jail, frankly it might make both of them realize that there are *laws* in this land and that they can be enforced." Allison Burnet was really getting going. "The Canadian courts have an abysmal record of enforcing their own access orders. In my view there is a way to deal with it. When an order such as yours was made, it should have stated that the access will occur or custody will revert to the other parent. If the court had had any sense there would have been an order that the *minute* access was denied a capable parent, there would have been a reversion of custody. It works. It's just that most judges don't seem to want to do it." The only remedy now was for Dash "to be in the primary care of his mother for long enough for him to be reprogrammed. This child has been programmed, and he has been programmed on a regular basis. It will *not* stop unless there is a change in primary placement. . . . This child has no major grievance with his mother. None. And the ones that he does have he can barely remember. Some of them lack all credibility when you determine his age now and his age when he alleges some of the things happened. The things she had done are the same picayune things that have been raised in this court for an extended period of time. They have nothing to do with his capacity to have a relationship with his mother. They have to do with his *father's* incapacity to have a relationship with his mother. The barrier here has nothing to do with his feelings for his mom or anything that his mom has done. The barrier is excessive loyalty to his dad, which *I have no doubt* has been actively encouraged by his dad. Mr. Hart cannot actively encourage this child to go to the mother's home. Without that active encouragement, there is no alternative but for the court system to do something about it."

Allison Burnet believed, as I knew, that Dash wanted to be able to love me, that his rejection of me was skin-deep. He melted too quickly when he was with me for it to be anything but a programmed response. "If this child were brought into this courtroom today and you told him that he was going to spend time with his mother and that his father had agreed and endorsed the plan, that child would go and have a lovely summer holiday with his mother. I have *no doubt*." She had seen the PAS in Peter's willingness to involve Dash in his battles with me. She had seen it in his badmouthing of me. But she had seen it most clearly, as Justice Brenner should have, as Dr. Elterman perhaps did, in the near-complete lack of access I'd had since the sole-custody decision eight years before. "I think it's long overdue that Mr. Hart recognizes that this child should have an opportunity to spend part of his childhood with his mother. His trouble is that he has a loving mother who wishes to see him and he is unable to break free and see her." Justice Brenner watched as this veteran child advocate, this woman uninterested in the desires, needs, and rights of Peter or I, fingered Dash's father as the sole director of the alienation.

Allison Burnet knew who to empower. The judge. He needed to stop vacillating and listening to a programmed child and start bearing ownership of Dash's fate. "Obviously quite an extended time ago, this child's wishes should have been overruled by the court," she scolded. "We are long past the point where we should listen to Dash. I think it's time Dash listened to you. *You* represent the best interests and welfare of this child and it is *you* who I want to deal with this."


"Now will Dash get help?" I pleaded to my lawyer's assistant, Jo-Anne, at the lunchtime recess.

"The family advocate knows what she's doing, and so does Jamie," she replied, reaching out and enveloping my cold hands in her own. I looked down at my hands, then up at Jo-Anne again and saw her compassion, felt her support. This caring mom who had sat in court with me day after day over the past two and a half years hadn't once wavered from the belief that something wrong was happening in Peter's home and that it was dangerous to my child and worthy of our fight. I was struck then by just how much I had always liked this smiling, curly-haired girl and how lonely I would have felt sitting in court without her all this time. Sandy came as often as she could, but Jo-Anne was *always* there. As she held my hands so tenderly, like my mother would have done if she'd been there, I realized that one of the reasons we had become so close was that she *wasn't* involved in my case in a legal sense, not really, not like Jamie had to be. She was there as the mother of three children, as a woman, and, now, as my friend.

Jamie walked over to us. "Come on," he said softly. "They're ready."


That day Justice Brenner made the first and only decision that acted in my son's true best interests. He didn't give me the interim custody

I was asking for, but he did give me what we had asked for in the alternative: ninety consecutive days of access — the whole summer — with police backup to bring Dash back to me if he ran home to his father, as both Peter and Ken assured us he would. I heard a cry of "It's house arrest!" from either Peter or Ken. To me the ninety days was time to show Dash what it was like to be part of a functioning family; what it was like to be fed regularly, worked with, and cared for. I wanted to show him what it was to be a child, not a cherished weapon of war. The access order was a "no-contact" order. Dash was allowed to call anyone, anytime, but Peter was not allowed to contact Dash for the first ten days of the ninety-day order. Beyond the ten days, Peter was to call no more than three times a week and for no longer than twenty minutes at a time. (Allison Burnet had recognized that Peter's incessant phone calls to Dash in the early years had been prime programming tools. Her demand for a no-contact order sought to limit their effect.) Ken Westlake, with his grandfatherly airs, promised the judge that he would respect this. "Oh, I have no intention of calling, Your Lordship," he said. I was to monitor all phone conversations between Dash and his father, and I, alone, was to sign any forms necessary to place Dash in the school's intervention program. Dash was going to have summer with me and start the one-on-one at Lord Byng when school restarted in September 1999. This was all Allison Burnet's doing. My gratitude couldn't be measured.

At two o'clock the next day, Peter brought Dash to the courtroom for the transfer. We all stood when the judge came in, then sat solemnly again. Jo-Anne was to my left, and once again Sandy had come. She had been with me through all these years, and I could see her pride now, her joy for me. I had tears in my eyes as I looked from her to the judge as he spoke.

"Now you know why you're here, Dash, don't you?" Justice Brenner asked. Dash nodded, eyes on the ground. He was pale. Peter looked mortified. "You're here so that you can go with your mother for the summer." Dash nodded again. "Now, when you're ready, I want you to say goodbye to your father and go with your mother."

Peter started crying. Dash burst into tears, too, and started sobbing, "I don't want to go. I don't want to go." He clung to his father and Peter clung back. The B-movie drama of the moment was astonishing. *Is this for real? This child is only going to visit his mother!* Jamie looked over at me. The four of us were speechless, and I wanted to shout at the judge for watching them so indulgently. *This isn't* Sophie's Choice! It was the only time I'd *ever* seen Peter cry. And yet I looked at Dash, red-faced, desperate, clinging to his father like he was his life raft. I watched them for as long as I could stand, then got up and walked over to them both. Peter had the devastated look of a man watching a lover leave. I put my arm lightly on Dash's shoulder.

"Come on," I said. "Time to go."

Dash and I walked out. He was crying in great, wracking sobs. *This is not healthy. This is not healthy!* I dared my will to crack. We walked and kept walking. I didn't slow my pace. Dash didn't slow his. And the moment we were out of the courtroom, Dash grew completely quiet. I glanced at him. His whole body had relaxed. He didn't look at me, but he was calm. I reached out and took his hand, which he held tightly all the way down the steps of the courthouse.

"Dash, how about we go to your house and pack some things to take up to Whistler. Maybe your skateboard and CD player?"

And, as if nothing had happened just minutes earlier, he said a level, "Sure, Mom." There was no anger in his voice, no venom. Just total acceptance, even a slight spark of enthusiasm. He spent five minutes inside his house packing some clothes and music tapes, then came out with his skateboard under his arm and jumped back in the car.

I drove straight home to pick up Mimi and the boys and the luggage I had packed that morning. Within minutes the five of us were piled into the car and on our way. Colby and Quin bombarded Dash with happy questions. *Dash, can you take us canoeing? Dash, can you jump off the dock with us? Hey, Dash, let's go fishing as soon as we get there! Can you ride a bike? Mom, can we light the fire outside and roast marshmallows? Dash, have you done that?* From the passenger seat Dash laughed and gave his whole, happy attention to each of the boys' questions. On and on they went as we drove over the Lions Gate Bridge and out of the city. I pushed back the sunroof and let the wind flow through my fingers. My body slowly calmed. Mimi's hand came to me from the back seat and squeezed my shoulder. I touched her hand and smiled at her in the rear-view mirror. We had done it.

Dash stretched his legs, reclined his seat, smiled out the window, and took in the exquisite scenery. We passed lakes, mountains, and hundreds of acres of forest swathed in brilliant sunlight. He was fine. The tears were all gone. He was just an ordinary boy going on a holiday. The performance had been for his father, and now he was free.

# Chapter 7
# Winged Angel

I hauled open the heavy Roman blinds in Dash's room. It was midmorning; the sun was high in the sky. "Dash, good morning. Look at the day! It's beautiful."

Dash wiped his eyes and blinked against the light. Sometimes he woke up feeling foul and hating everybody — other times he didn't. I took my chances each morning. He growled lightly. "Well, I can't see any clouds anyway, Mom."

"Right! And so guess what — I've got a great idea. Mimi's going to take the boys on a picnic and then swimming, so we've got a whole bunch of hours to ourselves. You know what I was thinking?"

"What?" He was starting to smile.

"Sailing. Just you and me on a boat. Out there." I pointed to the lake. "I haven't done it in years and years, and you haven't ever, have you?"

He nodded and shook his head at the same time. "Yeah, let's do it. I've never sailed before." His grin was broad now. Boys are so easy. Point them at a lake or a boat or a car and they're all yours. At the jetty, the dockhand took us through a brief explanation of how the little sailboat operated, handed us our lifejackets, and waved us goodbye.

"You got all that, right?" I joked with Dash.

"Sort of, I think so." He looked serious, found his footing, and glanced around him. He picked up the yellow rope the dockhand had shown him. "Let's see. You take the rope and sheet in —" And we were off. We shot over the steel-blue lake, shrieking with laughter. The wind blew in our faces and we squinted against the sunlight vaulting off the waves.

"I'm going to turn us around now, all right, Mom? I've got to put the boat in this direction and — Mom! Bend your head! The boom is coming over!"

I ducked, a little dramatically, and we laughed.

For an instant we lost our concentration and, while Dash was looking at me instead of where we were going, the wind picked up the sail and tipped the boat over. Sunny it might have been, but the water was glacial. We tumbled into it. "Oh, my God!" I shouted as Dash clamoured back to the boat, his teeth chattering. My legs screamed from the cold, but we laughed like the recently released as he pushed and then hauled the heavy wet sail out of the water and righted the boat.

"Mom, come on. You can do this!"

"Easy for you to say! You're already back in! Okay. One, two, three," and I hauled myself up. Dash stepped forward and took my arm. And over the boat went again. When we got going once more, I took the rope. "It's my turn now. I'm the captain and you're the passenger — you're my captive now!"

We swapped places gingerly and took off. "You got it, Mom! Hold tight and — oh, no!"

We'd spent more time in the water than on it. "Dash," I spluttered, clinging to the hull, "do you think we listened to the guy who told us how to do this?"


The good moments at Whistler that summer were exquisite. Sitting outside at night around the fire, staring at the stars, all of us trying to figure out which constellation was which. With Quin sitting so close to Dash he was almost on top of him, and Dash just smiling and putting his arm around him, we could almost forget everything and just be. Dash was sweet with me, kind to the boys. He was in every room I was. Every evening he wanted me to rub his back and feet, but while it was always something he'd loved, his demands had changed in quality. They came from something deeper. There was a palpable, almost desperate quality to Dash's need. At Whistler we slipped into a constant physical connection, watching television with our legs draped over each other, his hand in mine.

The bad moments shocked me: my child was a monster. Some days, maybe one in three, Dash woke up radiating hostility, and we all tiptoed around him until he shook it off. If he didn't want to do something, like help bring the groceries in from the car, he simply wouldn't. He would shout, "No!" and stomp off to his room, swearing, throwing his shoes into the corner, and slamming the door. Sometimes he refused to come out of his room for lunch or to get in the car when we were going on errands. He ignored my pleas for him to not dangle his feet out of the car window, so I had to pull over and wind the windows up. He would say things like, "Come now, Pam," when he wanted something, or "Get lost, I'm playing my game." When he was hungry he'd say, "Feed me now, Pam." When I picked him up from the skate park each day, he was often grumpy and critical. I would leave him be, and we would drive home in silence. His verbal assaults had an alarmingly misogynistic undercurrent, and they were always directed at me. Three times in those Whistler weeks he got angry at me over nothing and gestured masturbation in front of me. Once he pulled down his pants and showed me his bare bottom because I had "bugged" him about coming to the dinner table. Another time, when I asked him to help set the table for lunch he said, "Fuck off, whore." The word sounded impossibly vulgar coming out of a not-quite-fourteen-year-old's mouth. At first I was so shocked I couldn't respond at all, but within a couple of days I had worked out an active strategy: just keeping loving him, no matter what. "Dash, you don't need to say that," I'd say gently. Or "I know you don't really feel that way about me, Dash, so why say such horrible things?" I knew that, whenever he said such things, it added to the self-loathing that came with PAS. So I tried to neutralize it; take the shock value out of whatever he said by not fighting with him, by refusing to be provoked. It slowed Dash down. They never went away, but the number of incidents in our first week had halved by the second week and, despite Ken Westlake's dire prediction, Dash didn't try to run away either. He never threatened it, even when he was searching for horrible things to say to me. The stop for the Greyhound bus to Vancouver was only a stone's throw from our house. The bus ran five times a day, Dash had money in his pocket, and he knew I wouldn't stop him from going. Despite himself, Dash was having a good time. He even established a rapport with Dave again, who was easing himself back into Dash's life by coming up on the weekends. Dash asked me shyly if he could start calling him "Dave" instead of "Big D." Dash didn't want to phone anyone, and he avoided his usual lifeline, his friends. He declined my invitations to have them come and stay, and he didn't extend himself in their direction. When I asked him about it he got defensive and said, "My friends don't like you."

"They don't even know me, so if they don't like me it must be because of what you've told them about me. I don't think that's really fair, do you?"

He paused, then said, "I'm only joking."

Peter didn't call for the first ten days, as he had been told by the court. Every time I suggested that Dash call home, I received an emphatic "No!" or an enraged "I'm not calling!" When Ken Westlake and Greg Hart called, they didn't get much from Dash either. Ken had phoned just days into our time at Whistler, but Dash was at the skate park.

"I don't want you calling, Ken," I said. *Giving Dash his cues. Reminding him he's supposed to be mad.* "Dash will call you if he needs to."

I phoned Jamie straight away and told him to remind Ken of the promise he had made in court, but Ken called again and threatened to call "every half-hour until I speak to my client." I wasn't going to let this deputy ruin the progress Dash and I had made. "I'll call the police if you phone again, Ken," I said. I picked up Dash from the skate park and told him that Ken had called. He looked at me blankly, as though he didn't even know who "Ken" was, but on cue the next day, when Greg Hart called and asked Dash how he was doing, Dash flew into a rage. "I hate being here. It sucks," he said. "I'm not having any fun."

Beyond Dash's polarized and sometimes savage moods, we had other difficulties. Dash had failed Math and Socials that year and was heading for a fail in Grade Eight, his first year in high school, if he didn't retake them at summer school and pass. Dash had been enrolled in summer school but told me he had been "kicked out," because he had been late and "because I had to go to court." I called the coordinator of the summer school, Mr. Kerr. He told me that Dash had been so disruptive he had to be moved to a smaller class. Then, when Mr. Kerr interviewed Peter and Dash together to see if they could make some progress, Peter made so many excuses for Dash that Mr. Kerr finally asked him to "let Dash answer for himself." Peter called within days and said Dash had a dentist appointment and couldn't attend school that day, and Dash never showed up again. The amount of time that kid spent at the dentist, he must have had the shiniest teeth this side of Hollywood.

Thus we were stuck with an incomplete Grade Eight and an undisciplined, directionless boy. I went searching and found an American in Whistler with a Master's degree in Education (teaching special-needs children), who was tutoring that summer in Whistler while awaiting the birth of her first child. I talked with Janet by phone and, when she told me her specialization, I talked with her on a deeper level about Dash, telling her that he might be more difficult than the average tutoring assignment. She came to the house and met Dash, who seemed to like her immediately. They agreed to meet at the house twice a week, and Dash promised to do his math every day, for an hour each day. The two of them worked at the dining-room table together for two or three hours each time, and on Dash's first math test he got 92 percent, a far cry from the failure he had recorded at school. But after the first two weeks, it became increasingly difficult to get Dash to do his homework. He was resistant to his lessons with Janet, and eventually getting Dash to sit in front of his work became impossible. Trying to get him to do it piqued his anger and ate into our fragile connection, so among the three of us we decided to dump it for the time being.

I worked on other things with Dash under the guise of normal daily life. He was an insomniac, so we established a routine of lights-out at eleven o'clock, but I have no idea if Dash slept. There wasn't one day in those weeks that Dash didn't seem terribly fatigued, heavy. He didn't pick up a single book during those three weeks, but I had bought an armload of skateboarding magazines up from Vancouver, which got him reading — or at least looking at the pictures and engaging in one of his passions. Dash had told me a year before that he wanted to be a professional skateboarder, the first career aspiration I had heard from him in years. By then I leapt on any sign of passion, ambition, or engagement. I didn't care what it was. I believe in creative expression, and each signal that he was still artistic gave me hope that he was going to be okay. By then, if he had told me he wanted to be a tattoo artist, I would have rushed out and bought him his inks, needles, and studio space.

Dash had been interested in art even as a child, and I had nurtured it in him — taking him to Arts Umbrella, with all its creative-arts programs for children, and music and movement classes when he was four and five, a video-making class when he was twelve. I had always packed a bunch of coloured pencils and a sketchpad for him to use during road trips when he was young, and later he drew in proper art books I got him. Dash seemed to find it calming to sit and draw, and he did it for hours at a stretch. As we drove around Vancouver on our way to Westbeach for clothes or to his favourite record shop on East Hastings Street he always pointed out the graffiti in the city. One day I said, "Hey, Dash. I have a friend with an art studio. John Ferrie — remember Joan, my friend who helps me on the house? The interior designer? Well, her son. Why don't we visit him and see what he's working on?" We did and Dash's interest blossomed. I told him about two artists who had started out as graffiti artists — Jean-Michel Basquait and Keith Haring. We went and got some books on them and he flipped through them avidly.

"You mean these guys started out painting on the street? Really?"

"Yep, and look where they got to. When they were alive, galleries begged for their pictures. They were talented — like you, Dash. They started out with walls not canvas, too."

"Wow, Mom. I never would have thought that could happen."

"Now, how about this, Dash? Instead of doing your graffiti on buildings and public spaces, why don't I get some canvasses for you to paint on? Then you can work on it at home, too. It'd be like you having your very own studio."

When Dash was done painting his canvasses, he'd cover them with white paint and start all over again. And he'd call me out of the blue, when I hadn't heard from him for months.

"Mom, I'm out of paint. Can we go to the paint shop?"

And I'd rush out the door.

One afternoon after hamming it up in the paint shop, we pulled up outside Peter's house on West Fifth Avenue, shortly before they moved.

Dash turned to me and said excitedly, "Can I show you some of my canvasses, Mom? I've been working really hard on them."

"Dash, I'd love that!" I was astonished to be invited in. I hadn't been inside his house since he was five years old. "You run inside and ask your dad if I can come in and see your canvasses. I'll wait here for you."

Minutes passed. Dash came out again. Disappointment had crushed his happy face. "Dad says you can't come in."

"Oh. Well, Dash, another time then. I'd really love to see them."

"Yeah." He looked down and half turned to go. "Hey, Mom! I've got an idea!" He pointed to the corner of the house. "If you go over there, I can go into the corner room and show them to you through the window!" He ran inside and I walked around to where he had pointed; the window looked into a playroom in the basement. There were layers of grime and muck on the glass, and I knelt down on the damp ground and wiped it away. I cupped my hands on either side of my face to cut out the glare so I could get a better look, and there was Dash, so proud, standing next to a big canvas covered in graffiti art. I smiled and waved and gave him a big thumbs-up. He was beaming.

It was so important for me to support Dash's interests, no matter what they were and no matter what he was doing.

One of the strange things about having a PAS child for a son was that, although Dash was in some ways an ongoing "mental health emergency," he was also a boy, and that boy had grown up. He now lived in the world with other teenagers, and puberty had thrown up a vast array of opportunities for experimentation, rebellion, angst, and drama. So although we could curl up together on the couch in Whistler and toast marshmallows with the boys and laugh till we cried when we were tossed into the freezing lake, as far as trusting communication went it was still very early days. I plugged away, prying open the fields of communication so that Dash would get the counsel he needed as a teenager as well as the support and unconditional love he was missing out on as a PAS child with a dysfunctional parent. When Dash told me he had been smoking marijuana for a year, I didn't try to discipline him, and I didn't freak out, and I didn't attempt to change what he was doing. Many teenagers experiment with marijuana; I didn't want Dash smoking it, but I wasn't surprised that he did and, because I had no ability to discipline him, I tried just to talk it over with him.

"I guess the big thing that concerns me about marijuana, Dash, is that it's a drug and it affects the brain. For a young and developing brain, like yours, at fourteen years old, that's a big deal to me. I know that it affects children's grades and energy levels, even appetite. It can alter sleep patterns and might even make you feel down; blue, you know." Dash nodded, eyes on the ground. "It's also illegal, Dash. It's against the law."

"But it shouldn't be illegal. There's nothing wrong with it," he said quickly.

"And a lot of people think that, I know, and maybe some day the law will change, but at the moment it *is* illegal, and I think that should maybe be taken into consideration."

Dash looked unconvinced, but he didn't argue.

"Where do you get it anyway — the marijuana?"

Dash hesitated. "School."

"Really? From other students or kids that come to your school to sell it?"

"Mom, I can't tell you that. You don't rat out your source. They might get in trouble."

"Dash, I know you've heard me say this before, but if you're ever in a situation where you took something, or drank too much, and were in trouble or needed to get home, you can call me — anytime, any-where — and I'll always come and pick you up."

"I know, Mom."

"Don't be afraid to ask for a lift or help in a bad situation. Promise me that?"

"Sure, Mom," he paused. "Can we talk about something else now?" *Ah, teenagers.*

"Yeah, like what's for dinner maybe?" I said, smiling.

"Yeah, like what's for *after* dinner, too!"

Dash and I talked about sex the same way. I bought a couple of books on puberty and we read through them together. We looked at the pictures, had a laugh at some of them, and talked about respecting and caring for a girlfriend "whenever that happens, Dash, and there's *no rush!*" I laughed.

Still, Vancouver exerted its pull. Peter called home as we drove down from Whistler. "Is Dashiell back yet? Are they back from Whistler?" We had had three weeks in Whistler and, although they were tough, the intervention had started working. We had connected. I saw Dash improving. There had been no miracle — pacific Dash was not — but there had been real signs that, if we kept going, it would work. I had booked a week of horseback riding at a dude ranch in Bend, Oregon, for all of us after a couple of days back in Vancouver. But whatever Dash and his father had prearranged, or whatever unspoken agreement was in the air, when we stopped at a downtown stoplight ten minutes from home, Dash grabbed his skateboard and leapt out the passenger door.

"See you," he said casually. Like, thanks for the lift.

I had been watching him, anticipating it, and I waited him out, willing him to jump back in. The light was still red. Cars surrounded us. He kept his hand on the door handle and I watched his face.

"Dash, this is dangerous. What are you doing?"

He didn't look at me, but looked around, as if scoping out his trip home.

"Ha. Ha. Just joking," he finally said, and got in and closed the door again. When we stopped at another light, one block from our home, Dash leapt out again. This time it surprised me; we were so close to home. "I'll skateboard the rest of the way," he said.

"Dash, remember the doctor said after your fall you shouldn't put any weight on that foot," I said. *Please. Get in the car. Stay with us. We're going to the ranch. We'll be away again.*

"I don't give a fuck about my foot," he said, slamming the door and taking off the way we had just come, away from our house, toward his father's. I drove straight home, gave the boys some car-unloading tasks, and from my den called the police, then Jamie. "He's gone. I'm sure he's gone to Peter's." I swept back into the kitchen to organize snacks for the boys and take chicken out of the freezer to thaw for dinner — and I waited. I had an enforceable no-contact order. Dash couldn't stay at

Peter's and Peter knew that. But Dash didn't come home and, as the hours passed, I called all the friends I still knew and left messages at Greg's apartment and at Peter's.

"Peter, it's Pamela. Dash left my house on his skateboard. I've called the police. I'm considering filing a missing-person report," I told his machine. *That might do it.*

Peter called quickly. "Don't file a report," he said. "Look, I'm out of town, but I'll call his friends. See if I can track him down."

Day became night without word. I got up with the sun the next morning, had a coffee, and drove to Peter's house. For the first time — ever — I asked Dave to come with me. My neighbour Molly stayed with the boys, because Mimi had gone home for the weekend. This time the stakes were higher than ever. I was knocking on Peter's door and demanding Dash back, so I wanted Dave, but I didn't want to inflame anything either. I asked him to stay in the car unless it looked as if I needed him. I walked up the path and knocked on the door.

There was no answer. *He's harbouring that boy.* I waited, then we drove to Greg's apartment. There was no answer there either. I went home, made us all breakfast, and tried to stay calm. I drove to Peter's house alone at eleven o'clock.

"Who's there?" came Peter's reply when I knocked. "I'm on the phone."

"I'll wait, Peter. I need to talk with you." My stomach was already coiled when Peter opened the door. "Peter, I'm here to take Dash home."

"Well — he's not here."

"Oh, God. Peter he *is* here," I said. I was shocked when I began crying. It all started to pour out. "Why are you doing this? It's gone on too long and it's hurting our son. Can't you see that? I have tried so hard to make everything work between us, but you can't put the past behind you. It isn't healthy for anyone. And Dash — Peter, Dash is in so much pain. He wants to be able to see both of us." Peter looked at me as though I were hysterical, neurotic. He was detached and looked almost amused, as though he were watching an absorbing movie. Nothing I said moved him. "Dash needs to be allowed to have relationships with each of his parents. He needs both of us. He's troubled, Peter. He's really troubled. You heard Bob Lewis. Dash's heading in the wrong direction."

"Do you have any idea how awful it was to have been separated from Dash in court?" he asked, coolly. "With Dash hugging me and crying like that?"

My voice rose an octave; tears streamed down my face. "He was only going to visit his mother!" I cried. "He wasn't going with strangers. He wasn't being sent to jail. He was going to—!" Peter shushed me. "He hadn't stayed with me for three and a half years!"

"Pamela, you're being hysterical."

"Why did Dash calm down the instant we left the courtroom, Peter? He took my hand as soon as we were out of your sight."

"I told him to hold your hand," he said confidently, and I wanted to strike him. Hit him for every day of Dash's childhood I had lost. I balled my hands at my sides. *I will never reach this man, never, because he doesn't want to hear. He can't hear this.*

"Look," he said bluntly, "I'll call you if I hear anything. I really have to go. I'll call around his friends again. I'm sure I'll find him." *No doubt you will.* Peter was already shutting the door.

"Peter! Dash wants — Look! Please. Listen to me. Don't close the door on me! I've booked a week at a dude ranch in Oregon. Dash wants to go. We're leaving in a couple of days. He wants to come water-skiing at Lake of the Woods, too. Please, please let him come back. You have to let him get to know—"

"Hush, the neighbours will hear you," Peter said, gesturing with his hands.

"What did you just say?" My body stopped shaking for the first time since I had arrived. My mind blanked of noise and my vision sharpened. I was suddenly dead calm.

"Just . . . can you quiet down? The neighbours will hear you."

Peter didn't care about the neighbours. He had never cared about the neighbours. It was *Dash* he didn't want hearing my desperate pleas. Dash was upstairs and awake and listening. I backed up and walked slowly to my car, watching Peter as though he might suddenly pounce. I called 911 from my cell phone, quoted our case number, and said, "Dash is inside his father's house." I had a court order with police backup — they were there in five minutes. I stayed inside the car and let them do their job. They knocked.

"Who is it?" Peter asked innocently.

"Vancouver Police."

Peter came out and closed the door behind him.

"We're looking for Dash Hart and have reason to believe he is here with you."

"Oh, no, officer. I don't know where he is, but I'm sticking by the phone. I'm sure there's nothing to worry about."

The police asked him for a photograph of Dash, and Peter went back inside to get one. He'd left the door open and, although they couldn't cross the threshold, the officers looked inside the entrance-way. Dash's skateboard was on the stairs. A note to Dash sat next to it.

"Mr. Hart, would you mind if we came inside to look around?"

"Well, yes I would, actually. You don't have a warrant to do so."

There was nothing more the police could do, so after Peter closed his door, they came to my car. "He's lying to us," one of them said.

The other said, "And he knows exactly what to say. He knows we can't go in without a warrant. We can write an affidavit about what just happened if you want, Mrs. Richardson."

"I think we've had enough court."

"Then I don't think there's anything else we can do. Why don't you just go to Oregon like you've planned and let things settle down here? See what your lawyer can do to get the child back."

I turned the key in the ignition, shot a look at the downstairs windows, and drove away. I never, ever knew what my limits were. I never knew if this time or the next time or the time after that would be the last time I could bear being beaten up by these people. I felt as if my bones had been shattered and shaken up inside my skin. I was sapped. I had to get home to my family.

The next day Peter called, his voice slurred and slow. "Dash has called," he said. "He slept overnight with a friend, a new friend, I don't know his name."

I played the game. "Okay. I'll go and get him. Where is he? What's the address?"

"You don't know the friend. I don't want to tell you who, right now, anyway."

I sighed. "Then can you tell me—"

"Look, Pamela. Dash doesn't want to go to the ranch, so you should go ahead and make your plans. He's pretty ticked off."

And when Dash called that night to nonchalantly, matter-of-factly, lay out his lines, I wasn't devastated. I wasn't even surprised. I was too exhausted. I had seen Dash for three weeks in three years. Square one was an awfully familiar place by now. "I don't want to go to the ranch, Mom," he said. "I'm mad at you. The court order is crazy. I don't like it. I want to live with my dad. If you send police over, I'll run away from them, and if you start doing more court stuff, then I won't see you."

The next day, Dave and I packed up the boys and drove ten hours through majestic mountains to a horseback riding ranch near Bend, in the foothills of Oregon's Cascade Mountains. This was our third trip to the ranch, and we were meeting another family from Vancouver there. The horses were round, contented, and well-loved, and nickered softly at night so we could hear them from our cabin. The children had their favourite horses and were given carrots from the kitchen each morning to run downhill and feed to them. It was such a wonderful family time together, and Dave and I had hoped that this year Dash would join us. He would have loved the horses, the farm dogs, galloping over tumbleweeds, and the wide, open spaces. It wasn't to be. We hoped next year.

Back from an afternoon ride on the fifth day, I was handed a phone message. In a flurry of letters and phone calls back and forth between Jamie and Peter's lawyer, it was agreed — Dash was coming back to my house. I flew back on the next plane with Quin, and Dash walked through my door at half past four in the afternoon that Thursday. For once, Peter had brought him.

"Welcome back," I said.

I walked to him with my arms held loosely out and embraced him, but in contrast to our easy physicality in Whistler, now he was awkward and stiff. He told me he loved me but he didn't melt into my arms as he usually did when we were together. We sat in the kitchen and I hoped that the fragrant cut flowers and sunlight in that bright room, with the fridge and kettle close by, would all feel comforting and friendly to him. We talked lightly about what he wanted for his birth-day, horse-riding in Oregon, skateboarding, movies he'd seen over the past few days. Easy stuff. I made grilled-cheese sandwiches and tried to re-establish what we had begun building in Whistler, but he had been with his father for six days and nights and the connection was gone.

Dash was more dismissive and hostile to me than ever, and there were few moments of sweetness and consideration now to moderate his blasts of abuse. "Nothing is fucking wrong," he shouted when I asked if he was okay. "You're driving me there," he said when he told me he was going to a friend's. "What are you fucking going to do about it?" he asked when I asked him to please stay.

A school friend Dash had known since he was young was in the car during one of Dash's obscene rants at me. He told his mother later that if he were me he would tell Dash to "fuck off" and never see him again. The boy started to distance himself from Dash after that, and would soon cut off all contact with him. Dash's healthy friends all started to do it. Dash was whittling down the people in his life to just a few holdouts: his father, me, Greg.

Slowly, over time, his group of friends started to change. He started hanging out with kids two years younger, kids with whom he could still be a leader, and they were rougher than his old crowd. They had broken-down families and homes with no rules — just like Dash. He did what he wanted, when he wanted, with whomever he wanted to do it. Although part of him could still relate to a structured environment when we were up at Whistler, now that he was back in Vancouver it was impossible for him. When he stormed out of the house he didn't come back for hours. He spent more time at other people's houses — smoking dope — than at ours. He went to his father's, came back, demanded money from me, went away again. So I did what I could. I offered to drive him and his friends to the skateboard park. I picked up the taxi fares when he called me at mid-night and said he was ready to come home. I made his favourite meals, rented movies, and encouraged his friends to come over so that Dash would stay under my roof. After a couple of nights he would disappear again, staying at friends' then ending up back at his father's.

I needed to get Dash away or I would lose him for the rest of the summer. This was an intervention and it was drifting. I had to get Dash out of Vancouver. He couldn't function here. It was "Fuck off, whore" when we were together. Away, it was "I love you, too, Mom." Dash was nearly fourteen years old and what better place to sell a teenager than California? Universal Studios. Movie stars. Las Vegas, Nevada. Desert heat. American food. Theme restaurants. Magic shows. Roller coasters! *Thirteen hundred miles between us and his father.*

Dash had said he'd come. I booked tickets for two o'clock that afternoon and let him sleep as long as he wanted. That way he'd have less time to change his mind, less time to bleed back into his other life.

Sure enough, when Dash woke up, he wouldn't come. I waited him out. Finally he changed his mind: "Okay, I'll come." As soon as he said it, I flew into action, dragging a suitcase up from the basement and filling it with my clothes and Dash's few things. I organized meals for Dave, carpool pickups and drop-offs for the other two boys. I asked Mimi to stay with them for the nights I would be away. Dave couriered American dollars to the airport. I checked our passports and silently thanked my forward planning: when a judge had given me joint guardianship two years earlier, I had immediately applied for a passport for Dash. We would use it now and not need his father's permission to cross the border.

But in the rush, Dash panicked. "I have to get my skateboard from Rob's place," he said.

"You won't need your skateboard in California, Dash."

"Mom, I want it. I'm going to get it."

"Then I'll come with you. Out to UBC? Let's go!" I wasn't letting Dash get away. We drove to his friend's place and I stood with him at the front door as he knocked. I knew I was annoying him, but I didn't care. We had come too far this last month to let it fall away again. As Rob answered, I watched Dash. He was coiled, ready for action. He asked for his skateboard, then pushed past Rob to get inside. Too quickly, Dash had gone. I waited, hand on the door jamb, my heart hammering. At what point would I go in and look for them, I wondered, but a moment later the boys appeared. Dash looked around and then back at me. This was it: he was going to run. But I was still bigger. I was stronger. I lunged for the skateboard.

"Thanks! I've got it!" I said breezily and at a half-run repaired to the car with the skateboard under my arm. His prized possession was my hostage. Dash had hold of one end of it, and we tugged it back and forth. "Okay, Dash, we'll put it in the front, no problem!" I said, as I gave one final pull and slipped the freed skateboard under my arm.

I got in the driver's side and watched Dash climb warily into the other. When he'd closed the door, I handed him his board and drove out University Boulevard, taking the long way home, not wanting to get too close to his father's house. Five minutes from home, we pulled up to a four-way stop sign. Dash's fingers tightened on the board. As I moved forward, Dash opened the door.

I grabbed the end of his skateboard and held it tight. "Dash! What are you doing? Close the door!"

"I don't want to go. I'm not going. I'm getting out of here, Pam." He had one leg out the door.

I had to be firm. I had to be tougher than him. "Shut the door, Dash. We're going." I kept my eyes on the road and picked up speed. As Dash pulled the skateboard my fingers slipped on its smooth surface and I lost hold of it. Dash moved toward the open door. Using all my strength, I grabbed a handful of his arm and sweatshirt and hauled him back into the car. I took hold of the board again.

"Dash! Shut the door!"

He wouldn't. His eyes flashed, watching, waiting to yank the board away from me. I saw tension in the whites of his knuckles as they grasped the board's trucks. He said nothing, not a syllable — no "you whore," no "fuck this." He just held onto that board as if it were his lifesaver in a stormy sea. I drove as fast as I dared, mother of three and resident of tranquil Kerrisdale, struggling over the skateboard, calling to Dash to shut the door. A bus bore down on me and honked; pedestrians turned their heads as we passed. I swerved as a SUV pulled out in front of us. I missed a stop sign but just kept going. With my right hand holding the board and my left hand holding the steering wheel, I began to cry, pleading with Dash.

"Dash, you'll see. We'll have a good time. We'll go to Universal Studios and . . . " I struggled to think of our plans. "And the casinos . . . and Dash we have to get to know each other again. It's been so long. I love you so much. I love you, Dash." I said it over and over again, trying to convince him. The door swung wide open, then snapped lightly closed. Dash pulled on the handle and hauled on the skateboard again. *Be stronger than he is*, I willed myself. *Be his mom through this*. I was driving at forty kilometres an hour. The door was wide open. With my driving hand I reached through the wheel and grabbed my cell phone from the console. Forcing it down low under the wheel, I called 911. I had a ninety-day access order with police backup. They would come within minutes as they had before. But I hesitated when they answered. We were only three blocks from home. I hung up and called Mimi instead. "Mimi, we're one minute away from you," I cried. "Is the cab there? Good! Go down and press the button for the garage door!"

It started to pour rain. The jaw of the garage door opened wide as I wove the car downhill into the underground garage. With my left hand I turned off the ignition and jammed the keypad above my visor to bring the garage door down. Releasing my hold on the skateboard, I leapt from the car to catch Dash in case he ran before the door closed us in. I was panting and shaking; my body was wired. I was still crying. The door clanged closed into its lock and, still guarding the exit route, I turned to grab Dash but couldn't see him. Had he run? I raced around the car to his door and found it still closed. As I yanked it open, I braced myself, expecting a skateboard to come hurtling at me. Instead, I gasped at what I saw. Dash was still sitting in his seat, his face drained of colour. The black sky outside had darkened the garage, and in the dull light Dash looked pale and suddenly very young. Staring through the windscreen, he looked straight ahead, not at me, not at the window in front, just into space, at nothing. He was still frozen, cradling the skateboard weakly in one arm, his other arm lying limp at his side, and tears streamed down his face. His body was soft and his face was slack. His brown eyes were tired and small.

"Oh, Dash. It's okay. It's going to be all right," I said. "It's okay. We're going to have fun together, you'll see." He blinked a few times, as if slowly waking up. "Oh, Dash." I leaned into the car and held him. "I promise you it will be all right. You'll be okay." He turned to look at me, uncomprehending. "The cab is waiting to take us to the airport, okay? Okay, Dash? Let's go, now, and have our holiday. Let's just go. You'll see." Dash nodded slowly. He had given his all not to come. He had tried hard to escape, he could tell his father that. But with the garage door shut he could now accept his fate. It was *peace* I saw on his face, something I hadn't seen in years.

California glistened and gleamed from our airplane window. Our dramatic drive through West Point Grey and Kerrisdale seemed forgotten as Dash leaned forward to look out, a broad grin on his face. As soon as we touched down, he asked eagerly, "Where's our first stop, Mom? Universal?"

"You got it, Dash. We're going to see Jaws!"

"Jaws! Mom, that's so old!"

"The Psycho house?"

"Older!"

"Neverland?"

"That's Disneyland!" And so it went on. Dash and I romped around Universal Studios; helmeted up for the virtual-reality rides; got soaked on the Jurassic Park water ride. We lolled about for hours on end in the hotel's pool, then flew to Las Vegas, that overwhelming, otherworldly mirage. Our goal: roller-coaster rides and theme restaurants. The glittering hotel had a casino and a pool with a running river that we swam against. Dash loved it, hauling himself into it with strong strokes. When I got out, exhausted, he made sure I watched him swim. We ate junk food and slept every night in hysterical, Las Vegas–sized beds, which we dragged side by side so we could talk sleepily to each other as though we were at camp. We rode every roller coaster in Vegas. I have never screamed so loudly in my life, most of it from genuine and paralyzing fear. Dash and his teenage bravado took it all in stride, laughed at me. To him it was all a hoot. When my knees gave way after one ride, he grabbed for my arm, with another great boom. He had found his funny bone again. He laughed more on that trip than I had heard him laugh in a long time.

We went to a Lance Burton magic show that kept Dash mesmerized. I watched the simple, childish wonder on his face as he tried to calculate exactly *how* the magician had cut his assistant in half. When Burton made hundreds of doves appear out of his hat and beautiful ladies disappear, Dash turned and looked at me with a brightness on his face I hadn't seen for years. He was fascinated by the casinos and gambling. "I'm going to come back when I'm old enough and win lots of money!" he declared. When we walked through hotel lobbies, we made a game out of slowing down but never quite stopping to watch the gambling, lest a uniformed guard come barrelling over and remind me sternly that Dash was under age. "Keep moving, please, Ma'am," Dash joked, putting on a big deep voice.

Dash donned a jumpsuit and climbed into a flight-simulation capsule, then helped me choose a theme restaurant for dinner that evening. Over the week we had a "rainforest experience" and a red-and-white-checked-tablecloth Italian dinner, a 1950s burger night and a Japanese sushi night. We shopped for clothes as we always had. It was, by now, one of our favourite things to do together. I indulged his whims up and down "the strip." We did anything and everything he wanted to do. I wanted to spoil him, because he had missed out on so many great family times with us. I could never smooth away what Dash had lived, but at least as he lay his body down on the chaise longue by the pool, or laughed along with PG-rated stand-up comics, I could tell myself: *At least I got him here.*

It wasn't all easy, though. It was exhausting to be with Dash. I had to supervise him as if he were half his age. I didn't trust him to stay with me, and we were in too bizarre a town for Dash to be wandering off by himself. One night we had an early dinner before going to the Cirque du Soleil. Dash disappeared, saying on his way out, "I have something to do." He didn't come back for half an hour.

"Where did you go, Dash?"

"Yeah, well, I was in the washroom. So what?"

"Well," I put my palm flat on my chest to show I had been worried. "Dash, please. Would you let me know where you're going before you shoot off like that? It's not fair to make me worry about you."

He didn't seem to understand what I was saying. He shrugged his shoulders, and gave me a look that said, "How uptight are you? It's no big deal." The show started and the moment was up. Sometimes I had to push aside what had happened to Dash and remind myself that he was also a teenager. I leaned over and, with a smile, nudged him sideways and let it go.

Although Dash reacted poorly to criticism of any kind, I still called him on his bad behaviour. I was his mother. He had to learn from someone. Because I saw Dash as a traumatized child, I depersonalized his slurs, dismissiveness, and sudden impulses to get up and leave. It helped me to not overreact and gave me a base from which I could just keep pouring on the love. I used humour. It had always been an important part of our relationship, and when I used humour he understood. I said, "Baby, I am not your whore!" when he called me a "Ho" and "Do I look like a young girl to you?" when he called me "girl." Dash's charming habit of pulling his pants down and bending over to show me his naked bottom finally stopped, once and for all, when I said, "Do you think I want to look at your cellulite and pimples? Could you please cover up your bottom?" and laughed. He had neither cellulite, nor pimples, but I never saw his bottom winking at me again.

We had some long, grown-up conversations, but no miraculous epiphanies, and I didn't expect any. It was one tiny step at a time with Dash, and I was patient. I didn't push anything, or ask anything, and I let Dash begin most of our conversations. The only thing we had to accomplish during that intervention was reconnection. It had been there in Whistler. It had disintegrated in Vancouver. It was back now, and everything else flowed from that. Dash rarely mentioned his dad. Over dinner I asked Dash if he had any heroes, and he said "No," but then after a slight hesitation said, "Oh, my dad. And he's in AA now. To stop you saying things about him." It was a reflexive, protective line. I understood. "He's not an alcoholic any more," he said. I was surprised as ever at his naïveté, his utter lack of cynicism, after all he had been through. He truly thought that, if his dad said he wasn't going to drink any more, he really wouldn't.

I had been waiting with growing anxiety for what would happen once we went back to Vancouver, but it came a night early. On our last night in Las Vegas, Dash's growing agitation broke loose.

"The flight tomorrow is too early!" he shouted. "Pay the extra, change the flight."

"Eight o'clock is not too early, Dash," I said firmly. "I'm not changing the flight." Dash started calling me names, crying out, complaining. He shouted, "Pam, Pam, Pam!" over and over. He rolled around on his bed and made noises as I lay in the dark room trying to tune him out. It didn't last long, half an hour maybe, and he must have exhausted himself, because he fell asleep quickly once he calmed down. The next day, again, the moment was forgotten. Dash was fine. He got up without drama, got dressed and ready, wandered onto the plane still half-asleep, and we flew home. He lay his head in my lap and slept until we flew over the sprawl of San Francisco.

But off the plane, back only minutes at my home in Vancouver, Dash flew into action. "I'm going to a friend's place," he said, grabbing his skateboard from where it sat inside the door of our house. I followed him outside and took his arm lightly to get him to look at me. "Your friend can come here," I said. "I'll pick him up."

"Lick my balls!"

"Dash, I don't want you to speak like that to me. I don't want you to leave."

"No! Fuck off, you whore!"

Like I'd been slapped, I dropped his arm. I wasn't going to fight. Dave had heard the yelling and come outside. Dash threw the skateboard at him. Dash glared at me for a long moment, none of us spoke a word. Dash stalked off. I glanced at Dave. *Let him go.* I called the police, quoted our case number again, and told the officer that Dash was probably on his way back to his father's. I was shocked when the officer said, "Oh. I know Peter Hart. I hope he's sober."

The police called Peter. "Has he run away again? She drives him nuts," he said. "Dash isn't here." But in the meantime Dash had called me and told me he *was* there. He said he'd gone straight there from my house. Who knows if that was true, but Peter changed his story. He told the police that there had been "a big fight" at our house and that's why Dash had left. The next day, when Peter drove over with Dash, I thought I was dreaming. Hope surged in me. Peter was bringing Dash back to see out our summer. But no. They were here only to reclaim

Dash's skateboard. It was over. I hugged Dash. "I love you," I told him, and he was calm when he quietly replied, "I do, too, Mom. I'll be back on Tuesday in time for dinner, okay?"

But that wouldn't happen either. Peter had enrolled Dash in a skateboard camp, and they left the next day. What should have been a ninety-day summer access came abruptly to an end. Dash never returned, but I had broken the back of the alienation and re-established a fragile connection with my son. Dash had run away only when we were in Vancouver, and I had proved to the judge that Dash would stay with me if given half a chance. So I let it be. The intervention had worked.


I saw Dash a lot after that. We had proved that Dash and I could rebuild our relationship, just as Allison Burnet had predicted we could, if only we had unbroken time. I saw Dash every week, sometimes every two, but he didn't resist me any more, there were no more flimsy excuses. If I didn't see Dash for a week, it was just because I didn't live with him. He was older now and had plans with other people. I doubt whether Peter saw him much either. When they moved to their new house on West Tenth Avenue Dash got his own phone line, which gave us unfettered phone access for the first time in years. And it worked. We talked every night, lightly, easily.

But L.A. changed nothing for Dash on a grand scale. Our relationship had drastically improved, and that provided him with some mooring, someone to talk to and a mother's love and care, but the damage had been done a long while ago. Dash was an undisciplined and emotionally fragile young man. Though he was now in the intervention program at Lord Byng, he was still in a mainstream secondary school, and although Bob Lewis had bent the rules and let him start Grade Nine, despite his failed subjects, he began failing predictably quickly. Discouraged and isolated, he rarely went to school. In just one term he was absent forty-two times and late so often they probably stopped counting. When he did show up, he was exhausted and moody. In January 1999 he made a contract with Bob Lewis, whereby he would either attend and participate, complete homework, and behave appropriately, or drop out of school. Dash broke the contract every week. By early March, Dash's teachers were declaring they'd had enough, and although he did scrape through Grade Nine, it was a miracle and spoke more to the school community's support than Dash's work. Peter's illusions about his son remained intact. He wouldn't countenance the idea of finding an alternative program for him. Although, based on the sole guardianship order I received from Justice Brenner on September 23, 1997, legally I did not need Peter to agree to anything, I did need Peter to be onside emotionally, and over the past three years Peter had proved that he was totally incapable of seeing how badly Dash needed help at school.

I also asked for – and got – joint custody. Bittersweet victory, for it was too late to expect Dash to want to live with me. In fact, if he had joined our family, he was so badly damaged it would have affected everyone. It wasn't about me bringing up Dash any more. It was more that I had to somehow find a way for him to survive. The summer intervention had shown me just how directed Dash still was when his father was in the picture. Vancouver was where Dash failed to function.

When fifteen-year-old Dash entered Grade Ten at Lord Byng Secondary in September 1999, my fears were realized within weeks when he nominally dropped out of school. The vice-principal, Terry Howe, told me Dash was "screaming for help." Peter had fallen off the wagon again and Dash, who would have placed a lot of hope on life improving with his dad sober, was pulled once again under its wheels. Dash couldn't focus and no longer knew how to behave. As a mother, I had, for so long, wanted Dash to be happy, to thrive, and excel and become a success at whatever he chose. Now I just wanted him to function. No one but Peter thought Dash was thriving.

Dash had no boundaries and had become the sort of boy parents didn't want their children hanging out with. If there was any trouble, Dash would usually be leading the group. He thought he was dumb, but he wasn't, he just hadn't done school work for two years. He thought himself a loser, but he wasn't, he just hadn't been taught how to live outside the walls of his father's home. He thought he was ugly, but he wasn't, he just couldn't see the beauty I saw. Dash knew how different he had become from his peers. He had always been the class clown, the funny guy, but Dash knew his performances weren't funny any more.

They no longer bridged the chasm between him and the healthy kids. He couldn't concentrate for longer than a few minutes; he could hardly read what the teachers gave him. I could see in his face that Dash was beginning to feel frightened, knowing he was falling further and further behind the kids whose families had provided him with sanctuary for years and who were now drifting away from him. He dealt with it the way his father did — by denying, defying, fighting, acting out, demanding attention, or simply not showing up and staying at home sleeping, smoking dope, and festering.

A few days before spring break in 2000, Bob Lewis called a meeting at Lord Byng with Terry Howe, Peter, and me. I don't know what got Peter there. Bob talked through the options for Dash. None were good. Terry Howe said that Dash could stay at Lord Byng until he turned sixteen, because they could not legally ask him to leave until then. "But, Mr. Hart, Dash is not really here anyway. The contract that Dash and you and Mrs. Richardson signed about attending and doing his homework has not been honoured." Bob and all his support couldn't help Dash any more. He had needed specialized help, in a different sort of environment, for years. This was the end of Dash's time at Lord Byng. Bob looked squarely at Peter. "I have some things I would like to say to you." Terry and I fell dead silent. I felt a panic rise in my stomach. *What is he doing?*

"I am taking early retirement as you know, and I need to say this before I go and before Dash leaves this environment and starts up somewhere else. Your son is in this terrible situation because you have never given him permission to have a relationship with both his parents. I have met with you enough times over the years and I have talked to you on the phone many more times than that, and I have watched Dash very closely, and I believe that is absolutely true. Your child has been 'at risk' since the day he started here because you have not supported the relationship between your son and his mother."

*Oh, no,* I thought wildly, *now Dash will stop seeing me again.* I drew in my breath as Peter flew into a rage.

"This is none of your business!" he shouted. "You have no right to discuss my personal life! You have not formed your own opinion — this was given to you by Pamela. I'm not going to sit here and listen to this.

Not in front of her. Frankly, I have a few things I want to say to you, too. We can go into your office, but I won't speak here." Peter stood abruptly and they both left the room. Neither Terry Howe nor I spoke. I had had no idea this was going to happen. Every time we pushed against Peter I was terrified that things would go from bad to worse. But another part of me swelled: good for Bob. He called me that night, so exhausted that he had left school straight after his meeting with Peter. Bob told me that he and Peter had argued for two hours.

"He can't see what he's doing to his son," Bob said, strain evident in his voice. "I tried so hard to get him to understand that he's destroying this boy. But Pam, I just don't think Peter is capable of accepting that. He can't see it. He can't hear it. He can't conceive that this is what he's doing. I hope I've been able to reach him on some level."

Knowing we had to get Dash into a different school, I spent weeks researching, phoning, and doing background work before finding a special-education school in Vancouver called Glen Eden Multimodal Centre. It was run by a wonderful and caring man named Dr. Rick Brennan, who had started the school to help kids who had fallen through the cracks, children whose problems were too complex to be dealt with in regular schools. With a $20,000 yearly price tag that I assured Peter I would pick up and a maximum student population of forty, Glen Eden was a good next choice for Dash. I had already met with Dr. Brennan and toured the school. The school body consisted of adolescents with psychiatric, medical, and behavioural problems, but over 80 percent graduated from the program. Some 13 percent didn't graduate high school but found employment in their communities and functioned well. Only 6 percent of Glen Eden's students remained unable to function at a "socially appropriate level." That was a small enough figure for me. Dash was headed somewhere far worse. Not many children graduate from the streets.

If the idea had come from me, we all believed Peter would have rejected it, but coming from Bob Lewis when we met to discuss it, he didn't quibble. Bob and I had soft-pedalled Peter to ensure that he wouldn't walk out of the room and ruin our chances of moving Dash.

We hadn't talked about Dash's emotional problems. We had concentrated on Dash's academics and his need for one-on-one teaching like Glen Eden, which was tailored to each individual child. And so Peter agreed to let Dash try Glen Eden.

Dash had come around on his own after many conversations with me in the weeks before we decided. "There's no point is there, Mom, continuing at Lord Byng?" His clarity had surprised me. He was not living in a twilight zone. He was aware of what was happening in his life.

"Well, it doesn't seem to be working," I replied.

"I'll be better off at Glen Eden, won't I? I need that help right now." Dash was thinking about his future in constructive ways. He was thinking about a future.

I stuck with my positive message. "Glen Eden will get you back up to speed, Dash. It will get you through Grade Ten."

In March 2000 Dash agreed to come on family holidays with us. Ironically enough our trip to Maui was the first holiday for which I had not booked accommodation that included a bedroom for Dash. By the time he told me he really wanted to come, I couldn't change the booking and get a bigger place, and I hoped that wasn't an ominous sign. I didn't even let myself believe Dash would really come, and in fact the night before we left Dash must have panicked. He called a friend and asked him to come with him. Of course the friend couldn't come — it was expensive and no one had as free a life as Dash — and yet, when I called Dash late in the evening, he said he still wanted to come.

To this day I don't know how he managed to do it. *Why are you going anyway? You hate those people! Well, if you're going, you're on your own.* Dash jumped into my car with a bag packed for two weeks in Maui that brought tears to my eyes. He had brought ten dollars and some underwear. Maybe a T-shirt. I looked down at his bag and Dash shrugged his shoulders and said defiantly, "Whatever." I don't know any other parent who would send their child on holiday with ten dollars and some underwear, and I bet he didn't either.

Every time I was with Dash I was violently reminded of why I was fighting so hard for him. He was so badly damaged, and being confronted with that was very hard. In Maui he was often rude to me and rough with the boys. He played with them too hard now, pushing them; occasionally he punched one of them. Though Quinten still adored Dash, ten-year-old Colby was realizing that Dash wasn't the nicest guy in the world, and he didn't go out of his way to be with him or include him, which made my job even harder. The good times, the Maui sun, Dash's screams as he dive-bombed into the water, the fun we all had, the spear-fishing trip he took with Dave, the cuddles and endless back-rubs, never obliterated the knowledge that Dash had been changed so much as to be almost unrecognizable. When he watched TV with the boys, or slept, or lay in the sun, or was in some other way at rest, I watched him with an unbearable feeling of grief over all that had happened mixed with pure joy, at simply being with him.

I gained hope from the smallest of signals that he was looking to the future. He told me, "Next time, Mom, I'd like to bring a friend to Maui." Dash was already planning a "next time." He asked me if he could drive my Land-Rover when he got his licence, which was a year away, and when I said "Absolutely!" Dash smiled from ear to ear like any other kid. He was realistic. He knew he was in trouble and that education was going to be important for any plans he might make. An ability for Dash to contemplate any sort of future was all I hoped for. What he thought about in his black moments alone on his mattress on the floor with his father stumbling about upstairs I don't know, but these things he told me in Maui were like nuggets of gold in my hand.

Dash started at Glen Eden when we got back from Maui after spring break, cutting short his horrific Grade Ten at Lord Byng. Rick Brennan took an active role in each and every student's schooling and was good with Peter, but from phone calls and meetings with him, he quickly saw that Peter sabotaged and undermined Dash's progress. Rick said, "Our job is so much harder when a child like Dash has to go back each night to the same environment that produced the dysfunction in the first place." So Glen Eden didn't work just with Dash. They nurtured Peter along, too. He had to be treated with kid gloves, coached and con-vinced at every turn, lest he sabotage Dash. I used to joke that I was getting two for the price of one. Rick treated Peter respectfully, never rolling over for him, but managing him as I had tried to do for years. It was an intricate relationship, and Rick balanced it well, always with the view that, for Dash, we needed Peter. We needed him to listen to the results coming from Glen Eden as Dash went along. If Dash didn't do well, we had another plan, but we had to make sure the crumbs were out for Peter to follow.

Dash's Glen Eden tutor was a caring, gentle young man named Oliver Pavek. He was creative in his approach, and used both structure and flexibility to help Dash's learning. Sometimes he could keep Dash on track, sitting at work for hours, and when he couldn't they would go for a walk or go out. I told Oliver that Dash already went to the Jericho Tennis Club, and they should go there on my tab any time he wanted to see Dash in a relaxed, neutral venue. They went often. Oliver, just mar-ried and brown-bagging it, got a hearty lunch; Dash had a lesson even when he couldn't face Glen Eden. For a while, Dash made great progress. He attended classes and, for the first time in years, sat at his work for longer than a few minutes: Oliver's gentle encouragement often had Dash sitting in a chair for three hours at a time. But years of trauma-induced inattentiveness, absence, exhaustion, and low self-esteem had taken their toll. The Grade Four struggles Dash had with pen-and-paper tasks had never been properly addressed at home, and now they were full blown; his reading and writing abilities were way below his overall intel-ligence level. Dash's frustration and anger easily took over. He would only work on the subjects that he had traditionally been good at: Math and Science. Oliver allowed him this focus, realizing that the good marks Dash earned in these subjects would boost his self–confidence, and then they would tackle the others. Oliver inspired Dash to behave incremen-tally better and concentrate harder.

Peter's support was so critical to the process, but he started to pull back. Although toward the end of Dash's tenure at Lord Byng, Peter had participated in useful group meetings with me and Dash's team, when Dash shifted to Glen Eden, Peter once again refused to come to any meetings if I was also attending. Rick agreed to have separate meetings with each of us to keep Peter on-board, but it wasn't as constructive. Peter remained steadfast on one issue. He insisted that he be the one to drive Dash to school. He wouldn't budge, even though I told him many times that I badly wanted to do it — to make sure he got there, to encourage him on a daily basis, to see him — and that it was more practical for me to drive. "You're working so hard rebuilding your practice and I'm a stay-at-home mom. I drive right past your place to get Colby and Quinten to school every morning. I can easily pick up Dash and drop him at Glen Eden." But Peter remained adamant — and with that paralyzing control the seeds for Dash's failure at Glen Eden were sown.

Dash faltered just a month into the program. His attendance became patchy once more. Peter wouldn't drive him. Then Dash wouldn't catch the bus. Then he would want to do his lessons with Oliver at Jericho. Then he'd want them at home, but couldn't wake up in the mornings. Peter couldn't get him out of bed. Tensions within their household reached a peak and their internecine battle underwent a dramatic power shift. The monster roared back at his master. Oliver saw Dash abuse his father when Peter tried to get him out of bed. Peter took to spraying Dash with water to try and get him up. It was chaos again, and this only frightened me more, because, as controlling as Peter was, without him what did Dash have? I pleaded with Peter again to let me be the one to get Dash ready in the mornings, but he said, deadly calm, "Pamela, I told you. I'll do it." I was beside myself. I couldn't bear that Dash's great progress was falling away.

After Dash missed a number of days in a row, I phoned the house to offer him a ride. Dash picked up the phone and groggily agreed, but he must have fallen asleep again, because he didn't come to the car when I pulled up. I called from my cell phone, but there was no answer. I walked around back to the door that served as the entrance to Dash's half of the house, but it was Peter, not Dash, who yanked open the door. "I'm taking him to school!" he said, eyes red and blazing. *Peter's drinking again*, I thought as I backed away from the door. Oliver had told me he had smelled alcohol on Peter's breath in the mornings lately. After that Dash didn't speak to me for two weeks. He told me, "You got me in a lot of trouble turning up at the house like that." I had to back off. I left it in Oliver's hands. He started to go and try and get Dash to school himself, but soon Dash refused to go even with Oliver. The gentle-mannered tutor would not fight with him about it, so that fell off, too.

Dash withdrew again despite the support Rick, Oliver, and I all lavished on him. He stopped seeing me, which was hard, as I had been seeing him regularly by then and talking nightly by phone. He told me Glen Eden "sucked" and was full of misfits — which in a way it was, and I understood. "Mom, one of them wears a helmet all day and bashes his head on the wall," he told me. Dash missed his old friends. He sold bags of dope at Lord Byng about once a month for pocket money, and probably to try and connect with them. He didn't have much else.

He blamed everything on Glen Eden, but he was reaching. Dash was hard to be around and his social behaviour was immature and inappropriate. He came on to girls at parties by flicking condoms at them and saying, "Want to fuck?" It wasn't just his parents and teachers who couldn't handle Dash any more, his peers couldn't either. He wasn't invited to the parties thrown by his old friends, which upset Dash so much that one night he took a brick and smashed the window of a house after arriving at a party and not being allowed in. I continued to propose things that might engage him for even a few hours, but he couldn't raise the energy for anything. No longer shutting me out, he didn't resist me, he just couldn't get himself there. I begged him to come to Europe with us for three weeks that July, but he simply seemed too exhausted to make the decision.

I had organized two lunches that year for Peter, Dash, and me in the spirit of relationship-building and cooperation, and amazingly Peter had come to both and even acted graciously and with some of his old charm. So when Dash turned sweet sixteen, in August 2000, I called Peter and asked him to come to dinner as a family, just the three of us, to celebrate. But Dash couldn't decide where he wanted to go; he could hardly have a conversation about it, it taxed him so terribly to have to think. "Well, Dash. Where did you go on your other birthdays, with your dad?"

"One time we went to John Bishop's." It was one of Vancouver's best restaurants.

"Then shall we go there, then? If you've liked it before? It's a great restaurant." But Dash demurred and went quiet. His half-hearted answer took my breath away.

"What about the Blue Parrot, Mom?"

The Blue Parrot was a little muffin-and-juice bar at Granville Island Market that Dash and I used to go to when he was four and five years old. After grocery shopping we unwound with croissants there, and during the intervention summer, I took him to the Blue Parrot one day because he remembered going with me as a little boy and asked to go again. "I know I had a favourite sandwich there, but I can't remember what it was."

"It was ham and cheese! You could hardly get your mouth around it but you were determined! You ate the whole thing." We went back there again and again after that first time and he seemed to be delighted about it, but why did Dash suddenly want to go to a little muffin place for his birthday? I wondered, heartsick, if it was because we had gone there when he was a little boy?

The same thing had happened to his taste in clothes. Over the years Dash had always chosen lovely things for himself: good brands, hip gear, creative choices. He had a real sense of style and knew how to put clothes together. But now, when I asked him where he wanted to go shopping, he said, "Let's just go to Mark's Work Wearhouse, Mom." Each withdrawal frightened me more. All I wanted to do was take him in my arms, tell him that he was wonderful, tell him I loved him, and that he was going to be okay. But I couldn't, because Peter had built the walls so high around Dash that all I could ever do was stage-manage the peripherals: the schooling, the tutors, the birthday cakes, the bags of cookies and Valentines left on his doorstep, the encouragement. I wanted to tell him, "Dash, brown eyes to brown eyes, come on now, you're going to be okay. Hold on tight, I'll whisk you away." But Dash couldn't conceive of being whisked anywhere, let alone by me. It would have terrified him. He had been taught since preschool that I couldn't be trusted, yet a school friend of his told me that Dash was "frightened of his father." Dash had said, "I feel trapped in that house. I can't get away from my dad." A house full of lies. My child deteriorating before my eyes.

Dash's schoolwork and attitude began to falter by June, and by September his behaviour had become unacceptable even at Glen Eden, a school whose entire student body had severe behavioural problems. Dash was "totally non-compliant." Rick Brennan agreed early on that Dash's problems were rooted in his home, and by the summer he saw that, because Dash was still living with his father, he had stopped moving forward. Both Oliver and Rick had seen Dash's fundamental wonderfulness, his native intelligence, his sense of humour, his easy laughter. Oliver spent one-on-one time with Dash and didn't think he was a hopeless case at all. They saw that, far from being a class clown, underneath the PAS Dash was a wry, intelligent boy with an innate sense of audience and a natural desire to perform. A friend of his from Lord Byng, Lisa, told me about the way Dash had serenaded her on her birthday every year. He would perform the Barry White song from an episode of *The Simpsons* — "Can't Get Enough of Your Love, Babe." Lisa went into hysterics each time, and Dash soaked it up, beaming with the pride and glorious vanity of the performer. His graffiti art was beautiful. And on a skateboard, flying down Mackenzie Avenue, Dash looked, to me, like a winged angel.

The next step was radical. Glen Eden couldn't help Dash any more. He had turned sixteen on August 10 and had a Grade Nine education and no ability to function in the workplace. An immature, poorly socialized, undisciplined, semi-literate boy, Dash wouldn't have been able to hold down even a dishwashing job, because he couldn't stay on-task for longer than five minutes. He lashed out when challenged and was disrespectful toward authorities, just as he had been taught. How many employers would want a boy like that, even at minimum wage? What would losing his first job do to him? My choices were narrowing, and we had only a brief window. As Dash's sole guardian, I could make decisions for him only until he was eighteen years old. I had two years to implement something I could compel him to complete. After that he was on his own.

Peter still thought a bit of tutoring would be enough for Dash, and Rick Brennan agreed that Peter was so far in denial he would never help his son. Dash needed a therapeutic environment, out of his father's home, out of his father's city, far away from that stagnant influence. Both Oliver and Rick believed that Dash would be okay if he were away. It was in him to do the work. They believed he could commit. Rick said Dash's improvement "has not happened, it will not happen, in his current home environment."

The moment of decision had come, and the school Dash needed was in Northern California. It was an $80,000-a-year, two-year residential program for children like Dash. Cascade's program, said Rick Brennan, was the "right and only choice for Dash now." I visited the school, in Redding, California, and its rustic tranquillity blew me away. It looked like a small American college campus, sweet and homey. Set on 250 acres, adjacent to Lassen Volcanic National Park, the setting was extraordinary and the school had a loving, warm feeling. Since it took only 160 or so students at a time, the teacher-to-student ratio was one to six, and therapeutic counselling, both in a group and on an individual basis, was part of the daily routine for all of the children. I met the teachers and the headmaster, checked out the dorms, and had lunch with some of the children who were in the two-year program. Another boy was there from Vancouver. Everyone dressed casually and talked openly. None of them appeared to attend under sufferance, although I supposed some of them did. Most of them had been through really tough times in their lives, and I felt that Dash would be able to relate to that and fit in here. I noticed that on most of the beds were faded stuffed toys and, as touched as I was at seeing sixteen-year-olds who still had these reminders of long-ago childhoods, part of me felt saddened that somehow their childhoods had been traumatized and interrupted and they were here, in part, to reclaim them. The sprawling campus had many extracurricular activities in the arts and athletic areas, as well as a solid but flexible academic program. Although the staff often dressed like the students, in casual pants, golf shirts, hiking boots, and sneakers, they were experienced professionals. There was a full-time nurse and psychologist, and the students and faculty would gather in the evenings around a big stone fireplace in the main lodge.

It would be a hard adjustment for Dash, but at least he would be in a safe place. Eventually he would have to work through a lot of what had happened to him and, in such a positive, encouraging environment, with peers who may have suffered similarly, I felt he had a chance. A school for the non-compliant and defiant, Cascade had a built-in tolerance for children like Dash. He wouldn't be expelled no matter what. He would find boundaries, but he wouldn't be allowed to fall off. Flying home from California, I thought about my boys, and the education Dave and I had long ago committed to providing for them — private school, stimulating extracurricular activities, the best of everything — and how for Dash that had been for so long just a dream. Dash wouldn't be a Rhodes Scholar, he was headed for the streets, but Cascade could scoop him up and nestle him to its breast. The world-class education he would get along the way was a bonus.

Rick called Peter in and told him an appropriate school had been found for Dash. Although we faced a waiting list, Cascade's director of admissions had felt Dash's needs to be urgent enough to promise that a place would be found for him whenever we could get him there. What we didn't tell Peter was what Cascade had told me: They wouldn't take Dash as he was. Glen Eden *hadn't* stabilized him, he *wasn't* compliant. Most importantly, he hadn't been psycho-educationally tested. All special schools require testing so that they know exactly what issues they are dealing with for each student, and Cascade was no different.

"Then what do we do to get him there?" I had asked. "I'll do anything."

"Take him to Ascent. It's in Idaho. It's a six-week therapeutic wilderness program. It will stabilize him and they will test him. That'll meet our needs."

I flew into the research. I trawled Ascent's Web site, called them, spoke to their director and counsellors. I talked it over with Rick. Ascent was highly recommended. Between ten and twelve thousand children a year go through the wilderness-therapy programs that currently exist in the United States (of which Ascent is just one). Though there had been bad press generated by some badly run and unethical programs, independent studies, as well as parents of the children who have gone through the good programs, have lauded the results. Parents just like me get their children back. The six-week program — even at $20,000 US — was worth every penny to me. I couldn't fork it over quickly enough.

Ascent was the very beginning, a six-week preparatory program for children to then go on to other schools, like Cascade. It was an urgent-intervention program. I read a quote that said, "In many cases, we are literally reaching underwater and grabbing the hand of a drowning victim." For Dash, Ascent was a lifeline between the dysfunction in Vancouver that was destroying him and Cascade, which would put him back together again. Dash needed a caring home and, instead of mine, I was giving him northern California.

But, Rick warned me: Dash *had to* complete Ascent and he *had to* continue on to Cascade. "If he drops out of Ascent," Rick said, "it will be worse for Dash than if he had never gone. These programs don't work in a vacuum, and it will be disastrous if it's not followed by a long-term residential program."

I had sole guardianship. I could register Dash without Peter, and I did. But that's all. Even though I could have done everything, we had to tread carefully. This time we needed Peter and his influence over Dash. If Dash could be told that his dad agreed he should be in Cascade school, we all thought he would be able to commit to it. For once the loyalty inherent in the PAS relationship could be exploited to Dash's advantage.

Peter was his old affable self and agreed to talk with Cascade. He had had a two-hour conversation with the head of admissions at Cascade, Sunny Weir, but Sunny had worried that he was dithering and uncommitted. He was neither for it nor against it and instead wanted to ask Dash. If Dash wanted to go, then he would support it. The back door as always would be opened by Peter, and Dash had looked, his whole life, for the back door that pleased his dad. With the two of them turning to each other for cues, it was a perilous situation, and we had to work nimbly around it. Rick Brennan told me soberly, "We have to do this right, because Peter is going to sabotage Dash, somehow." I had watched for nearly twelve years as Peter pulled the rug out from under his son using the guise of "supporting his clear wishes." Dash was sure to say, "Fuck that!" to the suggestion of two years at a residential school. What child wouldn't, let alone one who had been programmed from the age of five to consider his dad his home. So I talked it over with Dave, Rick, and Bob Armstrong.

I phoned Allison Burnet, who expressed her concern that I would not be telling Peter until I was en route to Seattle with Dash.

"I have no choice, Allison. I wish Peter would cooperate for Dash's sake, but I've finally got sole guardianship and I'm going to do what I know needs to be done. We all saw for years that Peter is incapable of making or even agreeing to any decisions that are in the best interests of his son. Peter is in total denial that there is anything wrong with Dash. Maybe he doesn't want Dash to heal and become healthy because in the healing process Dash may blame his father. I don't know if that's Peter's reason, but I do know that Rick and Bob and Dave agree with me that Peter will not think Dash needs Ascent, and I can't take that chance. Time is running out — this could be Dash's last opportunity, and I will move heaven and earth to see him take it."

"Well, Pam, I believe you when you say this is Dash's last chance. Call Jamie and run it by him."

"Thanks, Allison. Wish me luck!"

I hung up and looked at the phone. Taking a breath I dialled Jamie's number and waited for it to ring — "No!" I said out loud, jamming my thumb on the phone's End button. I would not talk to Jamie. I didn't want to be warned. I didn't want Jamie's sage legal advice about the ramifications of not telling Peter what I was doing — because I didn't want to be stopped. I refused to be stopped, and if I called Jamie, I was afraid I would give in and play by the rules the way I had all my life. I would call Jamie afterward, when Dash was safe in the Ascent program.

The anxiety made me ill. I couldn't sleep. I had never lied to Dash — not ever — and I knew I was betraying him. But what overpowered my grief and panic was my fear that, if we didn't do this, something terrible was going to happen. I was not Dash's friend, I was his mother. I had an opportunity now to parent my child in a way that would give Dash back his life. Peter hadn't. The court system certainly hadn't. So I went over their heads. I empowered *myself* to be Dash's mom.

Then, by coincidence, Dash told me he wanted to go shopping in Seattle. "They have better stores there," he said. My heart raced. *Seattle. The United States.* Dash had asked me to take him there a couple of times over the previous months; the first time he had can-celled, and the second time I had commitments with my boys and couldn't carve out the time. Dash's request created an opportunity that I could capitalize on: Dash wanted to go over the border. When shopping day arrived, I was nervous and jittery, but on the drive over to Dash's house, I found myself fantasizing. It was two years in the future. Dash was smiling, his brown eyes were flashing. He launched himself at me in the awkward bear hug of a strapping eighteen-year-old. He had just graduated from his two years at Cascade. He had learned again how to feel and how to love. He was healthy, happy, and anchored, and he was coming home for the summer before going off to university, or the job he wanted to get on a cruise ship, or the Army, wherever. Cascade had saved his life, and I tacked the picture up on the wall inside my head and kept it with me that day.

Dash was restless for most of the trip. He ripped his seat belt on and off, tipped his seat back and forward. He hung out the windows and leapt from the front seat to the back. I had seen worse from him, and at least our conversation was friendly. We shared a couple of laughs. We had been silent for a while, amiably watching the road go by, when Dash spoke up. "I was in a fight with my dad," he said. I had presumed that they fought, but what shocked me was Dash's volunteering of the information.

"What sort of a fight, Dash?"

"A big one. Look at this." He pointed to a graze on his elbow; it looked like a rug burn. "I got that, and my jaw hurts from his left hook."

"My God, Dash!"

"Is there a bruise on the back of my neck?"

I looked.

"Yes, there's a bruise."

"I held a kitchen knife to dad's throat . . . "

"My God!" I was floored. I kept listening. *What is the message here? Is this all a lie? Or is this his life?* Dash was quiet for a second. "I shouldn't have told you that," he said.

"Well, now you have."

"Yeah."

"Was the argument about school, Dash?"

"Yeah."

And then he stopped talking. He looked out the window. We had crossed the border before he spoke again. Later that night he would tell me the fight was just in fun, and weeks later he would recant the story entirely, saying that they were just wrestling — "Greco-Roman rules." Dash said they had engaged in mock battles since he was little, but I didn't believe him. I think the wrestling was one of Peter's numerous methods of control, something that isn't uncommon among alienating fathers — the employment of physical tactics with their children, often under the guise of "fun," but always used to exert control and display physical power. I had never seen Dash with bruises before, but there had been long, long stretches in which I never saw him at all, so who is to know? Dash wrote in a later affidavit that he had made up the story of the fight to bug me, adding, with great satisfaction, that it did.

In Seattle we shopped and shopped. Weighed down with bags, we visited the Space Needle and the Frank Gehry Experience Music Project. We had a sushi dinner, then went back to the hotel for our last night together. We did our teeth, climbed into our pyjamas, and got ready to settle in for the night. The Sydney Olympics were on. During an ad break, I happened to looked down and catch a glimpse of Dash's toenails. They were curling all the way over the end of his toes and must have made it uncomfortable for him to walk. Dash didn't care how he looked, dressed, spoke, thought, or acted and it broke my heart because he wasn't normal any more. He had been *made abnormal*. He was at rock bottom, with no energy left to decide whether he was going to try and climb out again or just stay there and slowly disappear. I brushed Dash's cheek, then got up, took my nail clippers from my toiletry bag, held my son's feet gently in my hands, and without a word from either of us I cut his long nails.

An hour passed. I was engrossed in the Olympics when Dash said, "Pam, Pam! Look at me." He was lying on his bed, playing with his nipple, looking at me seductively. *Oh, my God.* "Look at my nipple, do you see, Pam? I remember how you breast-fed me as a baby." He made grotesque sexual gestures with his mouth and rubbed his nipples.

"Dash, stop it. You're being disgusting." I was horrified. I'd never seen this before. *How damaged is this boy? How can he bear it?* Dash smiled, stopped, and went back to watching the TV.

Half an hour later he rolled over onto his stomach and thrust his pelvis into the bed, groaning and moaning. "Mmm, that feels good," he said. "Does that feel good?"

"Dash, stop it now. You're acting repulsively. I'm your *mother*, and I don't want you to do that in front of me."

He began taunting me, chanting "Pamela, Pamela." Dash always found more and more shocking ways to express his pain, and in that moment, trying to remain calm, I swore to never forgive Peter for the damage he had inflicted on our child. After twelve years of slowly absorbing his father's names for me — slut, whore, bitch, fucking asshole — this was only logical. Just how bizarre would it become? Peter would say three weeks later in an affidavit, "Dash is an entirely healthy child. . . . He is very, very healthy, emotionally, mentally and physically." Dash eventually got bored and stopped. Everything was calm. At midnight, completely drained, I told Dash it was time for us to get some sleep. I curled up in my bed, turned off the light, and, with the room in a weird kind of silence, fell asleep.

At seven o'clock the next morning there were three knocks at the door and my heart stopped. I had already been up for half an hour. I had dressed in a cold sweat and sat in a chair staring at the door, expecting them. I knew they would be on time. I had done what Rick Brennan and the Ascent staff had recommended and had arranged the means by which the vast majority of Ascent's troubled teens get there. I had hired two personal escorts to take Dash from our hotel in Seattle to the wilderness camp in Idaho. I opened the door and saw two well-groomed men in their mid-30s standing in the hall. I went out and closed the door behind me to talk through the details of the day. Dash slept on. The escorts were gentle and soft-spoken, and I was immediately calmed by their professional manner and their obvious care. They wanted to know all about what sort of a child they were dealing with, and I told them, then breathed deeply and wrung out my hands. *This is it. We just have to do it now.* I went into the room, sat on the bed and gently shook Dash.

"Dash, I want you to wake up. I know it's early and you haven't had much sleep, but this is important. I don't want you to be afraid. Terry and Brian are going to take you to a wilderness program in Idaho. It's a six-week program and it's going to help you."

Dash's face filled with rage. "That ain't going to happen, Pam." His voice was like ice.

"It's time for you to get dressed, now, Sweetheart," I said firmly. He needed to know this was serious.

He rolled over languidly in bed. "You're cut."

Brian spoke. He was gentle but direct. He had seen this movie many times before.

"Dashiell, we would like you to get dressed, but we can dress you if you prefer."

Dash paused, then said aggressively, "I can do it." He ripped back the covers, pulled on his jeans and sweatshirt, and faced me. "I'm going to call my dad." It was his lifelong fallback position.

"Your dad knows all about the program, Dash," I said. "He thinks it will be good for you, too."

Dash sat down as if winded. "This is your last chance, Pam."

"Dash, it's a wonderful program. It's in the country. You'll be looked after there. You'll start to feel good again. Dash. You need *something*. It's only six weeks."

"I'm not going back to Glen Eden afterward," he spat. I was encouraged. On some level he was willing to do the six weeks and then figure out what would come afterward — as long as it wasn't Glen Eden.

"I understand, Dash," I said and I meant it. As much as Glen Eden had the staff and the program that Dash needed, it had also made him feel even more different and outcast than before. It hadn't worked. He needed Cascade, and I had just destroyed my relationship with him to give it to him. "I agree with you. Glen Eden's out. Now, Dash — Brian and Terry are going to make sure you get to Idaho safely, so don't be afraid."

Dash was calm. "I'm not afraid, Pam. I'm mad."

My mouth was too dry to swallow. No one spoke. I watched Dash for a long minute. His eyes were wet, and I knew he was frightened, despite his words. *Please forgive me for this, Dash. Nothing I ever do in my life will be harder than this.* He stalled for time, drank the glass of water by the bed, watchfully calm.

"Dash, this is how it's going to go," said Brian. "You can be taken with us one of two ways. You can go without cuffs — but I will hold the back of your pants as we go through the hotel lobby. I promise I won't give you a wedgie. Or you can be cuffed."

Dash listened, staring at the bedspread. Dash would later write an affidavit saying, "The men grabbed me and pushed me violently against the wall and forced manacles on my wrists. I continued to resist as best I could, but they were too strong. I was crying and protesting throughout, but anything I said or did to resist was ignored."

"If you go cuffed, then you have to stay cuffed until you get to Ascent."

Dash was quiet. "I want to go in cuffs." A heartbreaking piece of bravado.

I leaned toward Brian and said softly, "I don't think he needs to go in cuffs, Brian," and at that moment Dash sprang into life. He slapped me across the face. "Slut!" I turned away, shocked. By the time I turned back the three of them had left. I had heard the click of the handcuffs and the door gently closing, but I hadn't even seen them leave. Now my son was gone.

I sat on the bed and the burden of twelve years poured out of me. They became tears of relief. For the first time in all those years I believed that Dash was going to be safe. I wiped my face and got up. I had work to do. I had to get home. I had to make sure Peter was still on board. Rick Brennan was to have called Peter and told him everything the day before, as I was crossing the border into the United States. Peter hadn't called my cell that night, mercifully, and neither Dave nor Rick had called to report any problems. I looked at my watch. It was half past seven and Rick would have arrived at Glen Eden. I dialled the school. "Hi, Rick. It's Pam. How did Peter react yesterday when you told him what was happening?"

"He was really positive about it, Pamela. He said Ascent sounded like a great idea and he wished he was going to something like that himself."

Dash and the escorts boarded a plane at SeaTac airport, south of Seattle, and flew to Idaho. They drove north into the wilderness for an hour, and Dash was at the camp by lunchtime. Brian called me as soon as they had handed Dash off to the administrators. Dash hadn't resisted and he hadn't been any trouble. He had sat quietly through the flight, and on the drive through Idaho Dash had been calm. Stubborn, but calm. With that, I knew he would commit to the Ascent program. Dash could do it.

# Chapter 8
# Sabotage

Something was going to come undone. The air was thick with it. I had left the phone number of the Seattle hotel at my home with instructions to give it to Peter if he called asking for it, and I left my cell phone on all day and night in case he called. It stayed silent that entire day in Seattle, that whole night, the whole morning after Dash had been escorted to Idaho and the better part of the afternoon as I drove back to Vancouver alone. Finally, as I was picking up Colby and Quinten from school, Peter called.

"Where's Dash?"

"Peter, what did you just say?" I asked. I thought he was joking. My heart had started pounding.

"Where is he?"

*Think quick, stay calm.* Dr. Brennan had told Peter everything while Dash was still with me in Seattle. He'd had nearly twenty-four hours to call. "Dr. Brennan spoke to you yesterday, Peter. Dash is now in Idaho, at Ascent, the wilderness program."

"Brennan said that it was just something to think about, not that it had actually happened," he said, a hint of menace in his voice.

"Rick wouldn't have told you that, Peter. Dash is there *now*."

"Did he go willingly?"

"No, he didn't. He was escorted by the people Ascent recommended. They came this morning." Silence. "Peter, he's there. Glen Eden wasn't working, you know that. He needs this."

"What's the name of this place?"

"It's Ascent, in Idaho. It's a six-week wilderness program. Peter, you know all of this."

"I know nothing about this, Pamela."

A familiar, cold feeling came over me: *Peter is going to do something.*

"Look, I'm at the school picking up Colby and Quinten, but I'll call you later and answer your questions, okay?" I said.

I spoke to Dr. Brennan about it as soon as I got home, and he confirmed that he had walked Peter through the program step-by-step the day before and told him of the plan to escort Dash there. Brennan had faxed Peter the entire Ascent guide, which explained the program in minute detail and included maps and other information that Peter could follow up if he wished. He didn't know what to make of Peter's stance either. I left a message for Peter that night, but he didn't call me back. He never called me back.

The next morning Rick, Peter, and I were to meet at Glen Eden to further discuss the Ascent program and begin the delicate process of convincing Peter how desperately Dash needed to continue on to Cascade. I arrived with three lattes and waited with Rick for Peter to arrive. He never did.

Meanwhile Dash settled in. Orientation week at Ascent had just passed, and he was getting to know his counsellors and peer group. At first, the counsellors reported, Dash had trouble focusing, applied "little effort," had a bad work ethic ("although he would have you believe he was giving 100 percent"), challenged staff members' boundaries, and remained oblivious to the inappropriateness of his behaviour. But once he saw that the counsellors were serious — that they wouldn't offer him back doors or cower at his challenges — Dash had got serious, too. He began to complete daily chores and writing activities, and he even began to participate meaningfully in the talk sessions.

It is important to the work they do at Ascent that the child's parents are on the same page — they have to agree that the child needs to be there and then let Ascent do their work. Cascade had the same requirements. The parents need to commit just as much as the child, because they all have to work together toward healing. I was given the same instructions to follow and was sent the same information booklet that Peter received from Dr. Brennan — an extensive guide that walked us through every day of the program, what was happening to Dash, what he was learning, and what was expected. At no time did we not know exactly what Dash was experiencing at Ascent, and the regular contact with the counsellors reinforced this. I referred to the guidebook every morning to see what I was required to do, as a parent, to support Dash that day. Although the parents can speak to the counsellors directly, communication with their children is only permitted by letter, which is a safer method of communication than face-to-face visits or phone calls. Scheduled letter-writing times are crucial to the program.

Because most of the children at Ascent are not told they are going there until they arrive (and many are escorted as Dash had been), an important part of Dash's orientation week was dealing with my deception in Seattle. Dash's Ascent counsellor, Lana Galbraith, told me to write Dash a letter, explaining why I had done it, why I was worried about him, and why I believed he needed to be at Ascent. I knew from my research that children entering these types of therapy programs typically feel frightened and angry and view the intervention as a form of punishment. With that in mind, I dutifully faxed off a letter.

Dear Dash,

I am so sorry I had to deceive you in Seattle. I know you trusted me, and that had taken a long time to rebuild. There I was, destroying the trust of a son I love so very dearly. This is a chance I had to take, Dash. Sending you somewhere you don't think you need to go was a hard thing for me to do. Yes, I could lose you through this, but I would deal with that. I can't let you lose you. I would risk our relationship to see you mature into a person who can really make the best of his potential, someone who can enjoy life and make good decisions for himself, have positive relationships and a strong sense of who they are. Ascent is the start of all that and more, I really believe that.

Since early this year you have been in the Glen Eden outreach program because the public school system wasn't working, but outreach isn't working either. I am concerned about how withdrawn you have become. Yes, you have friends, but they're all in school. You can't get up in the morning for your tutor or for your dad. You haven't completed Grade Ten. You're bright, you can easily do the work, but still it doesn't happen. Not much does. We used to play golf together, shop, ski. Now you do nothing. It worries me terribly, Dash. I'm concerned about your inability to sleep. Remember the night in Seattle when you wanted to "chill" in the lobby at 2:30 in the morning?

Dash, you will be in Ascent for as long as it takes to complete the program. I want you to know that you have my full support and as always you have my unconditional love.

It's time for some positive changes.

All my love, and more,
Mom


The counsellors encouraged Dash to write back to me and "let it all hang out." That first letter was extremely important. It was an opportunity for Dash to express his frustration, fear, and anger at being at Ascent. Parents are told to be prepared for anything, as the children are typically in shock, and their mail is not censored. (Though the counsellors do ask that letters be rewritten if they contain obscenities or obvious untruths.) Lana Galbraith told me that Dash had written a vitriolic attack, marched up to her and asked her to fax it to me. Lana read Dash's letter and said, "Okay, I'm going to fax this now, Dash, so are you sure you want me to send it?" and Dash's bravado had given way. He hesitated and took the letter back. Some time later Dash gave Lana another letter for me. It was just a shade less stinging than the first one, and she asked the same thing. "Are you sure you want me to send this?" Dash hesitated again. "No," he said quietly. He never produced another letter for me.

By the second week, the children had already started opening up to each other in guided group sessions, where they listened to each other's stories and began to offer feedback. Lana had told me that these sessions would be crucial to Dash moving forward and that his best critics and advisers at Ascent would be his peers. Two counsellors monitored and facilitated the sessions, and during one of them something remarkable happened: Dash took the floor and began talking about his life, something unheard of for him. He still blamed me for all his problems. He said "Right now, I'm mad at her." He said I had sent him to Ascent "in cuffs." He said I had caused the "court battles"; his dad was wonderful, theirs was "the best relationship anyone could have." He said his home life was "perfect." But the other children saw right through him. They challenged him. One child said, "If your life at home is so perfect, why aren't you in school?" Others agreed. Dash could only look at them blankly. And a breakthrough occurred. Right there in front of Lana and his circle of peers, Dash let down his twelve-year guard and started to cry. He talked. He cried. He talked some more. He relived the entire "custody battle" from his earliest memories to the most recent.

"You're not going to believe this," is the way Lana began her conversation with me later. "The emotion was incredible," she said. Knowing his history, she had sat speechless, just listening to him. This was the boy about whom his Grade Seven teacher, Donna Andrews, had said, "I don't know *anything* about his home life. He *never* speaks about his father. He *never* speaks about his mother." Parents in the community who knew Dash had told me the same thing. He had never talked to anyone about his life. There was something about being at Ascent — the support, the care, the distance from his father and from me, the safety, that let Dash talk, cry, and remember. This is the boy who couldn't remember anything in court, but that day remembered *everything*. It spilled out without cease for two hours. His words might still have been of hate, blame, and his mother's treachery, but at least they were finally being released from that boy's body. Lana wasn't fooled either — her many conversations with Peter had revealed a striking resemblance to Dash's version of events: denial, blame, and the untrustworthiness and treachery of others (particularly me). Lana recognized the deep pathology that existed between the two of them. She knew Dash had a long way to go to begin healing, but his opening up — in front of near-strangers — was huge.

When Lana called me, I was driving to pick up Colby and Quinten from school before heading to Whistler for Thanksgiving weekend. I drove with the phone pressed close to my ear.

"Pam, we can work with him. His pain and grief is right there at the surface, ready to gush out," she said. "He needs this. He is in the right place."

I cried and cried listening to her. Having him taken from our Seattle hotel room just two weeks earlier, knowing I was shattering his gossamer-delicate trust, was the hardest thing I'd ever done in my life, and now, with Lana's few words, I poured out relief and grief and tears.

Lana reminded me of Dash's arrival-day comment, "I will die if I have to stay in this fucking place for six weeks." (Dash had been put on a twenty-four-hour suicide watch, and the next morning said he hadn't meant it. He never said it again, nor did he ever threaten to run away from Ascent.) Lana had begun to see just how enmeshed Dash and his father were, and how Dash's identity was entwined so deeply with Peter's. She saw how dangerous it actually was. "Pam, there are no quick fixes to this," she told me bluntly. "This will take years. We have to tread very, very carefully. Dash has deeply rooted emotional problems. He is in an extremely delicate place." He was like a seedling — the process of transplanting him into more fertile soil could kill him. Destroying the image Dash had of his father could destroy him, too, Lana said, because everything about Dash was wrapped up in who Peter was and what they believed they had survived together. So they had to unravel Dash slowly. If they showed him what had happened to him, or allowed him to discover it too quickly or in an uncontrolled environment, Lana said Dash would probably go under. He hadn't developed any tools to deal with the information that he would find.

The counsellors knew they were in a precarious position. Reckless intervention would do untold damage. Dash needed Ascent to start the work, and he needed the two-year residential program at Cascade to continue it, Lana said. I felt a fleeting, hollow victory, knowing I had been right about how sick my son really was, but mostly it just added another layer of fear to have it confirmed in such a clear way, by a specialist like Lana. I knew that, if Dash was to be free emotionally, he would have to be strong enough to withstand what he had been through, and I worried for a moment that he never would be. But I told myself that this was just my fear speaking. I knew he was being nurtured at Ascent. He was getting help. If he could do his six weeks there, then move smoothly on to Cascade, Dash would get there. I couldn't let myself believe anything else.

When Lana hung up, I tried to steady myself for the boys. My knuckles were white from gripping the phone as I drove, crying, through the October drizzle to the boys' school. I searched my thoughts. I was very frightened. My son was damaged beyond belief and had a long climb back to health ahead of him. He may not ever fully heal. But there was another thing, too; I felt it inside me. It sidled up alongside the hope I always managed to find. I felt *empowered*. Somehow I even felt strong. I knew Dash was in the right place. I knew he was going to be okay. It had taken twelve years, but I had made the right decision for him, despite the personal cost from which I would probably never recover. He might never speak to me again and was lost to me, at least for now, but he *wasn't* lost to himself. He *would* find his way back. I got to the school and my boys flew down the hill into my arms, brimming with their day's news and excited about our trip to Whistler. I hugged them tightly as they chattered on and let myself get caught up in their world. My family, for the first time in years, was *whole*. I had Dave, I had my boys, and Dash was finally safe. What I felt, more than anything else, was joy.

Dash was surmounting obstacles and had made that breakthrough, but that didn't mean he was performing any miracles. His life's lessons weren't going to go away that easily. Although I got nothing, Dash faxed his father some finely crafted messages. One the first week. One the second week.

Week 1:

Dear Dad,

I am adjusting at a low rate. This is hell! Did my mom tell you that I was going to come here? If so how come you let her. What can you do to help me home? Am I going to a boarding school after this? If so could you tell my mom that she is making a big mistake? There are too many rules hear. I am not allowed to draw or sing. I only get your letters once a week. ON WENDESDAYS. I hope to see you soon.

your ever loveing son,
DASH

Week 2:

Dear Dad, Sorey I did not wright you back sooner, but they only give you a limited time! I can't wright the truth because they say that I am being manipulative. Or that I am black-mailing her. Could you answer my question? Does my mom have full <u>CUSTUDY?</u> In other words does she own my LIFE!!!

As for what I do ALL DAY LONG IS wake up. Its every body is up within 5 mins or every one back to bed (ther are 15 to 19 people within a group). This can be repeated several times on a daily basis! Food, bathrooms, cut wood, bathrooms, food, bath rooms, cut wood, bath room, food, bathroom, journal time (<u>NOW</u>) then bed. The repetative life style leaves me in a motionaless time state thus makeing the past 2 weeks feel very short and the upcoming 4 feel very long.

Eternal Love DASH Your Ever Loving Son.

Dash was used to having the cavalry arrive whenever he didn't want to do something, and his letters were skilled attempts to manipulate his father into getting him out of there. Lana knew it, and she was worried. She called me, alarmed, one afternoon.

"Peter has been trying to speak to Dash," she said. "We're not going to let him, but he's calling constantly. I thought you should know."

Lana had told Peter over and over that direct contact was against the rules and might retard his child's healing. It was the same for each and every one of the thousands of children who completed the Ascent program each year: there is no contact by phone. Peter couldn't speak to Dash. For days in a row he called incessantly, demanding to speak with Dash, demanding to talk to Lana at all hours, flagging himself as a real problem and exhausting the staff, who needed to be left alone to do their work. But Peter was used to getting his way, and the tension was building.

At the end of Dash's second week at Ascent, and just half an hour after Lana had called to tell me about Dash's huge breakthrough in the group session, she called again. The boys and I were just turning onto the Sea to Sky highway.

"Peter is here to take Dash home," she said.

*Not now! Not after all this!* I wanted to shout out but I couldn't — the boys were in the back seat. Ascent's program director, Brian McInnes, and Peter were locked away in a room with a "DO NOT DISTURB" sign hanging from the doorknob. "That's all I know," she said, "but I'll tell you what's happening as soon as I do know."

Even in the warmth of my car I was suddenly chilled to the bone as I put the phone back in my bag. The boys chattered happily in the back, asking me mercifully mundane things that took my mind off what was happening in Idaho. "Can we have pumpkin pie with as much whipping cream as we want?" "Who's coming, Mommy? Uncle Davie? Warren and Georgia?" I couldn't erase what I had just heard from Lana, but I also couldn't do anything about it. I had to trust that Brian could convince Peter that Dash was doing fine and needed to stay where he was.

Two hours later Lana reported in. Brian had kept Peter locked away with him for two hours. He was adamant that Peter not see Dash. Brian took Peter on a tour of a secondary camp (it was empty), so he could see the facilities and grounds, and at the end of a long day, Peter finally told Brian he felt really good about Dash being at Ascent now that he had seen it. He said he had only come to see that his son was all right. Dash would benefit from the program, he said, and the upcoming backcountry camping experience would be exciting for him. Peter wrote a quick note for Dash, gave it to Brian, and drove the eight hours back to Vancouver alone. A sigh of relief went up from all the staff.

Such relief. The idea of Dash going back to Vancouver, back to his father's house, back to their Greco-Roman wrestling, and back to that mattress in his graffiti-lined bedroom would have been too much to bear. When the danger was over, when Peter was on his way home, that relief took the form of a strange and infinite fatigue. I just wanted to sleep. Sinking into my comfy chair, I stared at the fire, the embers glowing so hot they hurt my eyes. I heard the faint trill of laughter coming from Dash's old bedroom upstairs — the boys were playing their favourite video game, and I felt, as I had so often, the vast chasm between the life Colby and Quinten lived and the life Dash lived.

After Peter's visit to Idaho, his letters to Dash changed in tone, containing what Lana described as "mixed messages": general encouragement, but with an added, subterranean, message. Lana called me, worried. She had considered not giving Dash Peter's letters, but Ascent's rules don't allow that kind of censorship, even when the counsellors believe the child will be set back. With great trepidation she had given the letters to Dash, and although she wasn't allowed to show them to me, she did tell me about them. She described them as "ominous." There was enough embedded in them to give Dash a back door. The message, she believed, was: *Hang in there Dash, I may come and get you, so don't do or say anything you don't want to. Just hang on.*

And with that message, in whatever words it was rendered, Dash heard the same one he had heard in a million different ways throughout his life. His progress at Ascent disintegrated. He was going to be rescued. Peter and Dash had devised a sophisticated and largely unspoken code over the years, in which subtext was injected into every gesture or word: "Do you want to come home yet, Dash? Are they questioning you?" Or Dash's complaints: "I'm not having fun here, Dad. Mom isn't letting me watch TV" and "They're having people over for dinner and I don't want to stay." Peter had taught Dash that he could control his environment as long as it was for his father's benefit, and it continually gave Dash new ways to manipulate his father.

Dash flexed that muscle now, and his dad, who before had confidently left Dash at Ascent to finish the program, now flew into the fray, just as Dash knew he would. Dash had been surmounting obstacles and achieving small wins every day at Ascent. The journal writing was good for his mind, the carting of wood was good for his body. He was finally away from his parents' "battle," he hadn't smoked a joint in two and a half weeks, and he was sleeping solidly at night for the first time in years. He was looking healthy and strong. But Dash knew what "hang in there" meant, and with a casual "Fuck this," he stopped working and disengaged from the group sessions. He didn't come close to opening up again, because he guessed he wasn't going to be staying. Dash wasted that whole week before his backcountry trip, not moving forward and no longer interested in the hard work it would take to heal. *Don't worry, kiddo, no matter what your mother does, I'll rescue you.* Peter had done it time and time and time again. Dash may not have liked it at his father's house — particularly the "wrestling" — but it was the only place he had and he could fade out there. He could go numb again. When his father opened the door to him, Dash could do nothing but to go through it. He was about to go off into the wilderness with his counsellors and peers for eight days of introspection, self-reflection, journal writing, and intense counselling. It was the most critical eight days in the program, a time when Dash was to take his greatest steps toward healing. He was to leave on the weekend. But Peter's next moves were swift and decisive.

That Friday (the thirteenth, if you can believe it), Colby, Quinten, and I were just walking out of the comic-book shop on Fourth Avenue about to head to Blockbuster for our Friday-night movie, when Mimi called. "Pam," she said, "a courier has just come to the door. He has a package, but he won't let me sign for it. He says only you can. I told him to wait in the car and I would call you." Legal documents. I had seen this a hundred times. I bundled the boys in the car and drove home, my blood racing. *What is Peter doing now?* I pulled into the garage too fast and raced through the house to the front door. The "courier" climbed out of an old unmarked car and strolled to the door. He handed me a large envelope.

"Where do I sign?" I said automatically.

"Not necessary," he said, turning on his heel, striding at a half-jog back to his car. Something tweaked at the back of my mind — *that's strange* — but I brushed it aside.

I was expecting to find a notice of motion telling me that Peter was taking our case back to court, but it was half past four on Friday afternoon, and my gut screamed at me. *This is worse.* I tore open the envelope and stopped breathing. *This cannot possibly be true.*

Peter and Ken Westlake had gone to court a day and a half earlier, without informing me or my lawyer, or Allison Burnet, and got themselves an *ex parte* order to pull Dash out of the wilderness program. "She has abducted the child," Peter had said. Peter wanted his "rights as a custodial parent" enforced. He wanted to regain the access that had been "abruptly terminated." Dash was being held "incommunicado" and against his wishes in a boot camp in America, far from the custody of a desperately worried and loving father. And with those lies, Peter got an order to bring Dash back to Vancouver. Peter must have stacked the deck. The hearing had not been in front of Justice Brenner, who was still the judge of record on our case. Brenner knew our story and had seen Peter and Ken in action. He knew Allison Burnet was Dash's advocate. Ken and Peter knew that Justice Brenner, with his past history of not giving Peter an *ex parte* order without calling me to court, wouldn't have given them this order either, so they avoided him entirely and went straight to chambers, lined up in the cattle call, and got a judge who knew nothing about us. Any judge would have done the trick, as long as it wasn't someone familiar with the case.

Justice Jon Sigurdson had in front of him a custody case that had been before the courts in multiple guises forever and was again in court, this time for an *ex parte* order. The evidence consisted of Ken Westlake's affidavits, Peter's affidavits, and the manipulative letters from Dash describing the hell of having to get up at seven forty-five in the morning. Peter said, "You'll see from his letter if they don't all get up at 7:45 in the morning at the same time, they are all put back to bed again. And if they don't, you know, do all the dishes at the same time, then they don't eat." That was a lie.

Ken piped up, describing it as "autocratic." Sigurdson didn't say a thing; he was clearly moved. They used the tried-and-true character assassination of me: "She's got an enormous amount of money.

She's extremely litigious," said Ken Westlake. "When I've previously attempted to contact Dashiell and speak to him when he's with his mother, because he's left messages for me, I've not been able to speak to him. So she will actually cut him off from communication and even with speaking to me and so forth," Ken lamented.

Peter painted a picture, to a presumably horrified judge, of Dash being picked up in Seattle and dragged against his will to Ascent. He had found out where Dash was, Peter claimed with deliberate vagueness, only by speaking to "somebody who knew Pamela." He said, "It took me an entire day through information. . . . I looked through the maps and within a day I found out the place he was at. I called there." The "somebody who knew Pamela" was Dr. Rick Brennan, an expert, the man who had overseen Dash's educational welfare for the previous six months and who had recommended in the strongest possible terms that Dash go to Ascent and Cascade. He had told Peter all about the wilderness program. He had faxed him all the information. He had told him that Dash was going to be escorted to Idaho.

Ken said, "He was, in essence, taken by two men back to some form of camp or school setting in Idaho, which is basically a deprogramming school."

Peter summed it up, "They grabbed him, put him in a car, and drove him to Idaho."

Sigurdson must have believed them, because he later described Ascent as a "preparatory boot camp," rather than as a treatment facility for damaged children. Sigurdson never got on the phone to ask me if I had abducted Dash, and he didn't ask Peter why Dash was in the program in the first place. Peter and Ken Westlake used the words "taken by force" and "abducted" over and over for maximum impact. Peter said. "He was taken by deceit out of the country, and by force once out of the country, and then kept incommunicado." Peter didn't tell the judge that Dash and his father were able to write to each other. He didn't tell the judge that family involvement was considered crucial to the children's progress. He didn't tell the judge that direct contact was not permitted for any child. He didn't tell the judge that he was able to talk to Dash's counsellor every day, or that he had gone to Idaho, spent hours with the program director, and left having given it two thumbs up. The judge didn't hear about any of that. We have the transcript. What he heard were the words "abducted" and "incommunicado" — a dozen times in as many minutes.

Peter convinced Sigurdson that he only wanted an order for Dash to be returned to "the jurisdiction," so that Dash could tell the court where he wanted to be — in Vancouver or at Ascent. Sigurdson thought Ken Westlake's argument was sound, and set about writing an order that Dash be brought back. Along the way he did make some attempts at caution, but they were as weak as every other court order we had had.

"Judges are always concerned about *ex parte* orders," he said. "I am not being disrespectful to you, Mr. Hart, but there's often some other story or another twist or something even that you don't know about."

The only shot Peter had of getting the order he wanted was to go to court on an *ex parte* basis. If he had played by the rules, Allison Burnet would have been at the hearing and they wouldn't have got a thing. She had told Justice Brenner, two years earlier, that Dash's problem was his father and that he should be moved from his home. As Dash's full legal guardian, joint custodial parent, and mother, I could have told the judge what had happened for the past twelve years. I could have relayed Dr. Brennan's expert opinion on whether a safe, totally supervised, therapeutic wilderness program was better for Dash's welfare than an empty, graffiti-covered bedroom in a dysfunctional home. I could have told them Ascent was working.

"But," Sigurdson continued, "I don't see what the difficulty is making the order, and then if there's something your ex-wife can come forward quickly and say no, no, no, there's this and this, and this is why it's happened or whatever she might want to say. If she's got nothing to say, then you'll have the order."

Why did he trust Peter to do the right thing? Because he was a lawyer? Because he "knew everyone down there at the courthouse"? Justice Sigurdson should have shut the hearing down and demanded my presence. Peter even told him that I was in Vancouver. I was ten minutes away. But no one called me. Three times during that hearing the judge asked Peter to notify me of the order immediately, so that I could present my case before the child was picked up. But Peter and Ken didn't want that. They wanted Dash back in Vancouver first. He would be violently opposed to going back to Ascent, where there were rules and expectations and where no one believed his twisted version of their life story, and Peter knew from long experience that the courts wouldn't make Dash do anything — they never had.

Peter wanted to be the one to go and get Dash, but Sigurdson didn't quite buy it. The only order he was prepared to make, he said with finality, was one that directed *me* to bring Dash back to Vancouver. Peter leapt in, trying yet another tack. He used the same argument he had used for years, "He's not going to want to see her. He's hostile and angry. If you read his letters, they're . . . he's basically said, 'How could you let her do this to me?' He fought her. He hit her. He struck her, according to the Ascent people, when they put him in the car. This would be torture for him to have her go and . . . well . . . he won't even sleep over at her house!"

"I think it would be better off that I bring him back," Peter suggested innocently. *Why? Ask him why!* "He only has a relationship with me."

"Well," Sigurdson continued, "why not an order that she bring the boy back, and if she doesn't forthwith return him, then you can go down and get him?" he asked.

"Because it gives her the option of actually going there."

Still, Sigurdson didn't totally cave to their ceaseless "buts." He had decided: I was to be notified immediately of his order, to give me a chance to go before the court and have it overturned before removing Dash from the program, and if Dash were still to be removed, I was to bring Dash back to Vancouver, not Peter. It was the one concession to my sole guardianship, I suppose. But Justice Sigurdson wrote an order so close to what Peter had wanted that Peter made it all he needed. He didn't serve me for a day and a half and, as I held the order in my hands after the blue sedan had sped away, I was frozen. I had been utterly defeated. Here was an order ripping Dash out of the only protection he had known in twelve years, and the courts were now closed for the weekend.

All the hard work of the previous year — the decision to take Dash out of Lord Byng high school, starting him at Glen Eden, finding Cascade, crossing the border, lying to Dash, having him escorted to Ascent — took twenty minutes to undo, the time it took to make and drink a cup of coffee. Justice Sigurdson could have told Peter and Ken

Westlake to hold their horses, gathered up his robes, swept out the back, and called me to come to the courthouse. There was a child involved. He could have taken a look at our history. He could have checked with Justice Brenner to see what exactly was up with *Hart v. Hart*. He could have scratched the surface of the thin veneer that Peter and Ken had given him. Judges can do anything; Justice Sigurdson did nothing.

I don't believe a layperson would have been given the order Peter got that day. He knew from long experience that he could get away with his lies. He knew he could get away with serving me late, because he had never incurred any punishment for doing it before. None. He'd had a couple of slapped wrists and a whitewash in front of the Law Society a year earlier, when they had investigated his multiple contempts, but in all this time it had always been Dash and me who paid. Peter also knew he had to tread carefully. He waited until I had been served before doing anything with his order and meticulously planned every detail to ensure I would have no recourse until Monday morning.

Now, when I opened the order that was delivered to me, I saw that it had been stamped and dated much earlier. I was not served until after the courts closed on Friday afternoon. The "courier" had not needed a signature because not having one ensured there would be no evidence that I was not notified immediately as Justice Sigurdson had requested. Mimi had not witnessed the delivery because she left for the weekend as soon as she knew I was on my way home to accept the delivery.

At half past four Peter got the call from his courier — job's done — and then he acted quickly. He faxed the order to Brian McInnes at Ascent, and when I called Brian moments later he told me his hands were now tied. The order was legal. I called Ascent's lawyer, John Wohlgemuth, who worked out of California. Peter had just faxed him the order, too, and John was beside himself. "No judge in California would ever have given an *ex parte* order under those circumstances, especially when the absent party is the child's sole legal guardian," the lawyer said. "For a judge to have done that here, there would have to have been overwhelming evidence that the child was being abused; he would have to be black and blue all over before a judge would take a chance like that." But John warned me, "This is a legal order. It may be an appalling one, but it's real. You have to go and get it overturned. But Pam, if Peter goes to Idaho before you can do that, legally we have no choice but to give him Dash."

After all my years in court he didn't have to tell me that. I knew only too well that going back to court was the only way to question a judge's mistakes. I had to wait out the weekend. I sank into my writing chair at home, exhausted and traumatized. I could hear my boys' laughter filtering from the kitchen, where they were enjoying the snack Mimi had left them and playing with their beloved Westie, Bobbi. I needed to rest, just for a minute, before I went into the kitchen and pretended everything was fine. After three bunny-hops on a plane and a long drive, I had just come back from two days in northern California visiting Cascade in anticipation of Dash's arrival in three weeks time. I had called my travel agent to organize a plane ticket for Peter to go down there and check it out as well. I had so much work ahead of me now. And I was so tired.

I faxed Peter and told him I would withdraw my financial support of Dash if he took him out of the program. I knew that, first thing on Monday morning, Jamie and I would once again be strategizing and planning, rounding up Allison Burnet and Dr. Rick Brennan, writing long affidavits about what had happened, and preparing to go back to court. I was too tired to even cry, and all I could do was wait for the weekend to pass and try to function normally for my family. I felt beaten up. And now I was overcome with guilt: I had failed. I had failed Dash yet again. I couldn't even bring myself to call Dave, yet. I couldn't tell him what had happened. I had to just sit.

Peter got up early the next morning, and through a crisp October Saturday drove the eight hours to Idaho for a tearful reunion with his "abducted" son. I can't even imagine what lies Peter and Dash told each other on that long drive home, but I bet neither of them spent one solitary second planning anything constructive for Dash upon his return to Vancouver, something honest and achievable that would halt Dash's decline and address his depression. Ascent had been the one thing that had started to help Dash, and it had been pulled out from under him. What was Peter going to replace it with? Despite the hugging and crying that apparently took place when Dash ran to join his father, I believe Dash liked it at Ascent more than he ever let on. Lana felt strongly that Dash didn't really want to leave the program, but had to because that's what his father wanted. He was cared for there, and treated as though he mattered. He must have registered that, at the very least. Dash was only the second child in four years to have been taken out of Ascent by a parent. When Peter showed up that Saturday morning, both Brian and Lana tried one last-ditch attempt to get Peter to leave Dash alone. "He is showing the first signs of healing," they said. "It will be monumentally injurious for him to leave now, because he has started to open up." Peter just ignored them.

I was more worried than ever about what would happen to Dash once he was back in Vancouver. My relationship with him was over, I knew that. Without Cascade there would be no way in for me. Dash had nothing to go back to: no family, no goals, no self-esteem, few friends, no school, no structure, and the same home environment that had sent him into the deadly spiral that Ascent had been trying to stop. He was going back to that environment with fresh, open wounds and his father, his hero, once more responsible.

# Chapter 9
# A Final Statement

I didn't see the handcuffs on Dash when he left the hotel room in Seattle and I didn't see them five and a half weeks later when he was in them again. He had been brought to my house by the police, but the cuffs were removed while he was still in the paddy wagon, which was parked in the driveway. He had been back from Ascent for two weeks, and was brought to me only because his father wasn't home. The story of Dash's arrest was short and predictable: he and Stephen Frosch had climbed onto the roof of a house under construction near Dash's house to smoke a joint. A neighbour called the owners, and they arrived in short order and demanded that the boys come down. When they were down on the ground, Stephen and the owner began pushing and shoving each other, and Dash brandished a garden fork, yelling at the owner to leave them alone. When the police arrived, the boys ran, but were picked up immediately.

Where Stephen started crying, Dash became mouthy and arrogant. He didn't care. Authority was nothing to him. Dash said to the police officers, "My family isn't any of your business." Although he was known to the police from an earlier, similar incident, they didn't want to charge him — even one night in Juvenile Detention damages children, they said, and they tried to avoid it at all costs. So Stephen was taken home and, upon his mother, Melody's, suggestion, Dash was brought to me. By the time I saw him, Dash was once again the boy I knew so well — the other side of the sixteen-year-old tough-guy façade: he was polite, quiet, and subdued. He ambled down the path toward my front door in his uniform: baggy T-shirt, baggy low-slung pants, sweatshirt jacket, sneakers with laces that trailed the ground.

The police had already spoken to Dash at length in the car, so there wasn't much left to do but hand him off. "We're not going to charge you," they told him in front of me. "We're content to leave you with a parent." Dash stared at the ground and nodded. "Mrs. Richardson, would you take Dash into your care today?" one of the officers asked.

"If he'll stay with me," I replied. I turned to my son. "Dash, will you?"

I didn't want him to go back to his father's. Peter was frustrated — not even he could control Dash any more, and Dash had screwed up, publicly. I didn't want them to be anywhere near each other for a while.

"I won't stay with you," he said. "I want to go home." He was calm. He wasn't angry. He just wasn't interested.

The police used my phone to call Peter, and Dash talked to him for a minute. The police left, and Dash stood with his back to me on the pathway. I sat on the steps with my friend Teresa, a lawyer. I had called her after the police had called me, en route to my house. Like Sandy, she had sat in court with me many times, and she had come, within minutes, to be with me now. Dash hadn't caught my eye since he'd arrived, and now he just watched the street ahead of him. His dad was on his way.

The last time I had seen him he had slapped me across the face and called me a slut. He was a big boy now, and even though that slap had been light, he had such a great capacity to wound me with his words. I realized how afraid of him I was, afraid of his anger. Where there was one slap there were more. He had thought nothing of wielding a gardening fork as a weapon against that man earlier in the day. Dash came to inventive, violent blows with his father. I felt apprehensive around him now, as if he were a lover whose cruelty had finally become equal to his love, and whom I continued to forgive and reopen myself to. I couldn't even guess what Dash felt for me now. After Ascent any trust he had begun to feel had surely been comprehensively quelled; his disgust for those charged with looking after him had peaked. *This poor child, being brought in a police wagon to a mother he does not trust. Going home now to a dysfunctional, pathetic father.* How could I explain to him that Ascent had been the start of a new life for him? He wouldn't have believed me. How long could I continue saying, "You have to trust me," and then keep failing him by the help I promised not coming, or by his father coming instead and leading him back to nowhere? I got so angry then, sitting on my doorstep, Dash's back to me. Peter had brought him back — but for what? More court appearances, more sleepless nights, more directionless days, dope, isolation, fights, when he could have been protected and started on the journey to being well. If Peter could have just left him alone for six weeks — that's all Dash needed to get started.

And Dash shouldn't have been delivered here. The bond I had tried so hard to mend and rebuild over the past two years was wrecked utterly, and I couldn't do anything to take away his pain. Seattle had been the end. If he had got through Ascent, maybe. But there was a gulf between us now, so wide. I didn't have the courage to make any big move. I couldn't bear being spurned or attacked. Not today. Perhaps not any day now. Maybe I was changed, too. I could have reached out for him as I always had done, but I couldn't even bear his flinch, let alone a "fuck off." I couldn't take his rejection.

And so for now I thought of myself instead of him. I protected myself, as Dash was protecting himself. I didn't reach out. I didn't tell him I loved him and would always be there for him. I didn't say a word. The damage now seemed insurmountable, and my powerlessness complete. *God. I couldn't do a single thing.* I couldn't even engage Dash in conversation. What on earth could I say that wouldn't make his rage spike straight to the surface — or make him simply get up and leave? To alleviate the excruciating estrangement, Teresa chatted lightly with me. How it was still so warm out tonight. How her two girls were faring in their swimming lessons. How much fun their Halloween had been. I wasn't listening, though. My mind was on the next day's court hearing. I just hoped that the judge would listen to what had happened tonight, see how serious the situation was, and give us the order we needed, for Dash to go back to Ascent. I had to call Jamie as soon as Dash left and tell him what had just happened, so that he could work it into a last plea to Justice Sigurdson that we needed Ascent. Dash wasn't even under Peter's control any more. He was his own master, and it could only get worse from here.

I saw Dash's shoulders twitch. He moved immediately toward the front gate without looking back at either of us. Out on the road Peter's car had crested the hill in front of our house and was coasting down the hill. I got up and walked to the gate with Dash. Teresa whispered, "It looks as if he's out of gas."

"Goodbye," I said lightly as Dash opened the gate.

He said nothing to me. He helped his dad push the car around the corner. I didn't help, and I didn't ask them if I should call the service company for them, or go and get them some gas. I couldn't humiliate Dash any further.

I don't know how they got home that day. I turned around and walked back to Teresa. "Sigurdson has to order him back into the program, Teresa. There's nothing I can do here. *Nothing*. He needs Ascent. He needs to be confined now, and treated." She nodded and put her arm around me. I motioned vaguely, futilely, toward the street, tears finally coming. "He certainly doesn't need this."


Jamie and I had been in court four days earlier to overturn Peter's *ex parte* order and have Dash taken back to Ascent. We were hit with a brick from the first. Justice Brenner — our judge of record, the judge who had been on our case for four years and who had promised to micromanage us — abruptly took himself off our case. He didn't give an explanation. He didn't have to. People like me just have to deal with the consequences. Jamie was crushed. Back to well-worn square one.

In lieu of Justice Brenner, who had just become Chief Justice, Jamie asked for Justice Sigurdson, the judge who had given Peter his *ex parte* order. We hoped that, with Allison Burnet now back with us after missing the first rushed hearing, the judge would see what was really going on in this case. I wanted him to send Dash back to Ascent and then on to Cascade, or directly to Cascade. I wanted the judge to ignore Peter's claims for his "access rights" and ignore Dash's "clear wishes." Dash was incapable of making healthy decisions for himself. Even before Dash had arrived at my house in a paddy wagon, I had known that he was just steps away from Juvenile Detention, and yet again I needed a judge to cut off his omnipotent power — and *parent* him instead. In the absence of capability from either of Dash's parents, we needed the courts to take over. I wouldn't have my child on the streets because of Sigurdson's *ex parte* order.

But knowing that psycho-educational testing was one of the primary reasons Dash needed to complete Ascent — for Cascade to be sure it was the right school for him — Peter launched an offensive: he had already arranged for Dash to be tested at Edwards Thomas Learning Centre, he said. Edwards Thomas was a well-respected testing facility, but it was based in Vancouver — an "unsafe" environment as far as I was concerned. Peter had taken Dash out of a therapeutic program against the advice of the director of Glen Eden special school, Cascade's director of admissions, the director of Ascent, Dash's Ascent counsellor, and the child's mother and full legal guardian. Now he was planning to have Dash tested and sent back to a public school in Vancouver. Peter was willing to believe his son had one and only one problem — a learning glitch: Dash's known difficulty with pen-and-paper tasks. Peter would send Dash to a school in Vancouver that would help him with his academics. A stunned Allison Burnet told Justice Sigurdson, "This parent has not been concerned about Dash's education since the child was twelve years of age."

Every professional who had so far been involved with Dash believed that whatever learning difficulties he had were almost certainly caused by his years of emotional distress. The answer was *not* to send him off to fail at yet another school, while returning home to his father's house every night. Everything would go back to what it had been before: total, utter failure. With this new and reckless involvement from Peter, I saw Dash's life spinning out of control again right before my eyes. Peter hadn't involved himself until now — perhaps because he had to do *something* to stop Dash being sent away again — and, given his chronic state of denial, he would dabble, or do it half-heartedly, or head down the wrong path with Dash. Certainly he wouldn't have Dash tested in a secure environment like Ascent, where he was monitored around the clock and would be supported through the emotional fallout from whatever the tests revealed — academically or psychologically. Peter didn't want Dash going anywhere, and neither, of course, did Dash. "They treated him meanly," Peter told the judge, of Dash's experience at Ascent. "He was handcuffed and treated like a delinquent." Dash had requested to go to a public school in Vancouver, "so he can remain at home," Peter said. "Ripping him out of here because he's having troubles — has had troubles, I should say, and is trying to turn them around — to just rip him out of the only parent he's ever known . . . " Peter broke off dramatically.

We needed Dash psychologically tested but Peter simply wanted Dash's "writing, learning style and learning profile assessed by a proper educationalist," he told the court. After all Peter had heard from Allison Burnet, Bob Lewis, Rick Brennan, and Lana Galbraith of Ascent, he still needed to believe that Dash's problem was schoolwork. "His self-esteem is wonderful," he said, "it only suffers at the schooling level." When the judge pointed out how incongruous this was with everyone else's opinion, Peter countered that Rick Brennan had met Dash for only "about an hour and a half" and "you can get an expert to say anything." Allison Burnet, Peter said, didn't know him. The Dash who said he would "die" if he had to stay at Ascent, the boy who had fought a stranger with a garden fork, who couldn't get out of bed in the morning for school, and who simulated sex with his mother was a "happy" child, "really happy. He sings in the shower . . . he sings all day long. He's very cheerful. He's very, very healthy, emotionally and mentally and physically."

Allison Burnet was incensed. She told the judge, "This child has a problem. And I don't think it's a little problem with not liking school. I think it's a major problem." Dash's problem wasn't that he inverted his letters, couldn't spell, read more slowly than most of his peers, and had difficulty putting his thoughts down on paper, it was that for years the only parental involvement he had had in his life was abusive and neglectful. I don't spell well either, and my youngest boy Quinten in his primary years needed extra help, but I worked with him constantly, and now his is a good solid student. His report cards had said, like Dash's always did, "extra reading at home required, extra work during the summer required, nightly reading, help at home with his spelling." Quin got it, but Dash had *no help*. And it had been the same in every aspect of his life. Allison Burnet said, "Dash has been caught on the horns of a great dilemma for years, and that is how to keep happy a father to whom he is, in some respects, devoted and his concerns about some of the things that have happened in his father's care." Dash hadn't been supported in that home. And on some level, Dash knew it. That, on top of the profound trauma of PAS, had snowballed to such an extent that Dash could no longer function in a normal environment, let alone thrive.

Things had moved far beyond his lack of relationship with his mother; it had moved beyond the "custody battle." *Dash* was the problem now. "This child has been precociously empowered," Allison Burnet said. "We've been hearing for years that we can't force this child to do anything because he's eight, because he's twelve, now, because he's sixteen. . . . Well, now Dash is a lethal weapon in the making. His behaviour is outrageous and it needs to be modified if he is not going to be a threat to other people, particularly females. This is a child whose behaviour is so outrageous with his own mother that it gives me pause for thought for the kind of havoc he could wreak in any relationship with any other woman if something isn't done soon.

"Mr. Hart is in denial," she said. "He's in denial about many things in his private life. He's certainly in denial about this child. And at some point, somebody with some capacity to bring him to his senses should be telling him." Peter couldn't look after Dash. He hadn't, because he was too busy fighting me, and now he couldn't. Dash's will had grown bigger than him. "Only if Mr. Hart gets some insights into his own attitudes and behaviour and his child's and actively supports a program which will modify this child's behaviour is anybody going to have much success with this child," Allison said. "I have doubts whether Mr. Hart loves this child. A parent who is truly loving rises above a power struggle with the mother, rises above blind indifference and does something about the child's problems." *Someone* had to help Dash and, to a man, everyone involved with Dash believed he needed to be away in order to get better.

Justice Sigurdson had asked for the weekend to make his decision. Meanwhile, Dash had been picked up by the police. When we returned to his courtroom two days later and told him what had happened, he said he wasn't willing to alter his decision in light of it. He did make special mention of the fact that he was "not fully aware" of all the circumstances of this case when Peter and Ken Westlake went before him for their *ex parte*. "On reflection," he said, "I wish that I had the benefit of full submissions from Mrs. Richardson's counsel and the family advocate before making the order that I did, even though I expected to hear from Mrs. Richardson promptly if she was opposed to the order."

He gave me that admission but he wouldn't give me Ascent. He wouldn't give me Cascade. He had reams of material in front of him about the internecine battle between Peter and me over this child. He believed Dash was having a "very, very serious problem." He liked the idea of Cascade. But what he wanted, after all that we had been through, was for Peter and me to go off and work out together where Dash should be tested and where he should go to school. The last two years of working with Bob and Rick and Oliver and Allison Burnet and the Ascent people and the Cascade people to try and get Peter on board flashed before my eyes. And even that wasn't enough. It wasn't enough that Justice Sigurdson had ignored Peter's wreckage of his son's progress at a well-respected therapeutic program. It wasn't enough that he paid only lip service to his own rhetoric when he said, "Testing and tutoring for Dash's writing difficulty alone does not seem to be the solution, because his schooling difficulties have gone on to such a degree for so long it seems apparent to me that while he is living with his father he cannot, whether in a public school or on a one-on-one tutoring basis, properly pursue his education." It wasn't enough that he brushed aside all that he had been told about Peter's denial and sabotages — he said, "I think Mr. Hart knows that he can effectively veto any plan or court order because of the influence he has on his son."

He wanted to give Peter an opportunity to redeem himself. "I think the time has come for Mr. Hart to put aside certain grievances and animosity in the best interests of his son," Sigurdson said, glossing over nearly twelve years of history and giving Peter yet another chance to fail his son. Instead of taking away the last vestige of Peter's power and *forcing* him to act in Dash's best interests, Sigurdson said, "I think that the parents will have to show some leadership," as though we were squabbling children. As though Peter was *able* to come around. Sigurdson wanted to make us work together, but he couldn't see how far beyond that we were. It was as if we had been cast in Kafka's *The Trial*. We had been in court for *twelve years*. Dash's child advocate was there not to oversee a family picnic but to have Peter taken off the grounds entirely and have me *re-empowered* — after the debacle of Dash's removal from Ascent — to take care of my sick son. I had to get the legal power to keep Peter from interfering with any decisions, unpleasant and long overdue, that had to be made for Dash. That's why Allison Burnet was there. That's what we needed.

But Peter had suggested casually, in the middle of a grand speech at our hearing days before, that my sole guardianship be rescinded. He wanted to be Dash's joint guardian again. "It has been, in fact, de facto that way for the past two years in any event," he had lied. (Allison Burnet and I had begged for my sole guardianship because of Peter's incapacity to act when Dash had spiralled two years earlier.) Peter had thrown it out as a shot in the dark, and Justice Sigurdson said he was going to give it to him. As an incentive to act better, perhaps. As a reward for even wanting it. My sole guardianship had allowed me to host the successful interventions of 1998, get Dash to Glen Eden, get Dash across the border and into the wilderness program, and in the blink of an eye it was gone again.

Jamie is far too professional to be outwardly demonstrative, but he stood mute for a second or two, utterly shocked. My own shock was almost physical; if I had been standing I would not have stayed on my feet. As it was, I closed my eyes and looked down at my hands crossed in my lap. A deep, leaden exhaustion filled me. *Now I have no tools to help him with.* Dash's future, like so many grains of sand, had fallen through my fingers again. Peter would go right back to doing everything on a unilateral basis, or do nothing at all. He would again facilitate nothing, sign nothing, and support nothing but his own mercurial and haphazard ideas. We could forget Cascade. We could forget anything that would require mutual agreement and Peter's commitment. By allowing us to share joint custody and joint guardianship — a "normal" divorce arrangement — Sigurdson had once more given Peter total control of our son's life.

The end began. Without asking me or even informing me, Peter took Dash directly to the Edwards Thomas Learning Centre to conduct the tests Justice Sigurdson had ordered. But in the same way that Peter sought to limit Dr. Leslie Joy's assessment of Dash back in 1993, he requested that Dash be given a battery of tests that were solely learning-related. Sigurdson had ordered "psycho-educational" tests; Peter ordered "educational" tests. He didn't want to find any emotional problems. He didn't want to find any trauma.

By the time I could get an appointment to meet with Stephen Thomas of the centre — it was already November — Dash had completed a number of tests, and both he and Peter had met with Stephen a number of times. Stephen was starting to form his own conclusions. As Peter and Dash were leaving his office the first time, they saw a car accident happen right out front. Peter rushed out into the street and gave out his business card, which struck Stephen as an odd move for this criminal lawyer who had been such a high flyer, going out into the street to rustle up potential clients. What had brought Peter down so? He had smelled alcohol on Peter and, in the short weeks that he knew the two of them, believed Peter to be an alcoholic. He told me, "I presume Dash has home issues based on that alone."

"Alcohol is one of the issues there, Stephen." He listened intently as I told him about what Dash had lived since he was five years old. Stephen added that information to details he had taken from his meetings with Peter. In front of Peter, after one of Dash's sessions, Stephen said to Dash, "You know your mom loves you very, very much," and Peter called Stephen as soon as he and Dash got home and told him, "Dash hates it when you say things like that. 'Your mother loves you.' Don't say that to him again." Stephen, astonished, replied, "Peter, I think it is important that Dash knows his mother loves him and that she has been to see me and is here to support him." Stephen was concerned that Peter had made it such a priority to call him and that he claimed to speak on Dash's behalf. Stephen told me, "The person who hates me saying things like that to Dash is Peter." When I told Stephen about Dr. Brennan, Glen Eden, Ascent, and Peter's *ex parte* order he said, "You know, I've seen this before — when courts not only give but *continue* to give the child to a dysfunctional parent."

Still, the tests had shown that Dash did have learning problems. "Look, I've met the two of them a number of times now. I have no difficulty believing that Dash has suffered a great deal of trauma in that home, but the results of his testing still stands — there *are* learning difficulties here. Dyslexia and ADD have shown up, and while there are certainly other things going on here and Dash's self-esteem is very poor, they do need to be dealt with."

In Stephen's view everything would improve for Dash if he attained some success at his studies. Stephen was a dyslexic himself, and its discovery, he told me, had changed the course of his life. He couldn't speak highly enough about a school he had attended in New York State that had specialized in learning disabilities and had helped him overcome his own. He had talked with Peter and Dash about the school but, well-intentioned though he was, the lens through which he was looking at Dash was wrong, wrong, wrong. Not only did his approach focus on the *result* of Dash's trauma — the by-now-significant learning disabilities — over the *cause* — his emotional state — but the school he recommended to Peter wasn't a therapeutic environment. It was a regular boarding school in every sense. It even had uniforms. And so Peter began, or at least looked as if he began, an elaborate process of enrolling Dash in the New York school.

I panicked. We had come so far in the right direction and this was wrong. Dash would recoil violently from a structure like that, from anyone telling him what to do. He had learned years ago to rebel against any authority that wasn't his dad, or opposed his dad. He would run away, or be quickly expelled, or be quietly asked to leave, and then just enter a new spiral. How much more failure and anger could his already crushed self-esteem take? I was so convinced that Dash needed a school for non-compliant children — Cascade, or at the very least an academically focused *therapeutic* environment, something non-coercive and tolerant of children like Dash. As Rick said, "Dash needs to not be able to get kicked out." We had to fix Dash's head and heart, not sit him at a desk in a starched uniform. Would Peter follow through and jump through all the hoops I had already gone through with Cascade to get Dash into the New York school? He had taken Dash out of the wilderness program protesting that he couldn't get access to him — could he really bear to send him all the way to New York State? If so, why had he pulled him out of Ascent? Dash was there. I had paid the $20,000 tuition. I had now withdrawn my financial support, the only strategy I could think of that might have made Peter think twice about taking Dash out of Ascent. How was Peter going to find the money? Would he get halfway down the track and lose interest? Tell Dash they couldn't afford it, because I still owed them a million dollars? Would Dash be left in the lurch again? He needed an environment like Cascade, where counsellors and teachers were available twenty-four hours a day, seven days a week.

"I am not minimizing the learning difficulties, Stephen. It's just that Rick and I feel that the therapy has to come first. Dash has to go to a school for non-compliant children because that's what he *is* now. He needs to heal. Rick agrees. Everyone I have spoken with agrees. His learning problems are interrelated and integrated with his emotional straitjacket, the PAS. Until Dash is stabilized, I don't see how we can tell how bad, or even *what*, his learning issues are. He needs to get away — yes, definitely, and we've been working toward this for years — but in a regular boarding-school environment he'll get kicked out or run away. It will just set him up for more loss and more failure."

"Pam, I just don't agree. Maybe it'll be a tough adjustment at first, but positive results from his academic successes will bolster his self-esteem and motivate him."

"Stephen, can you please run some psychological tests on the side? Ascent was about to do this testing when Peter took Dash out. Cascade needs to see the whole picture, and the psychological testing is an important component. It will put the learning issues in the right balance. I have been to Cascade and I talked extensively with their admissions department and with the principal. They already have Dash's academic history and acknowledge how trauma has influenced his ability to learn."

"Peter hasn't ordered psychological testing. Listen, Pam, Dash is dyslexic. He has ADD. Does he have low self-esteem? Yes. Emotional problems? For sure. But, as I say, a school geared toward solving his language-based learning problems and bringing him some positive results ought to bring him up."

I wasn't turning Stephen's head. Dash's chronically low self-esteem didn't come from an inability to think and write coherently (although certainly it didn't help). It came from hopelessness and rage. Stephen's treatment of the symptoms would again submerge the PAS and Dash's depression, to be stumbled across at some later, perhaps catastrophic, time, like the breakup of Dash's first romantic relationship or the death of a friend, or in a devastating moment of truth with his father. Or maybe it wouldn't be discovered at all, but simply be left there, waiting to explode. Peter had set the parameters again. It didn't matter a damn what Justice Sigurdson had actually ordered. It didn't matter that Sigurdson had ordered Peter and me to agree on which professional was to do Dash's testing and then what school he should be sent to. Peter had gone right ahead and ordered himself up another expert to say exactly what he needed him to say. I was in the same position I had been for so long — playing catch-up. Stephen had his opinion and, although it was different to Rick's, Bob's, and mine, it *was* a professional opinion. "I've talked to Dash and Peter about New York, and Peter is very keen on the idea," said Stephen. "Dash has agreed to go, and they are both flying out there to take a look. That sounds positive to me."

"It does sound positive, but Stephen, I hope you don't mind if I get Rick Brennan to call you anyway? He has worked with Dash for over a year, and perhaps it would be best to hear from him why Cascade is the best place for Dash."

They did talk, but Stephen still believed his approach was the best one. When I went back for a second appointment, Stephen dropped his bomb: "I phoned Sunny Weir at Cascade today to discuss Dash's test results." I went cold. *Oh, no, Stephen.* "She told me that Cascade cannot accept him if my results are correct." *Of course they can't.* Cascade was a school where emotional issues were paramount. During my visit there, I had asked the staff for a profile of the average student (if there was were such a thing as "average"), and learned many children were like Dash. They came from broken homes, either through divorce or drugs and alcohol or some other form of family dysfunction. And while I was comforted by the fact that Dash would be able to relate to many of them, I was also saddened that so many children had to suffer because of issues beyond their control. What I saw and what made Cascade extremely effective for me was the school's ability to recognize and supply the care and nurturing that was missing in these young peoples' home lives. More than anything in the world, Dash needed to feel loved unconditionally in a safe, nurturing place. In my research, Cascade was the only school that wouldn't punish Dash for who he had become, because people there believed it was not his fault but the fault of his circumstances. I did not want Dash to suffer any more. He needed to be where having a childhood toy on your bed was okay. He needed to be where it was okay to feel the pain you were in. He needed to be where it was okay to share and work through his pain and be with other children who may have gone through something similar.

Stephen had not tested Dash psychologically, and so Cascade was not told about the trauma and depression that would have certainly shown up on test results. But, there was something else; the elephant in the room once again was Peter. In my heart I knew that Sunny was reluctant to accept Dash, not because of the dyslexia or any other learning issue; I had spent too much time talking to her about Dash's history for that. She knew, as I did, that both parents needed to be on the same page and will-ing to support Dash on his journey for the next two years; otherwise his ability to succeed would be sabotaged. I was praying that I could get Dash into Cascade, because I knew it was a safe haven, and then I would have gone back to court and begged for a court order that supported Dash being there, and if necessary secured an order that protected Dash by having Peter's phone conversations and visits monitored. Sunny and I had already discussed the importance of those court orders, because, after talking to Peter for over two hours, she knew that he would not be able to commit to Dash going to Cascade.

I was buying time. I knew Stephen would not believe me when I told him I had to get Dash to a safe place as quickly as possible. I knew if I had gone into detail about Sunny's concerns, it would not have helped the situation. So I took a deep breath and hoped that I could just get him there and then deal with everything else. One telephone call ended all that, though. All the research, the hours of talking to Rick, the phone calls with Sunny, the trip to Cascade, and endless con-versations with both Rick and Sunny to strategize about how to bring Peter along. Gone. What I hadn't counted on was that, without the context of psychological test results, learning issues combined with negative family dynamics equalled trouble, and, in a school already full to capacity, this combination was a no go.

I called Rick as soon as I got home. "Oh God, Rick. Stephen called Sunny at Cascade and told her the test results and said Dash was severe-ly dyslexic and had ADD, and they said they do not have the resources to handle such severe learning issues. Please call him, Rick. Cascade was our only chance. Now what are we going to do? Where do we start? Stephen continues to feel that Dash would thrive in a school that specializes in learning issues."

Rick gave a long sigh. "Pam, a non-compliant child like Dash needs a specific environment that can treat him in a safe but secure place. He has tried that and he didn't even do well here with our flexible program and home-school set-up."

"There has to be another school, maybe not as ideal as Cascade, but somewhere? A school that combines learning issues with counselling? There are other schools?"

"There will be some with everything we need. Something Stephen and Peter will buy into, that address the learning disability but also provide the therapeutic side and won't expel Dash for non-compliance. I'll start looking." He went silent a moment. He knew things had slipped a little.

"Rick, I've lost control of this again," I said. "Peter is dead set against Cascade. Stephen doesn't mean to, but he's bolstering Peter with these test results. If we find another school we can go around them again. If we can find a school that deals with learning disabilities, too, then Peter can tell everyone it is for Dash's academic problems. Whatever gets him on board. As long as the school understands PAS and trauma, I can accept it. Even a ranch in northern B.C., or Arizona, or something for a year. No schooling, just ranch-hand stuff. Something. If he is away from here for a good whack of time, he might stabilize. What's a year if it means a second chance for him? If he can start to heal . . . the school and other things can come after."

"I agree. I have a colleague in the States I can call. I'll track him down and get the names of some schools or alternatives."

In the meantime, while Dash had agreed to go to New York to look at the school, when Peter had gone to wake him the morning of their flight, Dash had run away. He didn't stay away long, but he made sure they missed their flight. When I spoke with Stephen later that morning, he was sceptical as to whether Peter had even bought tickets or not.

For once I was glad about Peter's inaction. It bought me time to work on Stephen.

"Do you see, Stephen? Even Peter can't get Dash to go see this school. It is not going to work. I think Peter is clinging to Dash's learning disabilities because that lets him off the hook. Or maybe Dash is now so difficult to live with that Peter will do anything. Maybe he's only doing it to justify his renewed guardianship. I don't know, it doesn't even matter, but suddenly it's chaos there again. Dash could have finished the wilderness program and be in Cascade by now. It was all done. It was all paid for."

I believed, after the missed flight to New York, that Stephen was coming around. He stopped advocating the New York school and seemed to finally concede that Dash was not truly willing to go anywhere, and that Peter wasn't on board either.

"When Rick finds out about these other schools, I really hope you think about them and perhaps help us work with Peter," I said.

"Well, let's see what else there is. Obviously we have to be able to get Dash to the school, whichever one it is, for it to be successful." He said he would speak with Rick's colleague in the United States, who knew of some special schools for non-compliant children who were also learning disabled, and I left Stephen's office feeling for the first time in weeks that we were finally on the right track. Peter would probably go with whatever Stephen recommended, and Stephen was now open to another school as long as it addressed the dyslexia and ADD. I tried to push away my frustration at the ticking clock, which had been picking up speed since Justice Sigurdson's decision. Everything took *so long.* So many days passed between waiting for the various experts and professionals on our case to get around to focusing on Dash — who wasn't their only priority in life — or returning my calls. Finding the right school, even with the influential and knowledgeable people I had on my team, might take weeks. Then I had to go and see them and speak with the directors; then we had to get Peter to go and visit and maybe Dash, too; then I had to apply and negotiate space for Dash in whatever program we all chose. They are always so heavily booked. Then we would have to get Dash psychologically tested, which all these school required, which would mean more chances for the whole thing to flounder or be sabotaged or for Dash's angry will to prevail and for Peter to let it. Now that we were joint guardians again, there would be no getting Dash there in secret. There might be no getting Dash there at all. As ever, it came down to whether Peter would truly support sending Dash anywhere.

How long did we have before Dash did something that had real consequences attached? As far as I knew he was just hanging out at home, sleeping the days away, staying up at night, waiting for his friends to finish school for Christmas. With all this time slipping away, I forced myself not to worry about how long we had before Dash got into real trouble and ended up in Juvenile Detention, or until his depression dragged him under, or until his drug-taking graduated from dope to something worse. I didn't know *anything*. I just had to focus on schools and getting Rick and Stephen and this American colleague all on the same page.

First, we had to find a school. Peter and Dash could come later. Over the next week, Rick and Stephen tried to connect again, but kept missing each other. Rick had a school in Seattle, too, and was shuttling back and forth between it and Glen Eden; he was also working on a book. We were days away from Christmas, and everyone was nailing up their shutters and going off on holiday. Dave and I were going up to Whistler with the boys, and although I planned to do another round of calling to get us all refocused on Dash in the first few days of the New Year, for now I had to accept that everything had to sit, untouched, for the holidays.

I spent my days anxious, though, because exactly what I had been trying to avoid for two years had of course happened during this whole process. Stephen and Peter had told Dash that he had real problems and they had done it in the unsafe and unsupportive environment of Vancouver, the home of Peter and Dash's *folie á deux*. I could have had Dash tested any time in the last two years — I had sole guardianship and I knew Dash needed it to get into any of the special schools I had been researching — but I had been unwilling to risk Dash being told any more bad news without a structure and proper support behind him. Dash's self-esteem had already hemorrhaged.

The relationship between him and his father couldn't sustain Dash's anger any more. Peter could control neither himself nor Dash now. I had deliberately, impatiently waited to test Dash until he was in the safe surrounds of the full-time, therapeutic program at Ascent because he wasn't *healthy* enough to deal with it otherwise. He couldn't take information in the way a healthy child could. Instead of him being bummed out by, but accepting, the testing results with a "Phew. So *that's* why I am struggling. I have dyslexia. That's why I behave this way and can't do my work. I have ADD," Dash was long past being able to deal with critical or negative information *on any level*. All his emergent fears about being "dumb" would be made true. And how do you treat ADD? He knew: with drugs. With Ritalin. He had talked to me about it years earlier, because a friend of his at school was on Ritalin. Dash would think he was going to be drugged up and sent off to boarding school.

He was so *fragile*. Why couldn't anyone see that? He would have seen Stephen's diagnosis as proof positive that he really was a misfit. A *loser* who would never fit into a school environment. A hopeless case. I knew intuitively that introducing *hopelessness* to a child who was depressed was a recipe for disaster. Dash doesn't "act" like a depressed child, Stephen had said, and Oliver had said the same thing to me. "He doesn't seem depressed." Dash still was a clown, fun to be around, sometimes. But that was Dash! He'd been born with a natural talent, but for a long time now had used humour to cover his pain. Bob Lewis knew it. He saw it. I *did* see Dash's depression. I *did* see Dash's pain. I saw it in his anger, his inability to stay on-task, his lethargy and insomnia. I saw a lack of hope when I looked into his beautiful but increasingly soulless, increasingly lifeless, brown eyes.

Telling Dash he was learning disabled, and then sending him off home back to daddy, did what I had dreaded: it pushed Dash closer to the edge. Taught to be the master of his own destiny, Dash was out of control now. When Peter took Dash out of the wilderness program, Dash's counsellor, Lana, had warned him that he was throwing away his last chance to draw the line with his son. Dash had spent years figuring out his dad and now could work him like a puppet to get him to do anything he wanted or get him out of anything he didn't want to do. The power struggle was over. Dash had won, and this was the result. He would no more agree to go off to a uniformed boarding school in New York than live on Mars, and there was no way Peter would rise above his son's opposition and put Dash's best interests before his loyalty to him. As well as simply running away, I am sure he fought with his father about it. From the bruises Dash had shown me driving to Seattle that day in the car, I was terrified of what would happen in that household now.

A couple of days before Christmas, around lunchtime, it started snowing. By the time I went to pick up my boys from school, it was snowing hard and the roads were slippery and slushy. I turned slowly onto Dunbar Street to take an easier route home and, as the car crawled along, I glanced over to the right at a little strip mall. There, outside a liquor store, was Dash, wearing the new snowboarding jacket he had chosen so proudly months before. He was with a friend, and they were talking amiably; Dash was smiling. They looked as if they were waiting for someone else to come out of the store with their alcohol.

"Look, Mom!" cried Quin, pointing. "There's Dash! Can we stop?"

I hadn't seen Dash since he left my house in his father's broken-down car weeks earlier, and my first instinct was to pull over, get out of the car, and call the name I had so lovingly picked for him at his birth. But a bigger part of me couldn't. Everything was still too fresh. I had felt the same way that day when the police dropped him off. What would he say in front of the ever-eager Quin and Colby? "Lick my balls"? Would he simply ignore me, ignore my eager little boys? I saw him jump up and down in the cold, then look around briefly toward the store, then onto the street. I had a new car that he wouldn't have recognized. I watched him for a few seconds, drinking him in, as we coasted slowly and then decided — no. I would let it lie this time.

"It looks too dangerous to stop right here," I told Quin. "It's so slushy! We don't want to get stuck. We'll see Dash soon, don't worry." I kept driving. Dash never even knew we had been there.

As we prepared to go up to Whistler I sent Dash a little Christmas card telling him I loved him. Dave and I had given Dash a new computer for his birthday four months earlier, and the card I sent showed Santa in deep frustration, trying to make his computer work. It had a funny holiday greeting inside, and I wrote some loving words, but I left it at that. I didn't beg him to spend Christmas with us the way I had every other year. I didn't buy him an armload of presents and ask him to come up and open them. No pressure.

Dash spent Christmas Eve at a friend's place. I was told that he had had "issues" with Peter throughout the Christmas period. Dash had left the house, stealing one of Peter's cars, and lived in it for two weeks, parked in a lane behind a friend's house. A long-time friend of Dash's told me it was a familiar thing between Dash and Peter for the two of them to fight and then for Dash to run away and stay away for days. A friend of mine had told me two years earlier that Peter once called her out of the blue and asked if she'd seen Dash around, giving her the impression that Peter hadn't seen Dash in days and had finally started to panic.

And so, when Peter and Dash had a big fight on New Year's Eve, Dash left the house and crashed a party in the neighbourhood. He didn't stay long, leaving, along with dozens of other kids, when the police were called to eject anyone who wasn't on the guest list. At the party, Dash had sat cross-legged, looking down into his lap, with his head sunk low. He was dejected and morose. Dash told a boy called Nick, "I got nothing for Christmas. My dad kicked me out. And I have nowhere to go." To anyone who knew him, his cry for help was a scream. Outside the confines of the wilderness program, Dash had never, ever, expressed any negative feelings about his father and their life together. He had never said anything publicly to discredit the myth the two of them lived — and Nick wasn't even a friend, he was just a boy Dash knew from the neighbourhood. The "perfect" life Dash and Peter led had finally, after all these years, hit the wall.

At some point the group of teenagers broke up and went their own ways. Dash went back home. According to Peter, Dash asked him for five hundred dollars. Peter also claimed he and Dash toasted each other at midnight, but that seems unlikely. Peter said he went to bed sometime around two, and when he awoke the next morning Dash was gone. These are lies. Dash and his dad had squared off. There were no Greco-Roman rules this time. The fight must have been physical and ugly. Peter had a big bruise under his eye for days afterward. Dash was a strong boy of 180 pounds, and he was *filled* with rage.

Somehow Dash managed to put on his pyjama bottoms, two pairs of sweat pants, a T-shirt, four shirts, a sweatshirt, a jacket, and a purple toque. I'm told children do that when they are planning to live on the streets. What Dash's state of mind was when he left that evening we'll never know. Where was he going? All his friends had gone home; it was too late to try and stay with one of them. Another cold and damp night in the back seat of a car? Would he walk or hop the free buses that run the length of Broadway on New Year's Eve? He chose the bus and was probably heading downtown, where all the other teenage runaways go.

But somewhere along the way Dash changed his plan. As he was crossing Granville Street Bridge, right above Granville Market, Dash stopped, took off his toque, laid it down, and climbed the handrail of the huge steel bridge that spans the water there. At four in the morning on New Year's Day, 2001, that silent, sober, and endlessly brave boy opened his arms wide and threw himself off.

The coroner on duty got the call and went straight to the scene. A cyclist had seen a body fall; the police had been called and were already there. Dash lay face down on the ground. The coroner walked up to his body and whispered, "Please, God, let him at least be in his twenties." She turned him over and saw he was just a kid. My Dash. More than three and a half years shy of twenty, he was only sixteen. The police officer on duty called it one of the clearest cases of suicide he'd ever seen. No alcohol. No drugs. Arms wide open. No noise. The coroner, who told me there had been an altercation after seeing Peter's freshly bruised and bleeding eye, would later say what Dash did was "a final statement to his father." Dash's broken body lay in the morgue for three days. Peter didn't look for him until January 3. Dash carried no ID. The John Doe suicide had been mentioned in the *Province* newspaper, but it was vague, suggesting only that the teenager might have been an aboriginal boy.

The same day that Peter finally started looking for our son, my family and I came home from Whistler. Dave had gone into work and Colby was at a friend's place. I'd spent the day unpacking, doing laundry, settling the boys back into our home, and thinking, as always, about Dash and how his Christmas had gone. I was going to call Stephen Thomas and Rick Brennan first thing the next morning. I was in my study checking the mail that had come while we were away, when, at two o'clock, the phone rang. It was Ken Westlake.

"How are you, Pamela?" he asked. He had his professional lawyer's voice on. Flat, emotionless.

"You know exactly how I am, Ken," I replied icily. I was suddenly incredibly anxious. *Why is this man calling me?*

Ken's voice was devoid of any emotion — utterly matter-of-fact — and when he said, almost lightly, "Well, I have some bad news," I knew. I knew my son was dead. Reeling straight backward from where I was standing, I shouted into the phone, "I will hold that child's death over your head as long as you live!"

"But I didn't do anything! Dash jumped off Granville Street Bridge!"

*Oh, my God. Oh, Dash. You jumped. Oh, God. You poor boy. I'm so sorry. Oh, my God.* I had lurched over and leaned on the back of a leather armchair, a million tons of weight suddenly pressing me to the floor. "You facilitated his death, Ken. Peter is sick, but you're not! You could have stopped this and you didn't. You didn't do anything!"

Ken hung up on me, and I dropped the phone and screamed. Mimi came running. "It's Dash. He's dead," I sobbed. "Call Dave. Oh, God. Dash. Mimi — don't let Quin hear me. Go be with him. I have to go and pick up Colby. Oh. Oh, no. Dash is dead."

Mimi tried to hold onto me, but I was too consumed and confused to be comforted. My hands shook so violently I misdialled Dave's number. I got through the second time and wailed, "Dave. Dave — Dash is dead. He jumped off Granville Street Bridge three days ago."

He said, "I'm on my way," hung up the phone, and ran out the office door for the car before his emotions could catch up with him and render him as incoherent as I was. I called Sandy. Terry answered, and he couldn't understand what I was saying. My voice was jagged and inarticulate.

"Oh, no. Oh, no. Oh, no," he said, relaying what I was saying as best as he could to his wife, who called from the background, "I'm coming right now, and I'll stay over. I'm just grabbing a few things."

Mimi called our neighbour and dear friend Molly, the boys' old babysitter, and she ran out of her house and down the road to me. My friends Joan and Lois were in their cars within seconds. From his car Dave had called my brother, who was working on a house just a few minutes from us in Southlands, and he was coming, too. Dave pulled up and jumped out of the car. With the phone still clutched in my hand, I ran through the house, opened the front door, and fell into him.

"Oh, Pam. We lost him. We lost him," he cried, holding me as tightly as he could. His body enveloped mine as his grief poured out and mixed with my own.

"He's at the city morgue," I got out. "Jamie called Ken. Dave, I need to see him. I need to put my arms —" I couldn't finish. *Dash is gone.* "Help me dial, Dave. I can't dial, I can't —"

When the coroner answered, Dave passed the phone to me.

"I need to see him," I sobbed. "I need to see Dash."

"No," the coroner said, as gently as she could. "Don't come. Pamela, he is not viewable."

# *Epilogue*

How do we even begin to describe the size and shape of the great love we feel for our children? And what would we do if we couldn't use the word "love," and instead had to describe that overwhelmingly *large* feeling without using adjectives? Could we ever get it right? Each time I try to define my love for Dash, I end up feeling suffocated, as though I had ten dictionaries bound to my back, all utterly empty of words. Dash was made up of a million sights, sounds, and smells, all of them as life-sustaining as air and water. Big brown eyes, long lashes, milky skin, join-the-dots freckles across his nose. Silken threads of tousled, mousy hair, long graceful arms, perfect fingernails. Even caked to the elbows in dirt and muck, he was a beautiful boy, and his fresh-out-of-the-bath little-boy smell was so soothing I can still conjure it up. He had squeals for excitement, squeals for delight, and squeals for happiness, each one different. He had a particular singsong voice for story time and a sharp shout of surprise when his favourite dinner appeared on his bunny plate in front of him. The effervescence that he saved for Dave, in the early days, gave me my greatest joy each day. Dave would arrive home from work and call out, "Little Buddy!"

"Big D!" Dash would shout.

Dave would crouch, so his six feet four-and-a-half inches were nearly halved, and say, "How was your day, my friend?"

"We went swimming and then to Granville Island for ham-and-cheese sandwiches!"

"Wow — that sounds like a full day. Any energy left for me?"

"Yeah!" And off they would tumble.

I had watched Dash's personality grow from the day I first met him, thirty seconds old. I had seen his first step, heard his first word, watched as he formulated his first questions, and observed him calibrate his responses and reactions to stimuli and emotions. I was there at his swimming and music classes, I was there cheering him on at his pre-school sports days and baking cookies for his kindergarten class. He had come with me to the fashion shows and luncheons I'd organized as part of my work and been strapped to my back as we traipsed across the Italian countryside during a year abroad. I came to know that boy's heart so well. I spoke for him in court when he lost the ability to judge what was good for him — *because* I knew him. A mother's knowledge doesn't just disappear as her child grows up and away. Even after all that time apart, I still *knew* the spirited young man who leapt off the dock into the icy waters of Alpha Lake or flew down MacKenzie Street on his skateboard. That same boy played gently and happily with our Westie Bobbi's new puppies when he was sixteen years old. His fronts only thinly covered the son I bore, and no matter what happened, I knew how to make him laugh, smile, and melt. The essential Dash was still there, quieter and dropped into shadow, but there. I focused on the boy I knew, not the boy his father created, and he responded as I always knew he would, faded and worn out as the years went on, but the amber flame of the little boy who shouted "Wheeeeeee!" from the apex of his swing was still burning.

In the black months after Dash's death, I cast about for ways to release the soul-splitting rage. I needed to find something to work hard at, something physical, something that *hurt*, something that would release my poison. With Dave I signed up for the Vancouver half-marathon and began training. And I hate running. I always have. It's boring and repetitive. It's hard on my body. I signed up because I had to do something. I had vented a tiny portion of my rage writing angry, broken-hearted letters to Justices Brenner and Sigurdson (Brenner never replied; Sigurdson wrote a one-liner), and I had howled in tears till I was red and puffy, for days and weeks in a row. I knew I had to work *through* my anger, not dwell *in* it. I didn't want to become bitter or vengeful. I wanted it to leave me. I wanted a full recovery for me, for my children, for Dave, and for all those whose lives had been touched by Dash's life and death. And it had to start with me. Colby had said, during a grief-counselling session, with Quin nodding hard in agreement, "Mommy, when you are sad, we are sad. But if you are okay, we are okay." So Dave and I ran. Me, always alone, running and crying, for three months.

I didn't know what would happen to me, or my anger, or my grief, when I began training. I didn't know if I would heal, if running would release or relieve me, I just laced up my running shoes each day and believed in the process. Its usefulness was in its utter lack of creativity. My mind floated free. It wasn't consumed with intricacies. It wasn't working. It just *was*. The emotions my runs brought out were at times vast, exhilarating, and painful. Sometimes I ran and was filled, just *filled*, with euphoria, and with a calm, quiet mind, I ran on, drinking in the scenery, smelling the ocean, admiring the diverse houses that lined the streets. At other times I was undone by my grief. I would clench my fists hard as I pumped my arms, and my thoughts were black. I went to the questions that had nagged me for years: Why? Why? Did I do too much? Did I do too little? Why hadn't I seen it earlier? If I had been in Vancouver that Christmas and New Year's, instead of Whistler, would he have come to me? Did it pressure him when I called when he was five, six, eight years old? Should I have called more? Less? Should I have broken the law for him? Why didn't I get a child advocate earlier? Should I have never gone to court? Should I have gone back again and again until I got him? I had been working blind for years, until I was supported by professionals who believed in what I was doing. But, nevertheless, each time it was me making the decision. To pick up the phone. To not. To call my lawyer. To not. To have him escorted to Ascent. To let him stay lost in his bedroom. When the worst of it came during those runs, I cried and cried as I saw my little boy, lying in all his clothes, crushed on an empty street at four o'clock in the morning on New Year's Day, his dead body still warm. To this day when I sense the warmth of my son, it triggers that thought, and I convulse. When I make up the boys' beds in the morning or pick up their recently discarded clothes from the floor, I feel the warmth of their bodies within the cells and fibres of the fabric and I think of Dash, the life left behind after the spirit and breath were gone. Running was my time to grieve. It was scheduled, permitted, encouraged, and fully acknowledged — and then, when I got home, I had a shower and moved on. The demons were exorcised for that day.

While my Walkman kept the pace and my sunglasses hid the tears that streamed, without cease, down my cheeks, I ran and cried for two and a half hours on the day of the half-marathon. My lips were set in a grimace, and I knew that, if I loosened my face just the tiniest bit, the whole thing would collapse and I would drown in grief. I had just turned fifty-two years old. Dash had been dead four and a half months. And I ran the whole way. At the end, wrapped in a silver blanket by Dave, who had finished half an hour earlier, I felt worthy, accomplished, and cleansed.

Peter Hart was found dead, at home, in August 2004, just as I was finishing the final draft of this book. When he failed to appear in the court of appeal, the Law Society tried to contact him. They called and called and finally someone was sent to his house. Peter had been dead, undiscovered, his dog sitting beside him, for at least a week. He was sixty-one years old, and the date of his death was put at August 11 — the day after what should have been Dash's twentieth birthday.

To me it was just as Dash's undertaker, who had spent time with the Hart family, had quietly said: "I give Peter Hart two years. He will spiral. He will never acknowledge what he has done nor will he recover. But it is only someone wracked with guilt who would insist on seeing the body, like Peter did. No matter how hard I tried to persuade him not to, he had to see Dash. He and Greg."

When I called Peter after Ken's phone call, Peter had seen Dash at the morgue and asked if I wanted to go, saying: "You know, really, he's not that bad." Where do you go inside yourself to rationalize that? Essential parts of both Peter and Dash had died a long time before their bodies did. I had fallen in love with Peter in 1981 because he had elementally loveable things about him, but they were lost along the way to emotional problems and drugs and alcohol. And my therapist told me a few months after Dash died that "the little boy you brought into this world was gone a long time ago, Pam." His words were a comfort, my reality acknowledged.

The minister at Dash's funeral told me, "You don't have to forgive Peter. There are some things in life that you cannot do, and that is okay." I *don't* forgive Peter for what he did to Dash. I don't forgive Ken Westlake. I don't forgive the judges who saw their hands as tied. Maybe it was too early. Maybe it will never happen. That's okay. We all move on. When Dash was still alive, I was often asked, "How do you deal with so many years of struggle, and how do you stay strong?" I am not always strong, and I certainly never used to be. But you make your mark as a human being not by your wins and your successes but by the choices you make in the face of loss and failure. Do you choose condemnation or understanding? Inaction or action? Vengeance or compassion? Bitterness or peace? I choose peace. I choose peace for my family. Peace for me. Peace for all those who went through this. Dash has found peace. Even Peter has finally found peace. And I am getting there.

I co-exist with a beautiful beast — my rage, mostly tamed. I don't feed it and I don't try to keep it alive; it is just there, a part of me. Sometimes it paces its cage; but at other times it dozes in the corner, now and then languidly opening an eye and showing its teeth in a smile at some memory or other. Like when I got a small win for Dash in court. Or when I got him to Ascent. Or today, when I told Colby, now fourteen, nervous about standing on Granville Street Bridge to take pictures of the city with his photography class, "I think you should rise to the challenge and face your fears." I enveloped all five foot seven of him in my arms and whispered, "I am giving you all my strength with this hug, and I want you to remember that the strength you feel from me is inside you, too. I want you to think of that when you are up there on that bridge." Colby called me, proudly, afterward. "I did it, Mom."

We all go on. One thing I have learned over the past fifteen years is that there is a particular kind of energy that comes from properly managed anger, healthy anger, *listened-to* anger, that can and always has been put to good use. That energy, used in a positive way to get constructive results, fuelled the women's movement; it fuelled and continues to fuel velvet revolutions and social-justice movements all over the globe. Change takes energy. Peace takes energy. But the beast can pace and I am finding my way. It is uneasy and fractured at times, but peace has a perch in the cage of my soul and its territory is growing.

The death of anyone close, let alone a child, makes us sense our own immortality. Dash's death has made me more alive. I have a keenness to me now, like the sharpened senses of those who do not see. I am sensitive to and respectful of the fragility of life, and how quickly things can change, and Dash's death has taught me that. I was always conscious that the time I spent in court, or trying to see Dash, or shutting myself in my den to cry when I thought no one would notice, took time away from my family and they suffered not only from my absence but from the pain they saw in me and couldn't help. I know it ripped Dave apart to be able to do nothing for the woman he had married but to keep pouring money into the legal coffers. I always knew I had to stay as strong as I could for me and for Dash, but also for them. It had taken an enormous, seemingly insurmountable toll on my family. Dave and I don't talk about it much in this way, but we both cherish the fact that we survived as a couple. The whole experience, from the beginning of my marriage with Peter to the end, with Dash's death, taught me what a fine art it is to choose, as opposed to being chosen. I choose my family. I choose love.

I'm the child who went to seven different schools and can walk into any room with confidence — but once I'm there, I'm still trying to be liked by everyone. I try so hard to please, but I know now that the whole crowd *won't* like me. And now that's okay. I've done what I can. I tried so hard. I no longer have to "prove" Dash was an alienated child

— the family advocate knew it and a coroner's investigator, after a year-long case examination, confirmed it (even though the department report was subsequently changed to "not point fingers at a parent"). I bumped into Donna Andrews, Dash's Grade Seven teacher, at Costco one day, and she told me, "No one is surprised Dash committed suicide." I'm not surprised either. I had feared it for years before he did it, I just always thought I would have more time to turn it around. My missteps and mistakes nagged at me like an ulcer. What more should I have done? Should I have kidnapped Dash? If so, I would have taken him away from a parent he loved. I'd never let it happen again, though. Next time I would grab my children and run. Australia. France. And disappear. I wouldn't go near the court system that failed Dash. I saw things in the last fifteen years that have stripped away my innocence. Do right to others and they will do right by you. Tell the truth and you will be heard. If you go to the courts for help, you will be helped. I believed that children came first above all other considerations. I believed that judges were courageous and wise and that people would break rank to speak out if a child was in danger, no matter what. But there are no people coming out of the woodwork to say, "I saw this. I did nothing." None.

The closest we came was when Peter's sister said to me at Dash's funeral, "I'm so sorry." Sandra Scarth was the director of the Children's Services branch of the Ministry of Community and Social Services in Ontario when Peter got interim custody of Dash in 1989. At that time she wrote glowing affidavits about how wonderful a parent Peter was. She had told Dr. Elterman that *I* drank more than Peter did, which was interesting knowledge considering we rarely saw her during the eight years I was married to Peter. She had later moved to Vancouver Island and, in the last six months of Dash's life, I would occasionally see her through Peter's kitchen window as I dropped Dash off at his back gate. At the time, I wondered what she could possibly make of everything that went on there. At Dash's funeral I pleaded with her, "Why did you never phone me and tell me what was going on? You knew what was happening," and she started to cry, saying, "Maybe you're right, maybe you're right." She lowered her voice and said, "I'll call you," but Peter shouted, "No you won't! No you won't!" And she didn't.

It's hard to bear a loss of innocence like that with equanimity. Counting on a community to come through for a child in need shouldn't be unrealistic. Going to family court shouldn't be a crapshoot. My poor strategic decisions — and I am sure there were many — shouldn't have led to Dash's death. Whether I stopped going to Dash's soccer games or whether I hired the right lawyer, whether I was a good, compliant access parent or a tough, ballsy one, whether I wore high heels to court or sensible flats shouldn't have mattered. Judges have to pull up a pew and get comfortable with being "super parents," because there is no one else.

Meanwhile I will keep trying to raise awareness to make something good come out of an experience this personal and unbearable. Family, friends, and strangers have heard my story and in their own small way are advocates for change, whether it is around the dinner table or in their own relationships with their ex-spouses. Dr. Peggie Ward, who works with children ravaged by parental alienation; Catherine Meyer, who has been ceaseless in her advocacy for ten years on this issue and has just re-established contact with her own alienated children — we are a group, we live in a society, and there is work to be done.


If you asked me how a person survives the suicide of their child, my early guess is that we don't. Not intact anyway. But we do go on. We make choices: to live or to hide. To let go of pain or to wear it as a badge. To move on, or to become paralyzed. The minister at Dash's funeral told me, "Pam, you cannot grieve twenty-four hours a day. It is too hard. So grieve — have your moments — and then put them away and go on with your day." His words were liberating. A friend said, "We have to believe Dash is in a better place now." And I do. I see Dash everywhere as I drive around this city. In my daily life I pass the places we used to go, the parks we used to play in, the shop where we bought his skateboarding gear, and the one that sells his favourite sandwiches. For years my two sons played soccer on the same field Dash did, and every morning and every afternoon, as I drive them to and from school, we pass Dash's old elementary, with its pretty red bricks and sweetly whimsical steeple. My heart remembers the struggle to see Dash. My whole body remembers how I clung to the wreckage that had been made of his childhood. But alongside that vast pain, I remember vividly the wonderful times I had with him and I feel his curly soft hair, see his sparkling brown eyes, his open smile, and his warm, happy being. I hear his laugh and the jokes we shared, and the magical evenings we spent watching the stars or cuddled up with the boys watching movies. And I can see him now. He is touching his two forefingers together, curling them inward and then curling his thumbs around each other. It is our little heart, the way we always said "I love you" and "goodbye" to each other when he was little. I have to think Dash is in a good place now, and I wish him peace. I wish all of us peace.